Re-reading the Salaryman in Japan

In Japan, the figure of the suited, white-collar office worker or business executive 'salaryman' (or, *sarariiman*) came to be associated with Japan's economic transformation following World War Two. The ubiquitous salaryman came to signify both Japanese masculinity, and Japanese corporate culture, and in this sense the salaryman embodied 'the archetypal citizen'.

This book uses the figure of the salaryman to explore masculinity in Japan by examining the salaryman as a gendered construct. While there is a considerable body of literature on Japanese corporate culture and a growing acknowledgement of the role of gender, up until now the focus has been almost exclusively on women in the workplace. In contrast, this book is one of the first to focus on the men within Japanese corporate culture through a gendered lens. Not only does this add to the emerging literature on masculinity in Japan, but given the important role Japanese corporate culture has played in Japan's emergence as an industrial power, Romit Dasgupta's research offers a new way of looking both at Japanese business culture, and more generally at important changes in Japanese society in recent years.

Based on intensive interviews carried out with young male private sector employees in Japan, this book makes an important contribution to the study of masculinity and Japanese corporate culture, in addition to providing an insight into Japanese culture more generally. As such it will be of great interest to students and scholars of Japanese studies, Japanese society and gender studies.

Romit Dasgupta is Assistant Professor of Asian Studies at the University of Western Australia.

Routledge/Asian Studies Association of Australia (ASAA) East Asia series
Edited by Tessa Morris-Suzuki and Morris Low
Editorial Board: Professor Geremie Barmé (Australian National University), Professor Colin Mackerras (Griffith University), Professor Vera Mackie (University of Melbourne) and Associate Professor Sonia Ryang (University of Iowa).

This series represents a showcase for the latest cutting-edge research in the field of East Asian studies, from both established scholars and rising academics. It will include studies from every part of the East Asian region (including China, Japan, North and South Korea and Taiwan) as well as comparative studies dealing with more than one country. Topics covered may be contemporary or historical, and relate to any of the humanities or social sciences. The series is an invaluable source of information and challenging perspectives for advanced students and researchers alike.

Routledge is pleased to invite proposals for new books in the series. In the first instance, any interested authors should contact:

Professor Tessa Morris-Suzuki
Division of Pacific and Asian History
Research School of Pacific and Asian Studies
Australian National University
Canberra, ACT0200 Australia

Professor Morris Low
School of Languages and Comparative Cultural Studies
University of Queensland
Brisbane, QLD 4072, Australia

Routledge/Asian Studies Association of Australia (ASAA) East Asia Series

1 **Gender in Japan**
   Power and public policy
   Vera Mackie

2 **The Chaebol and Labour in Korea**
   The development of management strategy in Hyundai
   Seung Ho Kwon and Michael O'Donnell

Re-reading the Salaryman in Japan

Crafting masculinities

Romit Dasgupta

LONDON AND NEW YORK

First published 2013
by Routledge
2 Park Square, Milton Park, Abingdon, Oxon OX14 4RN

Simultaneously published in the USA and Canada
by Routledge
711 Third Avenue, New York, NY 10017

Routledge is an imprint of the Taylor & Francis Group, an informa business

British Library Cataloguing in Publication Data
A catalogue record for this book is available from the British Library

Library of Congress Cataloging in Publication Data
Dasgupta, Romit.
Re-reading the salaryman in Japan: crafting masculinities/Romit
Dasgupta.
  Includes bibliographical references and index.
  1. Masculinity–Japan. 2. Corporate culture–Japan. 3. Men–Japan–
  Social conditions. 4. Men–Japan–Identity. I. Title.
  HQ1090.7.J3D37 2012
  305.310952–dc23   2012006765

ISBN: 978-0-415-74878-0 (pbk)
ISBN: 978-0-415-68328-9 (hbk)
ISBN: 978-0-203-10208-4 (ebk)

Typeset in Times New Roman
by Wearset Ltd, Boldon, Tyne and Wear

First issued in paperback in 2013

In memory of Professor Kamehata Yoshihiko, without whose support and encouragement this book would not have been possible, but who sadly passed away shortly before its publication.

Contents

Acknowledgements

This book is the culmination of a long, stop-start process, which often felt like it was more 'stop' than 'start'! It has taken over six years between the end of the doctoral research that provided the springboard for this book, and its final publication. Along the way, the book has had a rich and varied journey. It was drafted, written, and proof-read in a variety of sometimes quite unusual settings – university offices and libraries in Australia, Japan, and Singapore; cafes and hotels in various cities across Australia, Asia, and Europe; and at numerous airports around the world and on far too many long-distance airline flights! Most memorable of all, a little town in the mountains of northern Vietnam will forever remain etched in my mindscape, as that is where I started on what eventually took shape as the conclusion to this book.

Given the book's long journey over the years, innumerable individuals in different places contributed to its 'crafting' through multiple kindnesses. First, my biggest thanks go to Vera Mackie and Ines Tyson who guided me through the PhD research, and continued to offer me valuable support, advice, and friendship through subsequent years. In particular, without Vera's constant encouragement and affirmation, this book may well have not happened! I would also like to acknowledge the support of many other individuals, too numerous to name, in both Australia and Japan, whose support was invaluable during the early PhD stages of the research – in particular Yasuo Takao in Australia, and Kamehata Yoshihiko, Yamauchi Ryôji, and my close friend Aoki Norihiko and his family in Japan.

I also wish to thank my friends and colleagues at the University of Western Australia (UWA), where I was based for most of the time I was writing this book. Once again, there are so many individuals whose kindnesses I received, that it would be next to impossible to name everyone. However, I would especially like to mention my colleagues in the Discipline of Asian Studies: in particular, David Bourchier, Laura Dales, Stephen Dobbs, Karen Eichorn, Miho Masel, Tomoko Nakamatsu, Lyn Parker, Sachiko Sone, Kyu Shin, Gary Sigley, Leonie Stickland, and Wang Yi. I also wish to thank Susan Takao of UWA's Institute of Advanced Studies for her ongoing encouragement and support. Others at UWA whose friendship and support I have valued over the years include, Kirsten Abe, Andrea Emberly, Aaron Hales, Cecilia Leong-Salobir, and most recently, Abidin Mısırlı, Celeste Rodriguez-Luoro, and Anneli Strutt (who also helped with the index for this book). Elsewhere in Australia, I would like to thank the following individuals for their support and encouragement: Chilla Bulbeck, Raewyn Connell, Morris Low, Mark McLelland, Tessa Morris-Suzuki, Judith Snodgrass, among others. A special mention also needs to be made of David Chapman, Mark Pendleton, and Katsuhiko Suganuma – we share the common bond of being Vera's former PhD students, who all benefitted from her guidance and friendship. Mark also provided invaluable assistance towards the index, at a time when he himself was incredibly busy, finishing his thesis and in the midst of relocating countries and jobs.

In 2007, I spent one year on a Visiting Fellowship in the Department of Japanese Studies at the National University of Singapore, during the early writing stages of the book. The friendships formed there have continued long after the completion of the fellowship. I would especially like to thank all the colleagues I worked with during my time at NUS: in particular, Timothy Amos, Simon Avenell, Scot Hislop, Beng Choo Lim, Emi Morita, and Hendrik Meyer-Ohle. Others in Singapore whose support and friendship was invaluable include, Taberez Ahmed Neyazi (now at Kyoto University), Noor Abdul Rahman, Jiang Na (now in Hong Kong), Jean Bernard Sampson, and especially Chang Yau (CY) Hoon (previously at UWA, now at Singapore Management University). A special thanks also to Aki Honda (my good friend Tim Amos' partner); Aki kindly volunteered to design the book's very eye-catching cover.

In Japan, in addition to those individuals named previously, I am grateful for the support of the following individuals: Greg Dvorak, Toshiko Ellis, Alisa Freedman (who is at Oregon University, but spends her summers in Japan), Joel Mathews (previously at Kobe University, now at New York University), Osaka Eiko, Rio Otomo, James Roberson, Glenda Roberts, and Taga Futoshi. Also, although they cannot be named individually, I will always be grateful to the young men of the two organizations I have called 'Northern Print' and 'Northern Energy' in this book – it is their stories, and the friendships formed through my interactions with them, all those years ago, that has made this book possible.

A special mention needs to be made for all those involved in the editorial and production process over the months and years leading up to the book's birth: in particular, the series editors for the Routledge/Asian Studies of Australia East Asia Series, Morris Low and Tessa Morris-Suzuki; the anonymous reviewers approached by the publisher, for their very encouraging and helpful feedback on the initial draft; and Stephanie Rogers, Hannah Mack and their fantastic (and patient!) editorial and production team at Routledge. Also, as mentioned above, my friends, Aki Honda, Mark Pendleton, and Anneli Strutt provided valuable support with the book's indexing and cover-design.

Finally, my deepest appreciation goes to my family – my parents, and my brother and his family in the United States – for their constant support, patience, and unflagging (but perhaps misguided) faith in my writing ability.

Permissions acknowledgements

Some of the discussion in this book has previously been published either as academic journal articles, or as chapters in edited books. I wish to acknowledge these prior publications, and would like to thank their respective publishers for kindly allowing me to draw on these works for this book:

Journal articles

* 'Performing Masculinities? The Salaryman at Work and Play', *Japanese Studies, 20(2), 2000: 189–200; copyright © Japanese Studies Association of Australia. Reprinted with permission of Taylor & Francis Ltd.* www.tandfonline.com on behalf of Japanese Studies Association of Australia.
* 'Emotional Spaces and Places of Salaryman Anxiety in *Tokyo Sonata', Japanese Studies, 31(3), 2011: 373–386; copyright © Japanese Studies Association of Australia. Reprinted with permission of Taylor & Francis Ltd.* www.tandfonline.com on behalf of Japanese Studies Association of Australia.
* 'The "Lost Decade" of the 1990s and Shifting Masculinities in Japan', *Culture, Society and Masculinity,* 1(1), 2009: 79–95.

Book chapters

* 'Creating Corporate Warriors: The "Salaryman" and Masculinity in Japan', in Kam Louie and Morris Low (eds) *Asian Masculinities: The Meaning and Practice of Manhood in China and Japan*, London: RoutledgeCurzon, 2003, pp, 118–134.
* 'Cybermasculinities: Masculine Identity and the Internet in Japan', in Nanette Gottlieb and Mark McLelland (eds) Japanese Cybercultures, London: Routledge, 2003, pp. 109–125.
* 'Salarymen Doing Straight: Heterosexual Men and the Dynamics of Gender Conformity', in Mark McLelland and Romit Dasgupta (eds) Genders, Transgenders, and Sexualities in Japan, London: Routledge, 2005, pp. 168–182.

Note on Japanese names

In most cases, Japanese names, including names of authors of works published in Japanese, appear in this book in Japanese order – surname followed by personal name. However, in a couple of instances names of authors with Japanese names writing in English follow the English-language naming order – personal name followed by surname (for example, Kaori Okano, rather than Okano Kaori).

Macrons are used to indicate extended vowels, except in the case of place names commonly known in English (for example, Tokyo, rather than Tôkyô), and Japanese names of authors writing in English, who do not themselves indicate extended vowels in their names with a macron.

1 Introduction

Salarymen in the 'Lost Decade'

The 'JTB-Man'

In October 2007 I was at Narita Airport in Tokyo, at the end of a trip to Japan. Needing to buy a magazine, I stopped by the magazine stand near the departure gate. In addition to regular magazines, newspapers, and daily necessities, the shop also had on offer a range of touristy souvenirs. Along with the expected Hello Kitty mobile phone straps and inexpensive lacquer chopsticks-type kitsch was a selection of pocket-sized illustrated guidebooks published by the national tourism authority, the Japan Travel Bureau (JTB). Judging from the titles, these guides seemed designed to 'explain' Japan to first-time visitors – hence such titles as *Festivals of Japan*, *Eating in Japan*, and *Living Japanese Style*. Given the publisher and the series they were being published under, these publications were not particularly surprising. However, one guidebook did stand out a little from the others; it was called *'Salaryman' in Japan*.

At one level, the presence of such a title alongside works introducing Japanese festivals and traditions was not wholly unsurprising. After all, societies and nations come to be associated with particular tropes in the global imagination. In the case of Japan, the figure of the besuited urban, white-collar office worker/business executive 'salaryman' (or, in Japanese, *sarariiman*)[1] came to be associated with Japan's transformation from a war-devastated society in the years following defeat during World War Two to the world's second largest economy within a period of three decades. Typically the salaryman would be a middle-class, university-educated middle-aged man, with a dependent wife and children to support, working for an organization offering such benefits as secure lifetime employment guarantee for permanent employees, and a promotions and salary scale linked to seniority. He would spend long hours commuting to the office in a jam-packed train, from a house or apartment in a public housing estate in the suburbs. After spending the day toiling away at his desk, or visiting customers and suppliers on sales rounds, the salaryman would stop by a Japanese-style *izakaya* bar for a couple of drinks with colleagues, before returning to his home in the suburbs long after his children have gone to bed. This was a figure who came to be regarded as something of an 'everyman' of Japan's postwar social landscape, the 'corporate soldier' (*kigyō senshi*) who exerted a powerful influence on imaginings of Japan, both within the country and outside of it. Indeed, the ubiquitous salaryman came to signify both Japanese masculinity and Japanese corporate culture. In this sense, the salaryman embodied 'the archetypal citizen ... [someone who] is a male, heterosexual, able-bodied, fertile, white-collar worker' (Mackie 2002: 203). In other words, in the sociocultural imaginary of postwar Japan, the salaryman was the quintessential male *shakaijin* (literally 'social being', but more generally, a 'socially responsible' adult).

This seemingly powerful presence of the salaryman finds expression in the *Illustrated 'Salaryman' in Japan* guidebook mentioned above. The guide covers virtually every aspect of the salaryman's lifestyle. These include his daily schedule – how he commutes to work, what he reads while commuting, morning calisthenics when he arrives at work, what he eats for lunch, working overtime, and his after-work nightlife. The reader is enlightened about his leisure activities and pastimes, what he does on seasonal holidays, his conduct when attending weddings or funerals, what constitutes required reading for the salaryman, right through to the various health problems that plague him (headaches from hangovers and a weakened liver from drinking too much, haemorrhoids and stiff shoulders from sitting at his desk for too long, stomach ulcers from irregular diet and stress) (Japan Tourist Bureau (JTB) 2006: passim). Even the woman the salaryman is supposed to marry is depicted in some detail – ideally a so-called 'OL' (Office Lady) clerical/administrative staff, who, according to the stereotype, upon marriage to the salaryman, would quit work to become a full-time homemaker.

The packaging of the salaryman in this way points to the culturally iconic position occupied by him (and for that matter, the 'OL' he is supposed to marry). The Foreword to the volume highlights to readers that it 'is a historical fact that salarymen and the companies they work for have been the driving force behind the economic rise of postwar Japan'. Accordingly, it entreats readers who are 'tired of fragmentary or over intellectual reports of Japanese business ... [to] take a stimulating journey into the practical workaday world of the salaryman – a journey guaranteed to deepen your understanding and enjoyment of Japan' (JTB 2006: Foreword). Moreover, the description in the volume comes across as a deliberately crafted projection of the salaryman as being the embodiment of 'Japanese culture', in much the same way that the other cultural icons in the series (traditional food, architecture, the ancient imperial capital of Kyoto, etc.) are presented. This is reflected in the Afterword accompanying the guide, where the authors declare that 'the "salaryman society" is a realm possessing its own special rules and ethics, much like the worlds of politics or student life in Japan' (JTB 2006: 186). Attempting to 'explain why such a diverse range of people can be grouped together under the "salaryman spirit" heading' we are told is futile. Rather, ultimately, 'the old standby – "oriental magic" – may have something to do with it after all' (187).

Yet, we are talking about the *2006* edition of the guidebook, not 1986 or 1976. In the first decades of the twenty-first century, the discourse one is more likely to encounter, in the media or in the course of conversations with friends and acquaintances, rather than being about the 'oriental magic' of the 'salaryman spirit' is more than likely to be about Japan as an increasingly traumatized society characterized by a widening class divide (*kaksusa shakai*) and socially disadvantaged groups like long-term *furiitâ*, casual/temporary workers with little chance of finding permanent work, or NEET ('Not in Employment, Education or Training) or *hikikomori* ('socially withdrawn') youth with little hope of a non-dysfunctional future (see Allison 2009). Indeed, a casual observation of the media and social landscape may initially suggest that the suit-clad salaryman is no longer the embodiment of the 'archetypal' male citizen of modern Japan, an impression aptly captured by the title of a 2008 *Economist* feature on the changing corporate and social landscape in Japan – 'Sayonara, Salaryman' (*The Economist*, 5–11 January 2008: 56–58). Rather, thanks to the diffusion of the 'soft power' of Japan's popular culture, the signifier of Japanese masculinity is more likely to be the 'funky' commodified youth masculinity exemplified by the male stars of Japan's pop idol industry, or the 'feminized' masculinity of the so-called 'herbivorous men' (*sôshokukei-danshi*), or even the *otaku* 'geek cool' associated with visual culture products like *anime* and computer graphics, than the middle-aged (or even young), besuited salaryman. No doubt, the far-reaching economic, socio-cultural, and even political shifts that Japan has undergone since the 'Bubble Economy' boom of the 1980s and the subsequent recession plagued 'Lost Decade' of the 1990s and 2000s have undeniably had major repercussions for the salaryman and his position within Japanese society. Many of the earlier assumptions associated with the salaryman – the guarantee of employment for life, promotion tied to length of employment rather than merit, and a paternalistic regard for the employee, for instance – became increasingly redundant as a consequence of the corporate downsizings and restructurings of the post-Bubble years. Replacing the older model of the salaryman situated within its framework of corporate paternalism has been the emergence of a 'new' discourse of the salaryman, premised on significantly different corporate and life expectations (see Taga 2011b). This new discourse draws upon a globalized Euro-American-inspired neo-liberal corporate ideology, one emphasizing efficiency, individual ability, and performance over the group (and indeed, over the corporation). This newer style of corporate masculinity stands in marked contrast to the company-centred hard-working but not necessarily 'efficient' salaryman represented in the JTB guide described above.

An exemplar of this newer style of corporate masculinity would be an individual like Carlos Ghosn, the Brazilian born CEO of Nissan and Renault. Ghosn, after being appointed to the helm of automobile manufacturer Nissan in the early 2000s, was credited with turning around the flagging fortunes of the organization over a surprisingly short time-span, thanks to his introduction of a radically new, individual style of corporate leadership, quite different to earlier paradigms of Japanese corporate leadership (Nathan 2004: 84–98). As a consequence of the apparent 'miracle' he generated at Nissan, Ghosn became both a role model for a new style of management, and a popular culture icon – his autobiography was a bestseller, and he even became the hero of a popular *manga* revolving around his exploits. A more controversial (and notorious) exemplar of this new style of corporate masculinity in the early 2000s was the disgraced e-business entrepreneur Takafumi Horie, former CEO of the internet company Livedoor Corporation. Horie's meteoric rise to prominence, and his equally dramatic fall following his arrest, and subsequent conviction, on grounds of financial fraud, made him the centre of widespread public and media attention. Much of this attention revolved around Horie's unconventional business practices as well as his flamboyant personality and uniquely individual style of self-presentation. The image he projected (and continues to project despite his fall from grace) is quite contrary to the image of the conventional salaryman-style corporate executive.[2] Given such radically different projections of corporate identity, it is no surprise that the media discourse – particularly outside of Japan – about the 'death of the salaryman' seems convincing.

Yet, ironically, Carlos Ghosn or Takafumi Horie notwithstanding, the reality at the start of the second decade of the twenty-first century is that the salaryman continues to be pivotal to the ways in which Japanese corporate culture, Japanese masculinity, and indeed Japanese national identity continue to be imagined and framed. One of the most popular shows on the national broadcast network NHK in the mid- to late 2000s, for instance, was the series *Sarariiman Neo*, which took the salaryman and salaryman culture as an object of comical parody and even derision. Underlying the unexpected popularity of this series was perhaps its ability to effectively tap into feelings of (often uncomfortable) identification with the salaryman lifestyle which many in Japan still feel. A similar sense of simultaneous identification/parody also comes through, for instance, in the popularity of the J-Pop/hip-hop group Ketsumeishi's 2010 single, *Tatakae! Sarariiman* ('Fight! Salaryman'),[3] or in the continuing success of bestselling salaryman *manga* comics like *Sarariiman Kintarō* and *Shima Kôsaku*, which have been around since the 1980s and 1990s (see Matanle *et al.* 2008). Indeed, the salaryman's very visible presence in popular culture spaces as varied as advertising, television dramas, and *manga* attests to the salaryman's continuing presence in the collective national imaginary.

Even within the context of corporate culture, despite the media hype about the salaryman being an anachronism from the past, research evidence seems to point to, if anything, important continuities with the past. Peter Matanle, in discussing the shifts in employment patterns, points out that while changes have quite definitely occurred in many of the workplace institutions and practices, at the core the *ideology* of lifetime employment continues to underpin Japanese corporate culture (Matanle 2006; see also Inagami and Whittaker 2005). In a similar vein, drawing upon research conducted with mid-level managers across a number of large-scale organizations, McCann *et al.* (2006) note that despite the uncertainties and pressures faced by mid-level managers, the 'emphasis placed on seniority, loyalty and internal skills development in promotion decision-making remain largely unchanged' (100). Quite clearly then, there seem to be contradictory pressures and pulls at work in relation to discourses about the salaryman in contemporary Japan. On the one hand, what it means to be a sala-ryman in twenty-first-century Japan is seemingly quite different to what being a salaryman might have meant twenty, thirty, or fifty years ago. At the same time, it would appear that certain underpinnings and assumptions continue to inform and underpin the discourse surrounding the salaryman (see Taga 2011b).

The 'man' in 'salaryman'

There is a substantial body of academic and non-academic literature, in both Japanese and English, dealing with various aspects of the salaryman – as an indi-cation a search on the English and Japanese engines of *Google* for the term 'sal-aryman' (and 'sarariiman' in Japanese) generated close to 400,000 hits in English and over *14 million* in Japanese. Given this continued visibility of the salaryman in imaginings of post-World War Two (hereafter 'postwar') Japan, it is no surprise that over the years a not insubstantial body of popular and aca-demic literature has emerged around the salaryman and all that he signified (see e.g. Hazama 1996; Takeuchi 1997; Umezawa 1997; Tanaka and Nakamura 1999; Okamoto and Sasano 2001; Iwase 2006; Taga 2011d). Moreover, the sala-ryman was a visible presence in some of the early postwar studies of Japan which were to have an impact on academic and research circles in anglophone countries. These included works such as Ezra Vogel's *Japan's New Middle Class*, originally published in 1963, and Ronald Dore's *City Life in Japan*, originally published in 1958, which went on to become 'classics' within the emerging field of 'Japan studies' in the West. Subsequent works, including those by Plath (1964, 1983a), Ballon (1969), Rohlen (1974), Clark (1979), van Hel-voort (1979), Fruin (1978), Hamabata (1990), Allison (1994), Beck and Beck (1994), Ogasawara (1998), Sakai (2000), Matanle and Lunsing (2006), and Sedgwick (2007), have been concerned in one way or another with the salaryman.

However, only recently has the 'man' in salaryman started to come under some sort of tentative scrutiny. In other words, the salaryman as a *gendered* con-struct remained outside the orbit of scrutiny for many decades.[4] This is ironic, given that one of the core underpinnings of the discourse around the salaryman has been the equation of work with masculinity. Specifically, as reflected in the JTB guide mentioned in the opening pages of this chapter, the notion of being the *daikokubashira* (literally, 'the central supporting pillar'), the primary income provider for a dependent wife and family, was axiomatic to the salaryman dis-course.[5] Furthermore, despite all the apparent modifications to the contours of the salaryman discourse in the wake of the economic slowdown and restructur-ings since the 1990s, this core underpinning – work defining the salary*man* – appears to be as firmly entrenched as in the past.

A primary reason as to why the salaryman and all that he stands for had not been adequately addressed through the prism of gender has to do with the fact that until recently in Japan (as in other countries) the concept of 'men' as a category needing to be teased out and problematized was not given serious consideration.

'Men' were the default against which all other 'variants' – women, transgender persons, non-heterosexual men – were measured. Given the salaryman's position as a metonym for all Japanese men, the extension of the 'men as default' logic meant that the salaryman was studied from virtually every angle conceivable (class, income, age, lifestyle patterns, work habits, consumption patterns, etc.) save from the angle of his gender.

This theoretical blindness towards men and 'masculinity' started to be gradually remedied from the 1990s onward, both in the West and in Japan. There were several factors at work here. First, a growing body of academic and non-academic work, both in anglophone and European countries, as well as in Japan, interrogating and problematizing 'masculinity' as a construct, started to become visible.[6] Many of these works, both in the West and in Japan, emerged from, or were influenced by critiques of patriarchy by feminist scholars in the 1960s and 1970s (see, e.g. Brod 1987; Connell 1987, 1995; Kaufman 1987; Hearn and Morgan 1990; Morgan 1992; Itô 1993, 1996; Brod and Kaufman 1994; Inoue *et al.* 1995). Many of these were also influenced by the theoretical and empirical work carried out in the emerging field of lesbian and gay studies, and subsequently queer theory, particularly in relation to the pivotal role of homophobia and heterosexism in informing dominant gender ideologies (see Sedgwick 1985; Edwards 1990; Kimmel 1994; Connell 1995, 2000; D'Emilio 1997; Inoue *et al.* 1995: 235–262). What these studies had in common was their highlighting of the fact that masculinity, rather than being a biological given, constant over time and space, 'is historical ... created in culture ... [and] means different things at different times to different people' (Kimmel 1994: 120). Moreover, while many of these early works fully acknowledged the stake in patriarchy that many men have, they also drew attention to the fact that different men had differing degrees of access to the dividends of patriarchal power. Thus, this growing body of research and theorizing in the late 1980s and the 1990s brought to attention the fact that we need to recognize the plurality and diversity in men's lives and experiences – the existence of masculin*ities* in the plural, rather than a singular masculinity extending across all men, throughout the globe.

In the context of Japan, these theoretical and academic framings of masculinity cross-fertilized with indigenous scholarship to define the shaping of a body of research which came to be referred to collectively as '*danseigaku*' (literally, 'the study of men/males').[7] There is now a reasonable body of academic and semi-academic literature focusing on the construction and interrogation of masculinities (Itô 1993, 1996; Inoue *et al.* 1995; Toyoda 1997; Asai *et al.* 2001; Taga 2001, 2006a, 2011d; Kaizuma 2004; Abe *et al.* 2006; Miyadai *et al.* 2009).[8] At the same time, English-language studies on masculinities in Japan have also gained visibility since the early 2000s. These cover works that have a historical focus (Karlin 2002), as well as works on more contemporary masculinities, including edited collections (Louie and Low 2003; Roberson and Suzuki 2003b; McLelland and Dasgupta 2005; Frühstück and Walthall 2011b), monographs (Castro-Vázquez 2007; LeBlanc 2010), journal articles (Dasgupta 2000, 2009, 2010; Karlin 2002; Castro-Vázquez and Kishi 2003; Roberson 2005; Matanale *et al.* 2008), and PhD theses (Dasgupta 2005a; Hidaka 2006; Gagné 2010). Some of these works touch on the salaryman from an angle of gender and sexuality (e.g. Dasgupta 2000, 2003a, 2003b, 2005a, 2005b; McLelland 2005; Roberson 2005; Hidaka 2006; Matanle *et al.* 2008; Gagné 2010). However, to date, with the exception of Hidaka's ethnographically rich study of three generations of salarymen (Hidaka 2010), there has been no monograph-length published work looking at the salaryman through the lens of masculinity.

The salaryman and 'hegemonic masculinity'

In this regard, this book is both situated within and fills some of the gaps in this growing body of literature addressing and problematizing assumptions about masculinity. It looks at the contradictions of being a salaryman, through the articulated lived experiences of individuals caught up in the cross-currents of some of the changes in post-Bubble Japan, referred to earlier. Specifically, it focuses on the ways that individuals engage with these shifts as salary*men* – in other words, highlighting the salaryman as a gendered construct. In unpacking the 'man' component of 'salaryman' in this book, I deploy the theoretical construct of *hegemonic masculinity*. This is a concept, drawing upon Gramsci's conceptualization of 'hegemony' that is associated with the Australian sociologist Raewyn Connell (Connell 1987, 1995; Connell and Messerschmidt 2005). Hegemony, as Connell highlights, is 'a social ascendancy achieved in a play of social forces that extends beyond contests of brute force into the organization of private life and cultural processes' (Connell 1987: 184). Importantly, this ascendancy, 'embedded in religious doctrine and practice, mass media content, wage structures, the design of housing, welfare/taxation evaluation and so forth' (184), is achieved not so much through blatant domination and force, but rather in more subtle ways through interlaced ideologies and discourses circulating in society.[9] In this regard it is the very *ordinariness* of hegemony, its unproblematic, 'common-sense'-type circulation in discourse that underpins its efficacy and extent.

While Connell's early works on hegemony were in relation to class, it is her theorization in the context of gender, in particular masculinity, that has been especially influential (see Wedgwood 2009). It gained wide currency following the publication of her ground-breaking *Gender and Power* in 1987. The concept has since been elaborated on and deployed extensively, sometimes in quite loose and opportunistic ways (Connell and Messerschmidt 2005; Wedgwood 2009: 337). Nevertheless, the varied uses and abuses notwithstanding, hegemonic masculinity continues to be an important analytical tool.

Masculinity, as highlighted above, rather than being a fixed, biologically determined essence, is constructed, shaped, 'crafted' in response to socio-cultural, economic, political, and other conditions. Furthermore, rather than a singular form of masculinity, just one way of 'being a man', there are myriad masculini*ties*, at any one time, both within society *and* within an individual. These are constructed, represented, talked about, written about, given shape, embodied by individuals, as discourses of masculinity in society. These various masculinities do not just 'sit side-by-side like dishes on a smorgasbord' (Connell 2000: 10). Rather, there are hierarchies of power defining the relationships between these various masculinities. Of the various masculinities the discourse of masculinity that has the greatest ideological power and hold may be thought of as the *hegemonic* form of masculinity (Connell and Messerschmidt 2005: 832). The hegemonic form may be conceived of as a cultural 'ideal' or 'blueprint' which, by and large, cannot be perfectly attained by most men. As Connell highlights, it need not be the most common form, nor the 'most comfortable' (Connell 2000: 11; Connell and Messerschmidt 2005: 832). However, it is normative in that it does 'exert a powerful and often unconscious presence' (Kaufman 1994: 144) in the lives of men (and others).

Moreover, what hegemonic masculinity does have in its favour is power and ascendancy achieved 'through culture, institutions, and persuasion' (Connell and Messerschmidt 2005: 832). As Demetrakis Demetriou in his discussion of Connell's work highlights, this is a power and ascendancy over *both* femininity, through what he labels 'external hegemony', *and* over other forms of masculinity through 'internal hegemony' (Demetriou 2001). Drawing upon Gramsci's theorization of a 'historic bloc' (in the context of class), Demetriou argues that rather than outright domination or suppression, the more significant process at work is that of incorporation and appropriation of selective aspects of other masculinities. This 'internal hegemony' interaction between the hegemonic and non-hegemonic forms comprises what, drawing upon Gramsci's notion of a 'historic bloc', he terms a 'hybrid bloc' (Demetriou 2001: 345–348). I suggest that in addition to the dynamics of appropriation and incorporation Demetriou identifies, the hybrid bloc may also be shaped by dynamics of resistance, subversion, and playful engagement vis-à-vis the discourse of hegemonic masculinity.

Thus, it is through these 'external' *and* 'internal' engagements that hegemonic masculinity is constantly 'crafted' and 're-crafted', both at the 'macro' societal level and at the level of the individual male. This process of 'crafting' follows on from Dorinne Kondo's deployment of the term in *Crafting Selves*, her early 1990s study of intersections between work, community, and self in a Tokyo neighbourhood. Explaining her choice of title, Kondo noted that 'identity is not a static *object*, but a creative *process*; hence craft*ing* selves is an ongoing – indeed lifelong – process' (Kondo 1990: 48; italics in original). Accordingly, I argue that identity built up around being gendered as 'masculine' and/or 'male' is similarly a constantly shifting, re-shaping, re-enacting process occurring at the intersections of individual agency and discourses and ideologies circulating through society. This includes the discourse and ideology of 'hegemonic masculinity', at any given point in time – as suggested by Demetriou's theorization, 'hegemonic masculinity' itself is an ongoing 'crafting' *process*, in turn, part of an overall 'gender *project*' (Connell 2002: 81; italics added).

In the case of Japan, the discourse of masculinity within which the salaryman is situated could be regarded as having been the hegemonic form of masculinity for much of the postwar period. Salaryman masculinity was quite clearly the hegemonic form of masculinity during the glory years of the Japanese economy from the 1960s through the 1980s. Moreover, I contend that despite the apparent unravelling of this discourse of masculinity in the wake of the 'Lost Decade' of the 1990s, at the core, the basic assumptions around which the discourse of salaryman masculinity emerged, continue to be *ideologically* hegemonic in contemporary Japan. Despite the fact that only a limited number of Japanese men have ever fallen within the strictest definitional parameters of the term, the *ideology* (of gender, of class, of sexuality, indeed of *citizenship*) embodied in the salaryman and the discourse built around him has, over the postwar era, been far more extensive. The core of this ideology was, and continues to be, the equation of masculinity with the public work sphere and what Connell and Messerschmidt (2005: 848) term 'emphasized' femininity with the private, household sphere. Moreover, within this ideological framework, the two sides of the binary get linked together through the institution of publicly acknowledged and sanctioned heterosexual marriage. The discourse built around the salaryman represented, in a sense, the visibly hegemonic apex of these ideological expectations.

In light of the above, this book explores the ways in which the dynamics through which the discourse of masculinity embodied by the salaryman became the hegemonic form of masculinity in Japan over the postwar decades, and the ways in which these dynamics of engagement between hegemonic and non-hegemonic forms of masculinity have continued to operate into the present. The book explores these dynamics at both the 'macro' societal level, and at the 'micro' level of the individual. The former level of analysis situates the emergence of the discourse of salaryman masculinity (and the gender ideology underpinning it) within the context of Japan's project of industrial-capitalist modernization and nation building embarked upon in the final decades of the nineteenth century, and continued over the course of the twentieth century, and into the twenty-first century.

The second level of analysis explores these dynamics of the 'crafting' of hegemonic masculinity at the level of the individual. These engagements with the expectations of hegemonic masculinity occur as he moves through different 'life-stages' within his life-course, or, within what Roberson refers to as a 'life-path' (Roberson 1998). Or expressed in another way, these engagements characterize the individual's journey through different *masculinities* – in the playground as a primary schoolboy, as a junior high school student working out the complexities of 'first love', as a university student relatively free of demands of social responsibility, as a new *shakaijin*, who as a 'socially responsible' adult now needs to negotiate with the requirements of salaryman masculinity, as a married salaryman with the responsibility of being a husband and father, and as a retired 'honorary' *shakaijin*. Even if the 'life-path' taken follows a completely different trajectory – say, if he drops out of school and ends up far from the hegemonic 'ideal' (as a middle-aged unmarried day labourer, for instance) – this engagement with the expectations of hegemonic masculinity will be just as relevant.

Moreover, while these engagements occur over the entire 'life-path', they are arguably the most pronounced (and open to contestation) during the liminal years and months when the individual male is journeying through a sort of ambivalent 'no-man's land' between clearly demarcated life-path episodes (say, between 'un-sexual' child and 'sexual' adolescent, or socially insignificant youth/student and socially responsible *shakaijin*). It is during these periods of transition that the ambiguities, contradictions, and fissures between these various discourses of masculinity (including the hegemonic one) are especially pronounced, and hence, more readily prone to being interrogated and teased out. Such journeys through zones of transition are significant, both at the 'micro'level of the individual, and in terms of the wider socio-historical implications, at any point in time, since it is through these ongoing shifts and negotiations at both levels that the contours of hegemonic masculinity itself are 'crafted' and 're-crafted'.

In this book, I focus in particular on the first months and years following entry into the workforce, when the individual male is negotiating his transition to the status of a responsible adult, *shakaijin*. The discussion draws upon intensive interviews carried out with young male private sector employees in Japan. It explores the ways in which these young men, in passing through this threshold into adulthood, negotiated with the ideological expectations of salaryman masculinity, vis-à-vis their own masculine identities, in relation to work practices, consumer habits, lifestyles, articulations of sexuality, and imaginings of their future plans and dreams.

Millennial salaryman masculinity

The conversations with these young salarymen occurred at a point in recent Japanese history when the tensions between the expectations of the 'older', more conventional discourse of salaryman masculinity (as signified by the JTB guide salaryman) and the emerging new realities of being a salaryman in the leaner, economic rationalist environment of new millennium Japan were perhaps at their most acute. These were the closing years of the 1990s, just before the dawn of the new century. Historians of the future may well assess the 1990s as one of *the* watershed decades in Japan's trajectory of capitalist modernization and postmodernity. Indeed, there is already an emerging body of literature addressing the significance of the shifts and upheavals that occurred during these years (McCormack 1998; Iida 2000, 2002: 209–258; Yoshikawa 2002; Nathan 2004; Leheny 2006; Shimokawa 2006; Yoda and Harootunian 2006). What comes across in these various discussions is the sense of collective anxiety, indeed crisis, characterizing this decade. This was in stark contrast to the heady optimism of the Bubble Economy boom years of the 1980s, when it seemed that Japan had finally attained the socio-economic affluence and the accompanying international respect (however grudging) it had been striving for ever since the 1870s, when the power elites of the new Meiji regime embarked upon their ambitious project of nation building and modernization. Accordingly, during the 1980s the public discourse, both within Japan and, importantly, the discourse about Japan in the international press, had been all about the apparent collective confidence, bordering on bravado and arrogance, generated by affluence.

This Bubble-era confidence manifested itself in such phenomena as the snapping up of prime real estate in locations such as Hawaii and Australia, the purchase of major works of European art by Japanese buyers, the acquisition of iconic Western corporations, and a culture of almost frenzied conspicuous consumption. Japanese corporations were an integral component of this boom – by the late 1980s the ten largest banks and four largest security companies in the world were Japanese, and the Tokyo Stock Exchange was bigger than New York's (Nathan 2004: 17, 18; also Katz 1998: 7–9). Thus, the widely held perception across the globe at the time was that Japanese corporations (and by extension, all of Japan) must be doing something right, and hence there were lessons for the rest of the world. This 'learn from Japan' thinking, particularly pronounced in the area of management and organizational studies, was reflected in titles of works such as Ezra Vogel's 1979 *Japan as Number One* (with the subtitle, *Lessons for America*) and William Ouchi's 1981 *Theory Z* (with a subtitle along the same lines as Vogel's work: *How American Business Can Meet the Japanese Challenge*). The Japanese salaryman, as the basic building block of this seemingly invincible corporate culture, was regarded with a mixture of awe and suspicion in contemporary Western representations – the characterization of Japanese business executives in Michael Crichton's 1992 novel *Rising Sun* (and in its subsequent film adaptation) being one such example. Significantly, these years coincided with a seeming decline in the economic and geopolitical strength of the United States, in the wake of its debacle in Vietnam in the mid-1970s, and against a backdrop of a burgeoning trade deficit (particularly with Japan) and myriad domestic problems.

However, the bursting of the speculation-driven 'bubble' in the early 1990s put the brakes on the growing Japanese confidence of the preceding years, and ushered in the so-called 'Lost Decade' (*ushinawareta jûnen*) recession of corporate bankruptcies and downsizing, growing rates of unemployment (particularly among youth), a lack-lustre politics seemingly mired in indecision and bickering, and significantly, a growing national psycho-cultural despondency that stood in stark contrast to the collective smug self-satisfaction of the 1980s (see Iwabuchi 2008: 547, 548). This was a psycho-cultural despondency that was set against an international backdrop of, one the one hand, declining Japanese influence and prestige, and on the other, a resurgence of the United States' economic and geopolitical power in the post-Cold War global order. Arguably, the particular historical significance of the 1990s is underscored the most by this sense of a rupture with the past, a rupture symbolized through the succession of misfortunes and incidents which plagued Japan through these years, and which, at least on the surface, would appear to have little to do with the recession. The second-half of the decade, particularly the final countdown years into the new millennium, seemed to be years when this sense of anxiety reached its nadir, when any hope that the economic and socio-cultural woes plaguing the nation were just a temporary glitch seemed to finally fade (Uno 2008: 14, 15).

Marking these final countdown years were the two particularly traumatic events, both occurring in early 1995, which may well come to signify the collective anxiety of the 1990s (Nakanishi 2008). The first was the Hanshin earthquake on 17 January, which caused widespread damage to the area around the city of Kobe, and claimed over 5,000 lives. The second, and arguably the more psycho-culturally chilling event, was the poison gas attack on the Tokyo subway system by the doomsday religious cult Aum Shinrikyô on 20 March that year. Although the death-toll from the Aum incident was nowhere near the scale of fatalities from the Kobe earthquake, it was perhaps far more traumatic, in the sense that it was a carefully planned and executed *domestic* terrorist incident, bringing to the surface the human monsters – what Anne Allison (2006: 76) terms 'millennial monsters' – lurking within Japanese society. Indeed, the final years of the decade were punctuated by a succession of often extremely bizarre and seemingly random acts of crime committed by ostensibly normal, everyday (*futsû*) individuals, often teenagers or young people, who suddenly snapped (*kireru*) and lashed out (Allison 2006: 79, 80).

Such attention-grabbing incidents occurred against a backdrop of a collective anxiety, much of it centred around youth, about the impending social and cultural collapse of Japan. Frenzied media discussions about such social issues as Japan's falling birth rate, the growing visibility of the phenomenon of *enjo kôsai* ('solicited dating', where teenage girls would go on paid 'dates' with much older men), or the growth in the *freeter* ('freelance' temporary/casual workers) sector of the economy due either to the inability of young people to find permanent employment, or (as was often the *perception*) out of choice, all seemed emblematic of this impending social implosion and fragmentation. This collective social anxiety of the late 1990s was compounded by a string of highly publicized financial crises and corporate bankruptcies that occurred in rapid succession. Incidents like the *jûsen* (housing finance cooperative) financial scandal of the mid-1990s or the collapse of seemingly solid financial institutions like Yamaichi Shôken and the Hokkaido Development Bank in the late 1990s seemed to symbolize the tailspin into which corporate Japan appeared to be spiralling (Leheney 2006: 30–34; Yoda 2006: 19, 20). As a consequence, the initial perception in the immediate post-Bubble years, namely that the economic slowdown was merely a temporary aberration, had largely evaporated by the second half of the 1990s.

Viewed through the lens of these successive financial and social crises, these closing years of the twentieth century come across as a period of economic, social and moral disintegration, as popularly reflected in the 'Lost Decade' line of thinking. Moreover, in the wake of the Aum incident, the latter-half of the 1990s also saw increasing state encroachment into the private sphere, a trend that, as was the case with other industrialized nations, further intensified in the post-9/11 world. Legislation on issues ranging from schools' obligations towards symbols of nationalism like the national anthem and the flag, to the tightening of regulations surrounding residents' registration, through to the tightening of laws aimed at organized crime, were reflective of this trend towards greater state regulation and surveillance (Kohso 2006: 420). This dovetailed with the growing visibility and outspokenness of neo-nationalist intellectuals and politicians in the public domain – the charismatic, right-wing governor of Tokyo Ishihara Shintarô and revisionist historians of the Society for the Creation of a New History (*Atarashii Rekishi wo Tsukuru Kai*) being emblematic examples (Nathan 2004: 140–167, 169–202; also McCormack 2000; Rose 2006).

However, at the same time the 1990s may also be conceptualized, not in terms of decay and loss, and increasing social control and policing, but rather in terms of collective reassessment of the preceding half-century and, possibly, even in terms of renewal. In some respects these were years when important socio-cultural changes, in gestation for much of the postwar period, came to the surface and began to be collectively acknowledged in the public sphere. For instance, it was really during the 1990s that social and cultural diversity became visible – indeed in some situations celebrated – in the public arena, far more than had been the case in preceding decades. This diversity was best symbolized through the growing visibility and assertion of their rights by a range of groups in society – ethnic, cultural, and sexual minorities, for instance, as well as a range of citizens' groups and other NGOs and NPOs (see Kingston 2004). It was also a decade when, in the context of post-Cold War global realities, Japan as a nation moved on from its earlier exclusive foreign policy focus on its alliance with the United States, to a growing acknowledgement of Japan as being an integral part of Asia. Part of this 'return to Asia' was no doubt driven by a mercenary economic rationale of needing to tap into growing middle-class consumer markets in East and Southeast Asia. However, another aspect of this shift, notwithstanding the growing loudness of neo-nationalist voices in the public domain, was an acknowledgement of Japan's prewar legacy of aggression and brutality in Asia, and the first tentative steps towards some form of apology and redress for this legacy. One example of this was the emergence of the 'Comfort Women' issue into the public domain during these years, something greatly facilitated through the efforts of various community organizations, in particular a variety of women's groups, in highlighting the issue, and lobbying the state (Mackie 2003: 202–225; also Ueno 2004: 69–72).

Foregrounding many of these changes was the interrogation of aspects of the socio-cultural, political, and economic underpinnings of the postwar Japanese nation-state – the dominance of the political landscape by the Liberal Democratic Party (LDP) which had governed Japan almost continuously over the postwar period, the scandal-prone 'Japan Inc.' partnership between the LDP, big business, and the bureaucracy, an education system stressing conformity and stifling individual creativity, and a public discourse of gender which had simultaneously worked both against women entering into the public/work sphere in a significant way, and men participating more in private/family spaces. It is true that interrogations of these hegemonic ideological pillars of the Japanese state had been in circulation since at least the 1960s – the vocal, anti-establishment student movement of the 1960s being one example of a challenge to the status quo. However, it was really in the 1990s that a combination of factors, including demographic shifts and the emergence of a post-industrial, late capitalist society with more of an emphasis on diversity and individuality, not to mention the fallouts of the corporate downsizings and financial scandals of the post-Bubble years, enabled these underlying interrogations to find expression in the form of specific policies and enunciations. Thus, it was only in the 1990s that, for the first time since the late 1940s, the LDP lost government, albeit for relatively short periods of time. It was also during these years – particularly during periods when a non-LDP politician led the government – that Japan began its first tentative moves towards acknowledging and attempting to redress its prewar legacy of occupation and aggression in Asia (Nathan 2004: 154, 155).

It was also during the 1990s that many of the legislations relating to gender, including gender in the workplace, were introduced – among others, these included the Childcare/Familycare Leave Laws of 1992 and 1999, the 1999 Basic Law for a Gender Equal Society, and strengthening of the Equal Employment Opportunity Law, initially introduced in the mid-1980s (Roberts 2002: 75, 76). Ironically, the introduction of these laws aiming for an ideal of a gender-equal society were set against an on-the-ground reality of female employees being the primary victims of the corporate restructurings and recruitment cutbacks of the 1990s. In a similar vein, while on the one hand workplace pressures to perform became particularly intense for men in corporate Japan (including in the public sector), the 1990s was also the decade when government policy started targeting men to take a more active role in parenting and in family life – the 1995 Angel Plan, and modifications to childcare leave laws to include fathers being two such examples (Roberts 2002). Indeed, it was during the 1990s that men's groups were established in various regions throughout the country, and sought to draw attention to the ways in which men – in particular men falling within the rubric of the salaryman – were also victims of the patriarchal industrial-capitalist gender ideology of the postwar Japanese state. Significantly, it was the writings of academics and activists associated with some of these groups – Itô Kimio, Nakamura Tadashi, Nakamura Akira, Toyoda Masayoshi, and Taga Futoshi, for instance – that shaped the emergent body of scholarship of *danseigaku* (Men's/Masculinities Studies) referred to earlier in this chapter.

What emerges from the discussion in the preceding paragraphs then is the complexity of the various cross-currents at work in Japanese society during these years leading up to and immediately following the new millennium. Hence, what is required is a more nuanced evaluation of the 1990s than a simplistic judgement of the decade as a sudden reversal of direction in Japan's postwar trajectory of industrialization and post-industrialization. The reality was one where often seemingly positive and negative, progressive and regressive socio-economic, political, and cultural dynamics were at work in tandem – an example being the loss of some of the gains made by women in the workforce over earlier decades as a consequence of the economic recession, counterpoised against some of the seemingly progressive gender-related legislation enacted during the same period. Moreover, as Tomiko Yoda argues in her discussion of the 1990s, the decade cannot be regarded in isolation, as some kind of disjointed aberration or one-off blip in Japan's historical trajectory (Yoda 2006: 16, 17). Rather, at the very least, the 1990s (and the first years of the new millennium) need to be viewed as an integral part of Japan's overall historical processes of industrialization and post-industrialization set in motion in the late nineteenth century and continuing into the present, processes which in turn are intertwined with twentieth- and twenty-first-century discourses of modernity and postmodernity. Yoda stresses the fact that only by 'examining the decade in relation to the broader trends of globalization and postmodernization that followed the completion of Japan's postwar economic modernization' are we able to 'understand the profound sense of not only economic but also sociocultural disturbances in Japan with which the decade has become identified' (2006: 16). Also implicit in her comment is the need to take the situation in the 1990s and early 2000s into account in trying to make any kind of meaningful assessment of Japan as it is today, a decade or so down the track. Indeed, in the wake of the traumatic events of 2011, as the country may well move into possibly even more uncertain social, cultural, and economic conditions, looking back at the post-Bubble years of the 1990s and early 2000s becomes all the more important (see, for instance, Uno and Hamano 2012).

This book is situated within the above framework of the need to contextualize assessments of social and cultural shifts in Japan today in relation to the cross-currents of the 1990s (and earlier). To recap, the core of this book hinges around the notion of the negotiations individual men make with the ideological assumptions of hegemonic masculinity which, in the case of Japan, was, for much of the postwar era, signified through the discourse of salaryman masculinity. As highlighted earlier in this chapter, the late 1990s/early 2000s were particularly crucial years for the ways in which discourses of masculinity – in particular hegemonic masculinity – played out, and were experienced at the 'micro' level by individuals. It was over these years that the interweavings and collisions between earlier assumptions of salaryman masculinity (as embodied, for instance in the JTB-Man, discussed earlier) and the newer post-Bubble configurations (as embodied in figures like Carlos Ghosn) were at their most intense.

These collisions and tensions come out in the voices of the young men entering the workforce over these years, whose experiences I draw upon in subsequent chapters of this book. As their accounts will highlight, these young men were conscious of, indeed embodied, the contradictions and pressures of the shifts from one set of expectations of salaryman masculinity to another. Furthermore, this realization was articulated by them in ways that may possibly have been less pronounced had this book drawn on the experiences of men entering the workforce at the end of the first decade of the twenty-first century, men for whom earlier expectations of salaryman masculinity may be less relevant. At the same time, this sense of a shift within the expectations of salaryman masculinity may also have been less pronounced had the book been based on the accounts of an earlier generation of men, those entering the workforce prior to the economic slowdown and corporate restructurings of the 1990s.

Thus, the 'voices' that I draw upon in the book are in many respects voices from a significant juncture in the history, both of Japanese masculinity, and more generally, of the history of Japan's modernity and late modernity. At the same time, rather than merely representing a 'snapshot' from a moment in history, the analogy that should be made is of a deliberate pause in the ongoing narrative of hegemonic masculinity *situated within* the overall historical trajectory of Japanese industrial capitalism. In other words, any meaningful analysis of masculinity (or gender in general) needs to to take into consideration the socio-historical framework of the industrial-capitalist project in Japan. This has sometimes been overlooked in studies of Japanese masculinity. For instance, Hidaka's study of three generations of salarymen fathers and sons, while being richly detailed as an ethnographic study, does not sufficiently recognize the connectedness of the discourse of salaryman masculinity to the historical framework (Hidaka 2010). In contrast, this book takes as its departure point the argument that the salaryman was (and is) inextricably linked in with the emergence of the Japanese nation-state from the 1870s, with the state-propelled project of industrial capitalism over both the prewar and postwar decades, and with the unfolding of conditions of modernity from the early decades of the twentieth century onward. Thus, foregrounding the 'micro'-level stories of all the individuals who appear in subsequent chapters is the connectedness of their stories to these macro-historical forces.

'Micro' framings: the 'millennial salarymen' behind the voices

At the same time as suggested above, it is the narratives of the young men I was interacting with that, more so than any distanced, abstract theorizing, really gives voice to the shifts (and continuities) that were at play during these historically significant years. The conversations with them, in the form of interviews and discussions, took place over an eighteen-month period in 1998 and 1999 as the twentieth century was drawing to a close. Who were these men? Why did they so readily agree to share their stories (and indeed, their lives) with me at what would turn out to be a significant moment in Japan's historical narrative? These are questions we need to answer in order to get an appreciation of how the cross-currents surrounding salaryman masculinity were playing out and, indeed, being *personally* embodied, at that historical moment. In academic research-speak, these men were 'informants' who I interviewed and engaged with. However, as will become apparent through the richness of their accounts in subsequent chapters, the rather clinical term 'informant' does not really do justice to their identities as young *individuals* making the transition from pre-*shakaijin* to *shakaijin*. Similarly, the relationship that developed between these young men and myself over the course of our interaction transcended the limiting category of researcher/ informant. This needs to be borne in mind when occasionally, in later chapters, I do use the shorthand 'informant' to refer to these men for the sake of convenience.

These 'informants' were approximately forty young male employees of two different organizations in northern Japan – a profile listing details such as age, area of work placement, educational background, marital status, and number of years in the workforce is provided in the Appendix. At the time of my interviews with them they had been in the workforce for periods ranging from a few months to a few years. Hence, all of them were in the process of making the transition to the status of adult employees, and to varying degrees were dealing with the sometimes contradictory expectations of *shakaijin* salaryman masculinity. There was a representation of various academic backgrounds among these men – high school graduates, graduates of technical colleges, university graduates, and even a few with postgraduate qualifications. In terms of age they ranged from nineteen to thirty, with the majority clustered around the mid-twenties. Thus, for most of them, their transition from childhood through adolescence and student life into adult *shakaijin* had been in tandem with the unravelling of Japan's Bubble-era prosperity through the 1990s. The older informants had direct experience of the pre-Lost Decade years, and even the younger ones had memories from childhood and/or early adolescence of those years. While the majority were still single, there were some who were either married, or planning to marry in the near future. A few of the married informants were also fathers, or became fathers over the period of my interaction with them.

With one exception of an individual working in a public sector organization, all the informants were employed in one of two private sector corporate organizations, which had agreed to assist with my research by allowing me access to their employees. Both organizations were based in a prefecture in the north of Japan. This was an area with a history of migration from other parts of the country. Consequently, relative to many other regional areas, the prefecture did not have a particularly entrenched local 'flavour' or cultural particularities. In terms of the research this meant that the issues that came up in the course of the discussions with the informants, in many regards, mirrored similar dynamics at the national level. This is not to say that regional particularities were totally absent – for instance, the fall-outs of the 1990s economic slowdown were particularly acute in the prefecture, and this anxiety found expression in the voices of many of the informants, in particular those working in the smaller of the two organizations.

The (pseudonyms for the) two organizations were: 'Northern Energy', a large-scale corporation in the energy sector, employing several thousand employees in branches throughout the prefecture; and 'Northern Print', a medium- to small-scale firm (*chûshô-kigyô*) in the printing industry, based in a medium-sized regional city, and with around 200 employees. In many respects, they were representative of the two 'faces' of Japan's industrial structure presented in much of the literature on Japanese organizations. Northern Energy typified the kind of elite, large, bureaucratically structured organization often considered emblematic of Japanese organizations collectively, particularly outside Japan. Even after nearly a decade of economic slowdown and industrial restructuring, Northern Energy, like many other large corporations, continued to offer employees many of the guarantees associated with the lifetime employment model. Although not necessarily a major player on the national stage along the lines of giant trading companies or the major banks, Northern Energy, at the time of my fieldwork, was among the top three in the prefecture in terms of number of employees. Moreover, it was also one of the top employers as far as graduates' preferences were concerned. Consequently, it attracted graduates from top-ranked universities throughout the nation. However, as a firm engaged in the energy sector, it also employed a large number of its staff (particularly those in clerical or technical areas) straight from high school, junior college, or technical college.

Northern Print, on the other hand, was almost the antithesis of Northern Energy. In terms of its size, structure, and organizational culture it was fairly typical of the medium-small enterprise (*chûshô-kigyô*) sector, encompassing organizations. It is this sector, rather than the more high-profile large organization sector, that even at the high point of Japan's global economic power formed the 'backbone' of Japan's industrial structure, accounting for 80.6 per cent of total employment in the mid-1980s (Roberson 1998: 7). This sector is often the first to feel the impact of economic downturns, and this was the case with Northern Print in the late 1990s. Unlike Northern Energy, with its head office in the central precinct of the prefectural capital, branches throughout the prefecture, and sales offices in Tokyo and Osaka, Northern Print was located in a light industrial zone on the fringes of the prefecture's second largest city. In contrast to Northern Energy's corporatized, bureaucratic structure, the organizational structure of Northern Print was firmly in the hands of the Chairperson (*kaichô*) and President (*shachô*), sons of the company's founder. At the time of my fieldwork, the son of the current President – who was also one of my informants – was working his way through the different sections of the firm as part of his grooming towards taking over his father's mantle in the future. Reflecting this tighter organizational structure, the various sections of the firm – the print shop-floor, the administrative division, the sales and marketing sections – were all within the same premises. This tighter structure also translated into a relative lack of bureaucratic levels of hierarchy. Also in contrast to Northern Energy, Northern Print's workforce was predominantly locally based, as reflected in my pool of informants from that organization. Moreover, while the Northern Print informants did include a number of university graduates, they were all alumni of local or regionally based private universities of not particularly high academic standing.

'Micro' framings: research shapings and contexts

As mentioned above, the conversations with these young men were carried out over 1998 and 1999. It was through pre-existing academic and personal contacts that I was able to gain access to both organizations – initially the Human Resources divisions, and, through them, the young employees who were interested in my research. Following on from the initial trust building and 'groundwork laying' (including following the necessary protocols of obtaining consent), I was able to embark on the interviews, starting with focus group discussions in both organizations. This was valuable, in that it gave me the opportunity to observe interaction and exchange *between* the individuals. For instance, the dynamics of the senior/junior (*senpai/kôhai*) hierarchy would often be manifested here in a way that was not apparent in the individual interviews. The individual interviews with most informants, with the exception of a few who had quit or were unavailable, were conducted in two separate blocks over eighteen months, and followed a semi-structured format. This format allowed the discussion to focus around certain key themes or 'nodes' pertinent to the research. At the same time, a relatively loose, semi-structured format also opened up space for each interview to take twists and turns specific to that particular context, and to the relationship between myself and the specific individual.

Interviewing each individual on two separate occasions several months apart also contributed to the research in a number of ways. First, given the focus on the shift from pre-*shakaijin* masculinity to adult salaryman masculinity as an ongoing 'crafting' *process* that needs to be negotiated, returning to the same individual a few months after our first meeting allowed me to get a sense of this process at work. These shifts and changes were sometimes quite dramatic. For instance, as I discuss in later chapters, between our first and second interviews, one of my 'key' informants went from being a single, carefree young man with no major 'adult responsibilities' to a husband and father of a newborn baby girl, with all the cares and responsibilities that the shift in his circumstances had brought. Conducting the interviews in two instalments also allowed both sides to return to themes and issues raised the first time that may have required further reflection or clarification; a matter noted by other researchers conducting follow-up interviews (see McDowell 2001a; also Newton 1993). Finally, the lag between the interviews allowed for an appreciation of the significance of the broader social, economic, and cultural shifts occurring in the background, and the influence of these shifts on the informants (and on myself), in ways which may not have been apparent had the interactions consisted of a single interview. In this sense, interviewing the informants twice at different points in the ongoing narrative of 'Lost Decade' anxiety made the temporal flow of this anxiety, and the way it was experienced by individuals, all the more palpable.

In addition to the interviews with the informants from the two organizations, I also conducted interviews or discussions with selected individuals and groups. Among such 'one-off' interviews was one with a young salaryman working in a public sector organization who identified himself to me as 'gay'. I was thus able to explore issues related to sexuality and workplace hegemonic masculinity with him in ways I was not able to with the other informants. I also conducted 'one-off' interviews or discussions with a number of other individuals and groups – for instance, with the founder and coordinator of a men's group, with a human resources management consultant who provides training for new corporate recruits, and with human resources managers and supervisors of one of the organizations (Northern Energy).

Framing the 'micro' and 'macro': chapter construction

The interconnectedness of the personal and 'micro', discussed above, with wider socio-historical processes and currents informs the layout of subsequent chapters in this book. Chapter 2, 'Framing the "macro": historicizing salaryman masculinity', sets out the overall social and historical framework within which the discourse of masculinity pivoted around the salaryman, and emerged to become the dominant discourse of masculinity in postwar Japan. Specifically, it explores the ways in which the emergence of salaryman masculinity as the hegemonic form of masculinity in the postwar period was inextricably linked to the project of nation building and modernity that Japan embarked upon in the late nineteenth century. It looks at the ways in which state-sanctioned ideologies of nation, gender, family, work, and citizenship set in motion in the late nineteenth century worked in combination with socio-cultural and economic shifts to account for the emergence of a visibly articulated discourse of masculinity shaped around the salaryman. The chapter argues that although it was only in the postwar period that the salaryman became the embodiment of hegemonic masculinity, the forces shaping this emergence were already in operation over the prewar decades. Consequently, the discussion traces the shapings and articulations of salaryman masculinity from its early antecedents in the late nineteenth and early twentieth century, through the 'Golden Years' of the salaryman during the high economic growth decades of the 1950s, 1960s, and 1970s, up until the more recent shifts and re-shapings of the 1980s, 1990s, and early 2000s.

Having established the socio-historical crucible which shaped the discourse of the salaryman in Chapter 2, the subsequent chapters shift the slant of discussion to the 'micro' level of individual men negotiating with the expectations of salaryman masculinity amidst the various, often contradictory cross-currents of post-Bubble Japan. Chapter 3, 'Men's stories of becoming *otoko*', focuses on the ways that the informants constructed and imagined the process by which they 'came into *otokorashisa*' (maleness/masculinity; see note 6 above). In other words, the chapter explores the informants' recollections of the process by which they 'became boys', as a precursor to becoming adult men, being 'crafted' into salaryman masculinity.

Chapter 4, 'Becoming *shakaijin*: "Craftings" into salaryman masculinity', discusses the informants' transition into adult, salaryman masculinity in the first weeks and months after entering the workforce. Drawing upon both direct observation of new employee training workshops and discussions with individual informants, the chapter explores the ways in which informants negotiated this transition in the context of very pronounced efforts on the part of the employers to inculcate the ideological expectations of the organization and mould the informants to conform to these expectations. This is significant, as the backdrop to these voices and conversations was the reality that access to the dividends of *shakaijin* salaryman status was becoming increasingly elusive for increasing numbers of new graduates, ironically accentuating the ideological power of that status. In the context of the shifting socio-cultural and corporate cultural realities, the chapter brings out the ways in which individual negotiations with the 'crafting' process are characterized by a rich mix of conformity, co-option, appropriation, playful engagement, marginalization, refutation, resistance, and perhaps even subversion.

Chapter 5, 'Working with salaryman masculinity', further explores the connection between the work/masculinity nexus, as experienced on a day-to-day basis. As noted previously, the core axiom of salaryman masculinity was, and continues to be, the notion of the male as provider, as the *daikokubashira* (mainstay) of the family. Consequently, this chapter looks at the ways in which my informants constructed their sense of masculinity in relation to 'work', in the context of the discursive flux surrounding the concept particularly pronounced at the time. Specifically, the chapter explores notions of what constituted 'masculine' and 'unmasculine' occupations in the views of the informants, and where they situated being a salaryman on that scale. This is significant, in that these men were reflecting on the 'manliness' of being a salaryman at a crucial juncture in the history of the salaryman when the shifts from earlier expectations to newer ideals were particularly intense. The chapter also brings out the day-to-day 'micro-negotiations' of these men in their engagements with the shifts and continuities in the workplace demands of salaryman masculinity.

Chapter 6, 'Working with heterosexuality', looks at the intersections between sexuality and salaryman masculinity in the context of the socio-cultural shifts of the 1990s – specifically, the privileging of a discourse of regulated heterosexuality centring around the man as husband and father as a cornerstone of salaryman masculinity. The chapter thus explores the ways in which my informants engaged with the expectations of needing to publicly conform to this particular discourse of sexuality. Both single and married informants expand upon their views of what marriage and fatherhood meant to them. Moreover, the chapter also discusses the importance of these markers in defining access to the privileges of hegemonic masculinity, and importantly, the ways in which individuals who did not conform with the assumptions of publicly acknowledged heterosexuality negotiate with these expectations in the context of the workplace.

Chapter 7, 'Working with homosociality', explores some of the engagements with an aspect of organizational culture that has seldom been explored through the lens of *masculinity* – the significance of same-sex homosociality in the context of salaryman masculinity. Just as an ideology of publicly proclaimed heterosexuality articulated through marriage and fatherhood was (and continues to be) instrumental in the operation of hegemonic masculinity, so too were same-sex bonds within the organization. Intense homosocial bonds within organizations were especially important in earlier, pre-recession-era discourses of salaryman masculinity. However, with the shift in emphasis from the group to the individual in the newer shapings of salaryman masculinity in the post-Bubble realities of the 1990s and 2000s, the importance of these homosocial relationships seemed to be, on the surface at least, becoming less relevant. Accordingly, this chapter examines the ways in which my informants, caught in the shifts from one set of expectations to another, negotiated with homosocial relationships in the workplace, and the ways in which these intersected with the other expectations of salaryman masculinity.

The final chapter, 'Beyond "The JTB-Man": looking back from the 2010s', moves the focus back to the 'macro', and looks back on the narratives of the informants from the standpoint of the end of the first decade of the twenty-first century. In many senses, although the focus is on the final two years of the 1990s, the 'time-frame compartment' within which the discussion is situated could be considered to be book-ended on one side by the traumatic events of 1995, and on the other by the devastating earthquake, tsunami, and the subsequent nuclear crisis of 2011. With this in mind, the Conclusion returns to some of the territory covered in this introductory chapter, and reassesses the significance of the millennium years during which the conversations with the men in this book occurred, in relation to the shaping which salaryman masculinity is likely to take into the next decade of the twenty-first century, as Japan exits the post-1995 to 2011 era, into possibly uncharted socio-cultural and political-economic territory.

2 Framing the 'macro'

Historicizing salaryman masculinity

As highlighted in the Introduction, over the postwar decades the salaryman, in many regards, came to signify Japanese masculinity in its entirety. This was certainly the case over the high economic growth decades from the mid-1950s through into the 1990s, and even today, despite all the social and economic upheavals of the past two decades, to a surprising extent, continues to be the case. Hence, given this association with (hegemonic) Japanese masculinity, the salaryman, and the discourse built up around him, needs to be unpacked and viewed, not just for his position within Japanese corporate culture, but as a *gendered* construct. Moreover, as also stressed previously, any meaningful discussion needs to be situated against the historical backdrop framing the emergence of the salaryman as a prominent discourse of masculinity. Specifically, an appreciation of the interconnectedness of the salaryman with the state-sponsored *gendered* project of modernity and industrial capitalism embarked upon by the newly established Meiji regime in the late nineteenth century, and sustained and strengthened through the twentieth, is essential to understanding the dynamics of the salaryman in more contemporary times. Accordingly, this chapter lays the historical groundwork upon which the discussion of the lives of young salarymen at the dawn of the twenty-first century takes place in subsequent chapters.

The chapter starts off by clarifying and delineating the term 'salaryman' – as flagged in the previous chapter, this is a term that can be simultaneously inclusive and exclusive, thereby making it conceptually slippery. Having set out the definitional contours of the term, the chapter will then discuss the early shapings of salaryman masculinity – the influence on its shapings of earlier pre-Meiji forms of masculinity, the extent to which the ideology of the modernizing Meiji state was implicated in the process, and the socio-economic shifts that formed the backdrop to its emerging profile. The chapter will then go on to discuss salaryman masculinity during the period when it reached its 'full strength' – over the 'Economic Miracle' decades of the 1950s, 1960s, and into the 1970s, when arguably salaryman masculinity consolidated itself as *the* hegemonic ideal. The final section will explore some of the problematics and complexities underlying this hegemonic ideal, both during its 'glory days' in the 1960s and 1970s, and, over the 1980s and 1990s, as the contestations surrounding it became more visible and pronounced. This contextual background will then allow us to enter the lives of the young men who were making the transition into salaryman masculinity, during those crucial years of the late 1990s.

Defining and delineating 'salaryman'

As discussed previously, despite its ubiquitous socio-cultural presence, the term 'salaryman' is one that can be difficult to pin down and define. This 'fuzziness' comes across, for instance, in the JTB guide referred to in the previous chapter. The guide, as we may recall, tells the reader that the only explanation for 'why such a diverse range of people can be grouped together under the "salaryman spirit" heading' is through the 'old standby – "oriental magic"' (JTB 2006: 187). Yet, in reality, 'oriental magic' notwithstanding, even at the zenith of the 'Japan Inc.' model during the 1960s and 1970s, only a minority of men would have fallen within the strictest definitional parameters of the category of 'salaryman' – full-time, white-collar, permanent employees of organizations offering benefits such as lifetime employment guarantee, salaries and promotions tied to length of service, and an ideology of corporate paternalism characterizing relations between the (permanent, male) employee and the organization. The reality on the ground has long been a situation of the employment sector not necessarily dominated by the elite banks and trading companies and automobile manufacturers of which the typical salaryman was seen to be the archetypal employee. Rather, even at the high point of Japan's industrial strength, it was firms in the medium-small business sector (*chûshô kigyô*) that accounted for the bulk of employment for Japan's workforce, *male* and female (Kondo 1990: 50; Roberson 1998: 7, 8; also Yoshikawa 2002: 114–117). In 1986, for instance, this sector of the economy – firms that, in general, have fewer than 300 employees – accounted for over 80 per cent of all employment (Roberson 1998: 7). Obviously such firms would hardly be in a position to offer the types of benefits (such as long-term employment guarantee) associated with firms at the top end of the industrial structure (Allison 1994: 92; Cheng and Kallenberg 1997: 29).

In this regard, criticism by writers like James Roberson that the focus (particularly in English-language studies) on the large-enterprise sector of the workforce has led to a lopsided view of the actual picture of Japanese workers' everyday realities is understandable (Roberson 1998: 6, 7; also Kondo 1990: 49, 50). However, at the same time, the term 'salaryman' may be (and is) interpreted and deployed in a variety of ways, often well outside the narrow and even not-so-narrow definitions of the term as a white-collar, middle-class employee (see Okamoto and Sasano 2001; also Roberson and Suzuki 2003a: 6, 7). The term, as we will see when discussing individual narratives in subsequent chapters, is often applied by employees engaged in blue-collar or technical work, who also see themselves as salarymen (and hence, technically 'white-collar') because they are employed by an organization and receive a monthly salary.[1] However, it was (and continues to be) the discourse surrounding the salaryman and his lifestyle that has extended out to encompass large numbers of men 'into the totalizing image of the white-collar salaryman' (Roberson 1998: 6, 2005: 369, 370). In other words, the *ideology* associated with, indeed embedded in, the discourse of the urban middle-class salaryman has been far more extensive and pervasive in its reach, notwithstanding the reality that even prior to the 1990s, like the rubric of salaryman, the actual definitional reach of the 'middle class' was never as inclusively encompassing as was popularly believed (see Steven 1983; also Ishida and Slater 2010b: 6–8).[2] In this respect – regardless of what the *reality* might be – large swathes of Japanese men continue to identify with, and define themselves against, what the salaryman is considered to embody. Consequently, as Roberson and Suzuki suggest, 'as long as one is critically aware of the tensions and distinctions among ideology, ideal and reality, extending the discourse on/of men as salarymen beyond the middle class can be an important exercise' (2003a: 7; also Roberson 2005). In particular, it has been the centrality of work, of being the *daikokubashira* family provider, in constructing salaryman identity that has contributed to this sense of the attributes of the salaryman being applicable across the board (see Taga 2011c: 2, 3). More so than other attributes of salaryman masculinity, it was this equation of masculinity with work and being the family provider that was key to its emergence as the hegemonic model of masculinity in Japan over the postwar period. Moreover, as I argue throughout this book, this remained, and continues to remain, a core underpinning of hegemonic masculinity through the years of economic and social upheaval in the late 1990s and early 2000s (the time-frame of this book), and into the present. With this in mind, we can now situate the emergence of salaryman masculinity within the historical framework of Japanese modernity.

The modernizing state and 'crafting' emergent masculinities

As signalled above, the emergence of a distinct discourse of masculinity centred around the salaryman occurred within the framework of a state-sanctioned ideology of gender and sexuality. This ideology in turn was closely linked to the project of modernity and industrial capitalism initiated by the new regime that came into power through the 'Meiji Restoration' of 1868, replacing the Tokugawa *bakufu* regime which had been the ruling authority in Japan since the early seventeenth century. The 'Restoration' was ostensibly carried out to 'restore' the Emperor as the real and not just the symbolic/cultural focus of the political and social structure. The factors precipitating the overthrow of the old order were complex – a combination of domestic social, economic, and political conditions which had built up over the two and a half centuries of the *bakufu* administration, as well as a very real threat of military and/or economic domination by Western colonial powers, which at the time were collectively expanding their military and economic influence in East Asia.

Despite the rhetoric of 'restoring' the Emperor, power, in actual fact, was consolidated in the hands of the young *samurai* who had led the push for the Restoration, and who over subsequent decades would go on to become an entrenched clique of oligarchs dominating and regulating the body politic, and shaping the contours of state and society. Exerting authority in the name of the

newly 'restored' Meiji Emperor, these new leaders initiated a far-reaching programme of modernization and nation building which set the framework for the
emergence of Japan as an industrial and military power in the early twentieth
century. The various innovations and changes implemented included the creation
of a technologically modern conscript-based military that would soon go on to
spearhead the expansion of the Japanese Empire in Asia, and the establishment
of modern socio-economic and political institutions. The spirit of this project of
modernity was reflected in contemporary catch-phrases like *fukoku kyôhei* ('Rich
Nation, Strong Military') and *bunmei kaika* ('Civilization and Enlightenment').
Importantly, as reflected in the *bunmei kaika* slogan, integral to the creation of
the strong, new nation was the sanctioning and dissemination through instru-
ments of state and society of a discourse of 'civilised morality' (Pflugfelder
1999: 149), designed to create the new, enlightened Japanese man and woman.
This, as implied by another popular slogan of the time, *wakon yôsai* ('Japanese
Spirit, Western Learning'), synthesized *selective* neo-Confucian values from the
preceding Tokugawa regime, which had provided the prescriptive discourse for
the *samurai* and socio-political elites, with newly imported medical, legal, and
social discourses from the West. Importantly, the 'official' ideology that was
shaped out of these selective borrowings from the past was a *national* ideology
that in principle applied to all Japanese, not just to specific groups or classes, as
had been the case during the preceding Tokugawa order (Hirota 1999: 199).

This emerging discourse of gender and sexuality was inextricably linked to
the industrial-capitalist and military-nationalist enterprise – the Empire needed
pliant, productive workers and soldiers of its male citizens and 'Good Wives,
Wise Mothers' (*ryôsai kenbo*) of its female citizens (Sievers 1983: 110, 111), the
two sides of the binary linked together through the ideal (rather than contemporary reality) of monogamous, heterosexual marriage and the notion of family
centred around the husband–wife domestic pairing (White 2002: 45, 46). Thus
official and popular discourse, working through institutions like the military, the
legal system, the education system, and official and semi-official popular culture
media, worked to inculcate and reinforce these hegemonic ideals of masculinity
and femininity (see Kinmonth 1981; Sievers 1983; Roden 1980; Sand 1998;
Hirota 1999; Yamasaki 2001; Ishii and Jarkey 2002; Mackie 2003: 21–29;
Takeda 2005: 43–47).

The origins of the discourse of salaryman masculinity may be traced back to
these initial decades of Japan's industrialization enterprise. It was over these
years that the rudiments of an urban, white-collar, middle-class masculinity
began to emerge alongside the more visible contemporary expressions of masculinity such as the new conscript-based Imperial Army, rural masculinities, and
forms of 'elite' masculinity, such as the male student cultures discussed by
Donald Roden (1980), or the masculinity of the governing elites (Karlin 2002).
Although the term 'salaryman' (*sarariiman*) itself appears to have been coined
and popularized in the years following World War One (Umezawa 1997: 4; also
Gordon 2002: 110–116; Iwase 2006: 24–26), its antecedents can be traced back
to the *gekkyû-tori* (monthly salary recipient) of the early Meiji decades, and even

the *koshi-ben*, a somewhat demeaning term for low-ranking *samurai* bureaucrats in the late Tokugawa years, who had been reduced to dangling a lunch-box (*bentô*) instead of a sword from their waists (*koshi*) (Kinmonth 1981: 277–280; Suyama 1965: 135; Umezawa 1997: 4–6).[3]

By the Taishô and early Shôwa periods (roughly corresponding to the inter-war decades), socio-economic conditions allowed for the visible emergence of a distinct category of white-collar salaried worker (classified increasingly under the term 'salaryman', rather than the earlier *gekkyû-tori*) (Iwase 2006: 26). Underlying the growing visibility of this sector of the workforce was the intensi-fication of processes put into motion during the Meiji decades, such as urbaniza-tion and the emergence of a 'new' bourgeois middle class of professionals, small businessmen, white-collar public and private sector salaried workers, and service sector employees (Tipton 2008: 104–107; also Harootunian 2000: ch. 1; Gordon 2002: 110–116). As Ezra Vogel notes, for instance, by 1920, out of a total non-agricultural labour force of 12.5 million, white-collar workers accounted for 1.5 million (Vogel 1971: 6, n.3).[4] Furthermore, it was during these years that spe-cific features of the employment system which would come to be associated with salaryman masculinity, such as seniority-based promotions, implicit guarantees of lifetime employment for permanent employees, and corporate paternalism, gradually started to become entrenched, at least in large-scale and public sector organizations (Dore 1973a: 396–403; Beck and Beck 1994: 45–50; Cheng and Kallenberg 1997: 16, 17; Hazama 1997: 26–29, 76–96).

It was also during these years that the salaryman really started taking shape as a distinct form of *masculinity*, linked with the conditions of urban, capitalist modernity, and importantly, with anxieties about this emerging modernity. To his supporters, the salaryman was the embodiment of a new, modern, industrial-ized, urban Japan, and to his detractors all that was wrong with this new urban middle-class, modern culture. This period of Japanese history witnessed the sur-facing of the varied tensions and contradictions of modernity, as divergent dis-courses of 'Japanese-ness' competed in a socio-economic climate characterized by growing inequality, tension, and flux. For many of these circulating dis-courses – both celebratory and anxious – the reference point was modernity, and the implications were for Japan's future (Silverberg 1992; Minichiello 1998; Yano 1998; Harootunian 2000; Freedman 2011).

The emergence and circulation, both in the scholarly and popular press, of various discourses related to the figure of the salaryman, albeit couched more in terms of social class or lifestyle rather than with reference to the salaryman's *masculinity*, was set against this backdrop of articulations on conditions of modernity (see, for example, Harootunian 2000). The academic literature – reflecting the growing influence of Marxist theory – often tried to fit the salary-man within the framework of social class or in terms of lifestyle analysis (for instance, social commentator Ôya Sôichi's analysis of the salaryman and his lifestyle (Ôya 1981: 90–101)). The salaryman also started being represented in spaces of popular culture, such as Maeda Hajime's popular 1928 novel (and sub-sequent sequel) *Sarariiman Monogatari* ('Story of the Salaryman'), and cartoonist

Kitazawa Rakuten's popular *manga* depicting '*sarariiman no tengoku*' ('Salary-man's Heaven') and '*sarariiman no jigoku*' ('Salaryman's Hell') (Maeda 1928; Kitazawa Rakuten Kenshô Kai 1973, 124–125; see also Kinmonth 1981: 289, 290). 'Salaryman's Hell' consisted of such things as commuting on 'jam-packed' trams at peak hour, being gossiped about by colleagues, and having to work late at the end of the financial month; 'Salaryman's Heaven' included business trips, a walk with the typist, and long weekends.[5] Similarly, magazines targeting an urban, white-collar readership like *Kingu* ('King') or the monthly *Sarariiman* revolved around the daily concerns of a salaryman's life. *Sarariiman*, for instance, contained features on a range of concerns from the economy and issues to do with the workplace, right through to pieces on aspects of 'modern' life (everything from cafés through tips about fashion to advice about relationships).[6] *Kingu*, in Kinmonth's words, was 'a monument to mediocrity and middlebrow taste' (Kinmonth 1981: 321). Even the newly emerging medium of film engaged with the salaryman and his lifestyle – some of the early works of Ozu Yasujiro such as *Umarete wa Mita keredo* ('I Was Born, But') and *Tokyo no Kôrasu* ('Tokyo Chorus') had the salaryman at the centre of their narratives. These popular culture representations also served an important prescriptive and rein-forcing function – how to 'correctly' perform salaryman masculinity in terms of work, consumer habits, deportment, and lifestyle patterns. Significantly, this vis-ibility in public culture underscores the positioning of the discourse of the sala-ryman within the expanding conditions of capitalist modernity in 1920s/ early-1930s Japan (see Harootunian 2000; Iwase 2006; Freedman 2011: 31–35).

The emergence of the salaryman as hegemonic ideal

Despite the growing visibility of the salaryman as representative of urban, middle-class masculinity during these years, it was only over the decades fol-lowing the end of World War Two that the salaryman really became the over-arching embodiment of hegemonic masculinity as alternative/competing masculinities such as the soldier and farmer became neutralized as a con-sequence of Japan's defeat and postwar demilitarization by the Allied Occupa-tion Authority, and subsequent social and economic transformations.[7] The postwar socio-economic changes were pivoted around the 'Economic Miracle', the remarkable growth and transformation of the economy that occurred from the mid-1950s until the early 1970s (and, to an extent, until the early 1990s). This transformation, in turn, occurred within the economic growth prioritizing framework of the 'Japan Inc.' partnership between the ruling conservative Liberal Democratic Party (LDP) which dominated the political landscape over most of the postwar era, the government bureaucracy, in particular the Ministry of International Trade and Industry (MITI) and the Finance Ministry, and big business and industry (Nakamura 1981; Johnson 1982; Noble 1989). Import-antly, the success of this 'Japan Inc.' model, and indeed the ideology of postwar Japanese industrial capitalism, was inextricably linked in with Japan's postwar relationship with the United States of America. Specifically, the restrictions imposed upon military expenditure in the postwar Allied-imposed 'Peace Constitution' and Japan's positioning within the US defence and foreign policy umbrella in the Cold War global order facilitated the channelling of resources, which otherwise (as had been the case in the prewar period) may have been used for defence, towards economic recovery and growth (see Dower 1993). The emergence of the salaryman as the archetypal citizen of the postwar period occurred within this domestic and global ideological framework.

In many respects, as reflected in the term *kigyô senshi* ('Corporate Warrior') that came into circulation during these years, it would appear that it was the salaryman who had replaced the soldier as the new masculine ideal, while ironically, the representative of military masculinity in the postwar period, the Self Defence Force, did not really figure in imaginings of idealized masculinity. Indeed, as the noted feminist scholar Ueno Chizuko has observed, much of the terminology associated with the 'corporate warrior' over the key years of economic growth had strong militaristic connotations. These included terms and expressions like *messhi hôkô* ('Selfless Devotion'), *senpei* ('Advance Guard'), and *shijô senryaku* ('Market Strategy'), all conjuring up images of the military masculinity idealized in prewar Japan (Ueno 1995: 215–216). The application of such terminology suggests not only the salaryman's replacement of the soldier as masculine ideal, but also underscores his important role in contributing to the postwar Japanese nation-state's objective of *economic* (rather than military) strength.[8]

The sheer scale of the socio-economic transformations foregrounding the postwar emergence of the salaryman is reflected in a variety of socio-economic indices for the period. For instance, from 1954 to 1958, gross national product (GNP) grew at an average of 7 per cent per annum, 10.8 per cent over the period 1959 to 1963, and 10.9 per cent from 1964 to 1968. This was at a time when global GDP as a whole was growing at 5 per cent per annum (McCreery 2000: 17). In particular, the implementation of the 'Income Doubling Plan' under the Ikeda administration in the 1960s had significant repercussions for both society and the economy. Within that decade, Japan had quite definitely made the transition from a developing economy still mapping out its road to affluence, to an advanced industrialized nation, confirmation of this status being its admittance into the ranks of the OECD in 1964.[9]

At the ground level, this translated into very real improvements in the standards of living of large sections of the population – as an example, the average monthly income of workers in firms with more than thirty employees tripled between 1960 and 1970 (Duus 1998: 300). In terms of people's everyday *material* quality of life, there was no denying that there had been some very significant improvements. For instance, per capita personal consumption expenditure, which within the objectives of the Income Doubling Plan had been targeted to be increased by 6.7 per cent within the ten-year time-frame, actually increased by 9.4 per cent by 1970 (Uchino 1983: 112). Moreover, the nature of this household consumption shifted, as the share of household income spent on essentials – the Engels coefficient – decreased from 44.5 per cent in 1955 to 32.8 per cent in 1969 (Yano 1970: 67), allowing families to devote greater shares of their resources to non-essential and quality-of-life-related consumption. Indeed, it was during these years that the diffusion rates for many of the consumer durables that Japanese industry was producing really started to accelerate. For instance, by the end of the decade, in 1969, 88.9 per cent of urban households owned washing machines, 88.2 per cent possessed their own refrigerators, 18.1 per cent owned a private family car, and the diffusion rate of colour televisions jumped over one year from 6.3 per cent in 1968 to 16 per cent in 1969 (Yano 1970: 75; also Naka-mura 1981: 94).

Also foregrounding the growing visibility of the salaryman on the social and economic landscape were shifts in the composition of the labour force from the 1950s. One consequence of the rapid industrialization from the 1950s was an expansion of white-collar labour – Ezra Vogel, for instance, gives a figure of 7.3 million for the number of white-collar workers in 1959, an increase from 6.1 million in 1955, and 3.5 million in 1940 (Vogel 1971: 6, n.3). At the same time, changes in the countryside such as land reform programmes carried out during the Allied Occupation in the 1940s which had led to improvements in techno-logy and reduction in the labour required for farming, meant that agriculture no longer needed to occupy as large a share of the labour force as even a decade or so earlier. In 1949, for instance, it had still accounted for nearly half of all employment (Kelly 1993: 203), but by 1959 the primary sector's share of employment was down below 40 per cent, and by 1968, it hovered just above 20 per cent of the workforce (Cole and Tominaga 1976: 68). In particular the second and third sons of farm-owning families were now freed up to seek employment in the rapidly expanding factories and offices of an urban Japan undergoing, first, postwar reconstruction, and subsequently the 'Economic Miracle' of the late 1950s and the 1960s. From the 1950s through to the 1970s, Japan quite definitely became a nation of wage and salary earners, numbers increasing approximately threefold between 1950 and 1975, as the proportion of total employment increased from 35.4 per cent to 69.8 per cent (Levine 1983: 23). Correspondingly, proportions of various occupational categories within the employment sector reflected these increases. Professionals, managers, adminis-trative and technical personnel, clerks, and service workers doubled in numbers over the period 1955 to 1975, and transport and communications workers increased over three times during the same period (Levine 1983: 23). By 1970, Japan ranked seventh in a cross-national comparison of white-collar workers as a proportion of the total economically active workforce (Cole and Tominaga 1976: 74, 75). Significantly, it was really over these years that attributes associ-ated with Japanese corporate culture such as lifetime employment, seniority-based wages and promotions, and the ideology of corporate paternalism started extending out beyond just elite, large-scale organizations, as had largely been the case in the prewar years (see, e.g. Ballon 1969; Beck and Beck 1994).

Linked in with these changes was the rapid urbanization that occurred over these decades. Between 1955 and 1970, fuelled by the influx of migrants from regional Japan, the population of the six major urban centres increased at an average rate of one million per year. Thus, in 1964 Tokyo became the first city in the world to reach a population of ten million (Duus 1998: 303). By 1970, 72 per cent of the population was concentrated in urban areas, bringing Japanese urbanization rates up to the same level as the United States of America (McCreery 2000: 21). One immediate consequence of this rapid industrialization and urbanization was the impact on rising urban land prices (see Hein 1993: 101, 102, n.7; McCreery 2000: 22). This, in turn, led to the distancing of homes from workplaces, further accentuating the public/private dichotomy. The public/work domain became increasingly associated with masculinity, and the private/home sphere with femininity, motherhood, and nurturing. Indeed, the trend towards smaller, nuclear families in the postwar years, coupled with the rapid diffusion of household durables like vacuum cleaners, refrigerators, and washing machines, resulted, ironically, in focusing women's roles on motherhood and child-rearing (hence the female counterpart of the salaryman – the *sengyô shufu*, or full-time housewife). As Kathleen Uno (1993) points out, it was motherhood that replaced being a wife as the dominant image of the Japanese woman over the postwar era. Moreover, this image of woman as mother 'also contrasted sharply with the high and late postwar image of the Japanese male – a man in a dark blue suit commuting by train to a company, an actor in the public world, rather than a father or husband in the private world of the home' (Uno 1993: 304).[10] The hegemonic ideal of the family as a nuclear unit of a husband/wife with two children, which in the prewar period had been an ideal only for limited sections of the urban middle class, now became increasingly widespread and accessible to growing numbers of young couples and families. By 1970, 64 per cent of households in Japan were in nuclear family situations (Fujii 1995: 129).

Importantly, as had been the case with modernity in the 1920s, these social and economic shifts underpinning the strengthening of the salaryman discourse found expression through being embodied in, and performed through, the everyday practices of work, leisure, home life, and public life of citizens (see Mackie 2000b: 189–192). In other words, the emergence of the discourse of salaryman masculinity as the culturally privileged/pervasive hegemony was inextricably linked to the production and dissemination of the products – in particular consumer products – the production of which underpinned the postwar 'Economic Miracle'. Marilyn Ivy makes a similar point when she notes that not only did electrical appliances fuel the Income Doubling Plan-generated consumer boom of the 1960s, and become the sign of middle-class inclusion, but they also 'standardized the image of the average household … their presence and placement within Japanese dwellings … also homogenized Japanese domestic space, which became a "concretized metaphorical scene" of social equality' (Ivy 1993: 249). Thus, the salaryman/*sengyô shufu*-centred nuclear unit came to be both the target for, and to represent, all the catch-phrases coined to capture the various fads and trends that were the driving force behind the *akarui seikatsu* ('Bright New Life') of the 1960s and 1970s – the three Treasures (washing machine, vacuum cleaner, black and white television); three Cs (car, colour television, cooler [i.e. air-conditioner]); three Js (jet, [i.e. holiday overseas], jewels, *jûtaku*, i.e. own house); *mai-hômu* (own home, with the implication of privatized lifestyles), and *mai-kaa* (own car, implying mobility, consumption of leisure), to name a few (see Vogel 1971; Tobin 1992; Ivy 1993; Kelly 1993).

Compounding these social and economic shifts that formed the backdrop to the standardization of the salaryman/*sengyô shufu* pairing in the national psyche were demographic forces coalescing around the postwar 'Baby Boom' *dankai* generation (see Kelly 1993: 197, 198; McCreery 2000: 51–53; Matsuno 2001: 263–265). This was a generation whose trajectory into adulthood was closely intertwined with the material and social changes of the 1950s and 1960s. Moreover, as we will see later in this chapter, this generation continued to be closely associated with the fortunes of the Japanese economy over sub-sequent decades. Many of the present (and anticipated) socio-economic prob-lems and faultlines (including the unravelling of the salaryman ideal) are inextricably entwined with this generational cohort. At the time this generation was coming into adulthood, though – in the late 1960s/early 1970s – Japan was at the high point of the 'Economic Miracle' years. The 'miracle' itself was, at that time, strongly associated with the efforts of the *kigyô senshi* ('Corporate Warriors') and *môretsu shain* (intense/passionate company employees) salarymen of the preceding *Shôwa hitoketa* (Shôwa single-digit) and *Shôwa futaketa* (double-digit) generations. The former, those born in the first decade of the Shôwa era (i.e. 1926–1934), had come of age either during the war, or during the chaotic, hardship-filled immediate postwar years. As Kelly outlines, this was a generation that had:

> become the bedrock of postwar recovery and boom. They became, in the popular imagination, the workaholic company-men (*môretsu shain*) and the education mamas (*kyôiku-mama*), whose selfless efforts on behalf of company and children insured present and future prosperity.
>
> (Kelly 1993: 197)

It was men of this generational cohort who embodied the *kigyô senshi*/Corporate Warrior discourse. In contrast, the *futaketa* generation, those born between the mid-1930s and the mid-1940s, were, in Kelly's words, 'to many commentators the *mai hômu-gata*, home-oriented types, who nonetheless retain a commitment to the workplace, if only to secure the status and resources to enable a prosper-ous home' (1993: 198). Rather than being *kigyô senshi*, this cohort was closer to the stereotype of the *kaisha ningen* ('Company Person'), who while dedicated to the organization, lacked the same burning zeal as the previous generational cohort. The Baby-Boomer generation of salarymen came into the workforce at this juncture. As McCreery points out:

> [r]apid economic growth created jobs, making space for them at the bottom of growing organizations. Their fate would be to provide the army of subor-dinates that growing companies needed for the older generations whose members were starting to move up the corporate ladder.
>
> (McCreery 2000: 53)

The men of this generation went on to become:

> what both foreign observers and the Japanese man in the street would con-
> sider the 'typical Japanese'. In this familiar stereotype, we are talking about
> men who achieve the Boomer dream. They become successful, but not too
> successful, middle-class, white-collar workers. They are married, have one
> or two children. Their homes are in the suburbs. They commute long dis-
> tances to offices where, after working long hours, they go out drinking with
> their fellow workers. These are the men, it is said, who work so well in
> groups. They know the wisdom of the oft-cited maxim, 'The nail that sticks
> out gets hammered down'.
>
> (McCreery 2000: 52)

Thus it was against a backdrop of the various social, economic, and demographic
shifts and forces outlined above that the salaryman became the embodiment of
Japanese masculinity *and* the middle-class lifestyle that postwar economic
growth had brought within the reach of increasing numbers. On the one hand, in
many respects it *was* the legions of salarymen and their wives desiring access to
the products and cultural symbols associated with a middle-class lifestyle who
became the metaphorical 'foot soldiers' of the various economic White Papers
and plans devised by the economic planners and bureaucrats of 'Japan Inc.' to
chart the recovery and subsequent 'take-off' of the economy. This is brought out
quite clearly in the desires and aspirations of individuals in many of the ethnographic studies of urban life carried out during these decades, such as Dore's
detailed study of the residents of a Tokyo ward in the early 1950s (Dore 1973b),
or Plath's (1964) and Vogel's (1971) works conducted in the late 1950s, or even
Rohlen's study of white-collar bank employees in the early 1970s (Rohlen
1974). Consequently, the long hours of overtime put in by corporate workers, or
the bonus payments channelled into household savings in order to purchase a
house or consumer durables or to put aside for children's education,[11] or the
pressure on children (particularly boys) to study hard, translated, directly or indirectly, into the success of the economy on a macro level.

At the same time, this economic growth and expansion also allowed for
increasing numbers to enter into the lifestyles associated with this standardized
middle-class salaryman discourse. Thus, in contrast to previous generations
when only a small proportion of students finishing compulsory education would
have continued on to secondary and tertiary education (thereby gaining greater
access to white-collar occupations), the increasing ability (and desire) of parents
to send children on to post-compulsory education meant that by 1965 about 70
per cent of children went on to some form of secondary education, and 17 per
cent went on to tertiary education at either two-year junior colleges or four-year
universities (McCreery 2000: 157). One consequence of this was the entrench-
ment of the belief that Japan had become a classless society, with the over-
whelming majority of the population belonging to the middle class – according
to surveys conducted by the Prime Minister's Office during these years, 90 per

cent of Japanese citizens saw themselves as belonging to the middle class (Kelly 1993: 195). As I have argued earlier in this chapter, this claim needs to be treated with some reservation, and over the years, has been the subject of considerable debate and criticism. However, as I also noted earlier, regardless of the reality that the actual proportion of the population falling within the category of the 'middle class' was far less than popular perception suggested, it was the *discourse* (and indeed, the ideology it was based upon) associated with a middle-class lifestyle that was far more extensive in reach (Kelly 1986: 605).[12]

Problematizing salaryman masculinity

It was within the context of the social, economic, and historical framework out-lined in the previous sections, that the salaryman emerged as the 'ideal citizen' in the first two decades of the postwar period (i.e. over the 1950s and 1960s). He emerged as both the corporate 'ideal' and the masculine 'ideal', shaped by and embodying the hegemonic discourse of masculinity. Typically, he would be middle class and often university educated, entering the organization upon grad-uation from university in his early twenties. Once within the organization, he would be expected to display qualities of loyalty, diligence, dedication, and self-sacrifice. Everything about the salaryman embodied (and indeed, to a large degree, continues to embody) these values: his behaviour, deportment (white shirt, dark business suit, lack of 'flashy' clothing and accessories, neat hairstyle), consumer habits (for example, reading certain types of magazines), even his verbal and bodily language. Moreover, his success (or lack of it) would be prem-ised not only on workplace conduct, but also on his ability to conform to the requirements of the hegemonic discourse – to marry at an age deemed suitable, and once married to perform the appropriate gender role befitting the role of husband/provider/father. This type of 'Everyman' *kaisha ningen* and/or *kigyô senshi* hero figure featured prominently in spaces of popular culture – in con-temporary films like the 1960 suspense drama *Kuroi Gashû: Aru Sarariiman no Shôgen* ('The Black Album: The Testimony of a Salaryman') based on one of the works of crime fiction writer Matsumoto Seichi, or in the innumerable busi-ness novels (*kigyô shôsetsu*) or salaryman *manga* of the period.[13]

However, in many ways, the above description represented the 'ideal', albeit a hegemonic one. The reality, even during the 'glory days' of the 'Economic Miracle', was far more nuanced and complex. As signalled in the Introduction, hegemonic masculinity is far more tenuous and open to questioning and contes-tation than might initially appear to be the case. While the discourse built around the 'ideals' of hegemonic masculinity (for example, the 'ideal' of the selfless *môretsu shain*) may well exert a powerful influence on the lives of most males (adult men and boys), virtually no one matches it one hundred per cent – to echo Connell, '[t]he hegemonic form need not be the most common form of mascu-linity, let alone the most comfortable' (Connell 2000: 11). Thus, in terms of the discourse of salaryman masculinity, even in its heyday, there *were* alternate, subordinated masculinities that continued to engage and interact with salaryman masculinity in varying ways, ranging from outright hostility and opposition, to varying degrees of co-option, complicity, or subordination. Moreover, as also flagged in the Introduction, different discourses of masculinity often co-existed and interacted within the same individual, either at different stages of his life-path, or at the same point in time. An example from the period under discussion would perhaps be a student activist involved in the anti-establishment protests which punctuated the social landscape through the 1960s, who subsequently went on to enter private corporations and rise up the organizational hierarchy, a not uncommon occurrence (see, for example, Morris-Suzuki 1984: 312).[14]

While the discourse of masculinity embodied in the student activists of the 1960s may have been *visibly* the most oppositional and antithetical to what salaryman masculinity represented, there were also other less visibly flamboyant masculinities that continued to maintain a presence on the social tapestry. These included discourses surrounding working-class and rural masculinities, as well as non-heterosexual masculinities. If the figure of the *kigyō senshi* and *kaisha ningen* as depicted in contemporary popular culture of the period embodied and represented one face of the high-speed economic growth years, another face was presented by figures such as the 'anti-hero' cinema characters played by actors such as Takakura Ken and Ishihara Yūjiro, or the bumbling, ineffectual but endearing character of Tora-san (played by the actor Atsumi Kiyoshi), the protagonist of the enormously popular *Otoko wa Tsurai Yo* ('It's Tough Being a Man') series of over forty films, the first of which was made in 1969, at the zenith of the 'Economic Miracle' (see Buruma 1984: chs 10, 12; Standish 2000; Schilling 2000). Indeed, the appeal of these characters lay precisely in the fact that they represented a (possibly nostalgic) alternative imagining to the increasingly bureaucratized, regulated reality of lives of the expanding numbers of salarymen and their families. The success of Tora-san, in particular, may have been because he reinforced, in Ian Buruma's words, 'how lucky we all are to lead such restricted, respectable and in most cases, perfectly harmless lives' (Buruma 1984: 218). Similarly, accounts such as Kamata Satoshi's story of back-breaking, demeaning labour as an 'under-cover' production-line worker in a Toyota plant, or Robert Cole's ethnography of blue-collar workers, provide another decidedly less upbeat side of the 'Economic Miracle' and the machinery of Japan Inc. (Cole 1971; Kamata 1982).

Salaryman masculinity itself was not free from contestation and interrogation, both during the high-growth decades and in the decades following the maturation of the economy after the Oil Crisis of 1973.[15] Indeed, the very dynamics responsible for strengthening and expanding salaryman masculinity (both in terms of the discourse built around it, and in terms of actual *numbers*) – the expansion of the white-collar sector, the large numbers of the Baby Boom generation entering the ranks of the salaryman in the late 1960s and early 1970s – also contained counter-forces within themselves. The Baby Boomer salarymen had entered the organizations at a time when rapidly growing companies needed growing numbers of white-collar salarymen at the lower end of the corporate hierarchy:

Their fate would be to provide the army of subordinates that growing companies needed for the older generations whose members were starting to
move up the corporate ladder. For themselves, however, lifetime employment would turn out, at the end of their careers, to be literally, a pyramid
scheme. The end of high growth and a shrinking number of younger men
would make it impossible to continue the seniority-based promotions that
made a salaryman's life seem so attractively secure.

(McCreery 2000: 53)

This suggests that the seeds of the post-Bubble crisis of the 1990s were already
in the making in the 1970s and 1980s. At the same time, other challenges to
aspects of the salaryman and his lifestyle that would also become more pronounced a decade or so down the track – issues such as the personal cost and
burden on the family, for instance – started to surface during these years. This is
vividly brought out in contemporary representations of the salaryman, such as in
the 1970s *manga, Dame Oyaji* ('Stupid Dad'), revolving around the tribulations
of a 'typical' salaryman, who, 'after spending his days bowing at a nightmarish
office,... is tormented by his wife, a vicious, screaming harridan, nicknamed
"the devil woman"' and his two children, 'his son, a bald little horror and his
daughter, a whining sadist, [who] both happily assist their mother' (Buruma
1984: 196). In a less 'tongue-in-cheek' sense, Kumazawa Makoto's sensitive and
incisive account, 'Twenty Years of a Bank Worker's Life', based on the personal
diaries of a Fuji Bank employee over the 1960s and 1970s, conveys a real sense
of one man's frustrations and struggles as he tried to contend with the demands
of the corporate ideology, union bureaucracy, work responsibilities, and responsibility to his family. His attempts to balance these demands with his deep personal commitment to justice for workers, and defence of strongly held principles,
end up taking a toll on himself, both in terms of his career and his own well-
being (Kumazawa 1996: 205–247). The following excerpt brings out the burdens
imposed by hegemonic masculinity on someone who, in many respects, started
his career as an exemplar of the salaryman ideal (a graduate of an elite university, working for one of the top banks in Japan):

the time he could spend with his family or reading was extremely limited.
Every morning he left his house at 6:45 and did not usually return home
until 11:00 P.M. In this one year (1976), the entries in his diary in which he
mentions being busy because of work and being exhausted increased
greatly. There are over fifteen periods during which the only notations for
five or six days in a row are 'busy' or 'tired.'

(Kumazawa 1996: 236)

Inevitably, this man's health broke down, and he spent the remaining two years
of his life alternating between spells in hospital, and returning to a gruelling
work regime at the bank. In the end, he was knocked down and killed by a truck
on his way to work in January 1978. Although not explicitly spelled out, the

implication seems to be that his death was somehow linked to the psychological and physical toll of trying to be a diligent *kaisha ningen* ('company person') *and* at the same time trying to maintain his sense of personal integrity.

This interrogation and problematization started to intensify and become increasingly visible during the 1980s. The social and economic conditions during the 'Bubble Economy' years shaped the attitudes and values of a new generation of salarymen (dubbed the *shinjinrui*, literally 'New Humankind', generation). These conditions included a speculation-driven economic boom where even relatively small-scale companies embarked on ambitious expansion programmes, a labour shortage allowing university graduates to be discerning about employment conditions, and a culture of almost hedonistic conspicuous consumption. This was also a period when the *costs* of buying into salaryman masculinity started to enter into public discourse in a far more visible fashion. Issues such as *karôshi* (literally, 'death from overwork'), *kitaku-kyohi* (inability or reluctance to go home, partly due to a lack of communication between the salaryman and his family), *tanshin funin* (workers forced to live away from their families, sometimes for years, due to job transfers), *madogiwa-zoku* (literally, 'window-sill tribe' – middle-aged salarymen automatically promoted up the corporate escalator to junior management posts, but due to either personal inefficacy or a lack of available jobs commensurate with their status, being sidelined and relegated to the desks by the window, so they could pass their time staring at the scenery outside) entered the lexicon of everyday discourse, as a result of wide coverage in the media. *Karôshi*, in particular, received considerable attention due to a spate of widely publicized incidents, where corporate employees (generally males in their forties or fifties, but occasionally female staff, and younger male staff too) collapsed and died as a consequence of work-related physical and mental stress (Matsuno 2001: 41–44; Dasgupta 2002). This questioning and criticism seemed to coalesce around the key tenet of salaryman masculinity – that it was through work that a man's sense of self-worth and societal esteem was determined.

Accompanying this growing criticism of salaryman masculinity (or at least of some of its negative fall-outs) were wider socio-economic, cultural, and demographic shifts that started to become visible in the 1980s, and further intensified over the 1990s. These had considerable bearing on the discourse of salaryman masculinity. First, the shift to a mature, late-industrial society which had been triggered by the 1973 Oil Crisis became more pronounced through the 1980s and the 1990s. With the growing transition to an economy centred on the tertiary services sector, industries which had previously been less important started to occupy an increasingly influential role within the economy. These included areas such as fashion, tourism, media and communications, information technology, and education services. These areas of employment tended to de-emphasize attributes traditionally associated with the solid, respectable, corporate masculinity model of the salaryman, instead valuing traits like youth, creativity, flair, and sensitivity. Thus, for significant numbers of younger Japanese – male and female – there was now a greater range of lifestyle options than had been available to their parents' generation, when the choices had been more clearly defined. For males in the past, it had generally been a choice between either accessing the cultural ideal of hegemonic salaryman masculinity with all its associated dividends (lifetime employment security, middle-class respectability) or settling for other less economically and socially rewarding alternatives. Now, particularly during the heady years of the 'Bubble Economy' boom, the choices were less clear-cut, in that there was a far greater range of options available to choose from which offered the possibility of gaining social and economic dividends on a par with salaryman masculinity.

The 1990s 'Lost Decade' and salaryman masculinity

Intertwining with these shifts was the bursting of the 'Bubble Economy' in the early 1990s, and the various social, economic, and cultural repercussions over the ensuing years of the 'Lost Decade' (see Kingston 2011).[16]

One of the fall-outs from the economic slowdown and consequent corporate restructuring was a further dismantling of some of the mainstays of the organizational culture associated with the salaryman, in particular the implicit guarantee of permanent lifetime employment, even in the larger, elite organizations which had generally been considered to be insulated against sudden radical shifts in employment policy and practice. Indeed, more than just specific institutions and practices, this dismantling extended out to encompass some of the core ideological assumptions of corporate culture. The discourse around workplace success (even *survival*) started shifting quite emphatically to an ideology of *seika-shugi* ('performance-based') privileging individual responsibility (*jiko sekinin*) and entrepreneurial risk-taking, a significant move away from the earlier emphasis on consensus and generalist managerial skills (Miyazaki 2006: 150; Gagné 2010: ch. 3; Higashino 2011).

This had a particularly acute impact on that generation of men who had come to be most closely associated with salaryman masculinity: the Baby Boomer generation that had entered the workforce during the peak years of economic growth in the late 1960s to early 1970s. The implicit assumption was that the economy would keep growing and corporations would continue expanding. Hence, the expectation, within the framework of the lifetime employment/seniority promotions system, was that as this cohort moved up the organizational hierarchy, organizations would keep expanding, and by the time they reached the age when they would move into middle management, sufficient managerial posts would have been created to absorb them. However, in the wake of the unanticipated economic slowdown following the bursting of the 'bubble', corporations found themselves with excess capacity, particularly in terms of human resources, and it was this cohort of salarymen who were particularly troublesome for corporations. In the context of a seniority-based organizational structure that had tied promotions and pay scales to length of service, they were now turning out to be an inefficient layer of 'excess fat around the middle' within the organizational hierarchy. At the same time (partly due to the cost burden on organizations to continue maintaining permanent staff at or approaching middle management), organizations were increasingly forced to cut back on their new staff intake, particularly the intake of young female graduates into the workforce, ushering what came to be dubbed the 'Employment Ice Age' by the media at the time (Rebick 1998). One of the consequences of these cutbacks was that the burden of work and the pressure on middle management to 'come up with the figures' became even more intense, further exacerbating those negative aspects associated with salaryman masculinity, such as *karôshi* and the *tanshin funin* phenomenon, which had come under social and media scrutiny in the 1980s. Furthermore, as part of the 'restructuring' (*risutora*) of organizations and hierarchies that many corporations embarked upon, large numbers of middle-management staff found their very jobs under threat. As organizations sought to cut costs – even by shuffling around numbers, so that on paper there would at least be an appearance of reduction in staff numbers at the parent company – growing numbers of lower- and middle-management staff found themselves being shunted off to branch offices and subsidiaries, or even being 'outsourced' to other firms.[17] Others were asked to take extended leave, or only come in to work a few days a week, or, contravening everything lifetime employment supposedly stood for, were laid off (Roberson and Suzuki 2003a: 9, 10).

The implications of these shifts in corporate ideology were manifold. First, the unemployment rate continued to climb through the 1990s as a consequence of companies driven into bankruptcy due to the recession, or as a result of corporate restructuring – in 1992 the official unemployment rate had been 2.1 per cent; even in 1995 it was still at a relatively low 3.2 per cent, but by 1999 it had climbed to 4.7 per cent, reaching 5 per cent in 2001 (Japan Institute of Labour 2003: 22). The group impacted the most by the adverse employment conditions was males in the fifteen to twenty-four age bracket (with an unemployment rate of 11.1 per cent in 2002, compared with 4.5 per cent in 1990). However, these unemployment figures also reflected a rise in joblessness rates among middle-aged men, many of whom were the victims of corporate restructuring and lay-offs. The unemployment rate for men in the forty-five to fifty-four age group had been a mere 1.1 per cent in 1990; by 2002 it had climbed to 4.3 per cent, and for those in the next age category – fifty-five to sixty-four – the rate was 7.1 per cent, up from 3.4 per cent in 1990 (Japan Institute of Labour 2003: 44). For men in these age groups, the implications of being retrenched were particularly hard-hitting. Not only did they have to contend with the financial and economic strain imposed upon themselves and their families, but, given the centrality of work in defining their identity up until that point, their very *masculinity* was seen as being compromised. One fall-out from this was a marked increase in the male suicide rate, particularly among middle-aged men – as Roberson and Suzuki note, by 2000 the number of men killing themselves was over 2.5 times the 1970 number, and suicide was the second most common cause of death for men in their forties (Roberson and Suzuki 2003a: 14, n.7; also Itô 1996: 48–51; Taga 2006b: 179, 180). Generally speaking, for a significant proportion of salarymen in this age group, even among those who had not been laid off, there was a heightened sense of anxiety, stress, and a feeling of having been betrayed by the corporate ideology and system into which they had invested so much.

For younger men, those becoming *shakaijin* during the 1990s, while there was not the same sense of betrayal, there was a definite shift in the way the discourse of salaryman masculinity was being constructed. First, many younger men had firsthand experience of the toll which salaryman masculinity had taken on their fathers' generation. Thus, many of the old 'givens' of salaryman masculinity – stable, lifelong employment with the same firm, or corporate paternalism, for instance – were far less appealing *and* far less of an expectation. Indeed, the new corporate hero seemed no longer to be the *kigyô senshi* or *kaisha ningen*-type figure of earlier decades, but rather, drawing upon the new global realities of a world dominated by transnational neo-liberal capitalism, a more entrepreneurial, 'no-nonsense' economic rationalist-type figure (see Miyazaki 2006). An exemplifier of this seductive new globalized corporate masculinity over these years was someone like Carlos Ghosn, the Brazilian-born CEO of Nissan Motors. Ghosn had taken over the mantle of CEO of the then financially troubled organization in 1999, following Nissan's merger with French automobile manufacturer Renault. He had implemented an aggressive 'take-no-prisoners corporate restructuring' (Dawson 2002: 27), which was seen as being the key to turning around the fortunes of Nissan. Consequently, in the early 2000s, Ghosn became a hero both in corporate boardrooms and business management schools, *and* also something of a popular culture icon. Not only did his autobiography become a bestseller, but it also generated a *manga* based on his career and exploits (Dawson 2002; Roberson and Suzuki 2003a: 9). Another millennium poster boy for the new style of corporate masculinity was Horie Takafumi, the young founder and CEO of the internet company Livedoor Corporation, whose characteristic style of business, flamboyant personality, and sense of grooming appeared to be the complete antithesis of respectable middle-class salaryman masculinity (Gagné 2010: 103, 104; Takeyama 2010: 235). Although Horie was subsequently prosecuted and imprisoned for financial impropriety, he continued to be a powerful symbol of the new, post-bubble, 'un-salaryman'-like masculinity, a style emulated by numerous young entrepreneurs and even younger salarymen.

This shift in the ideals and expectations of corporate masculinity found expression through spaces of popular culture. These popular culture expressions ranged from 'pop management' literature highlighting the new, increasingly hegemonic attributes of success like individual responsibility, assertiveness and risk-taking, through to *manga*, such as the hugely successful *Sarariiman Kintarô* series, whose protagonist Kintarô, a former motorcycle gang member with only a junior high school education who almost accidentally becomes a successful corporate executive, embodied both the diligent, conscientious responsibility associated with middle-class salaryman masculinity *and* the brash decisiveness and aggression that were now being seen as desirable, indeed essential, attributes of success (see Matanle *et al.* 2008).

In addition, for large numbers of young men, the life of a salaryman was becoming less relevant, not only due to the apparent decline in the appeal of that discourse of masculinity, but for the simple reason that compared with their fathers' generation, the likelihood of finding employment in 'traditional' lines of white-collar employment was far more limited in the context of the 1990s 'Employment Ice Age'. As pointed out earlier, by 2002 the male unemployment rate in the 15 to 24 age cohort had risen to 11.1 per cent (Japan Institute of Labour 2003: 45). Conversely, the trend that first started becoming visible in the 1980s of an expansion of temporary and casual work (*arubaito*) among young people, particularly in employment areas like information technology, leisure, hospitality, and the services sector, became firmly entrenched in the 1990s, becoming a sustained source of income and employment for many. Thus, for a growing number of younger Japanese, the narrowing of opportunities in traditional employment areas, dovetailing with their own desires for more flexibility and personal choice in lifestyle, resulted in a sharp increase in the number of 'freeters' (*furiitâ*).[18] Moreover, while in the 1980s and early 1990s there was an association of *freeter* with choice and flexibility to opt out of a rigid employment system (Slater and Galbraith 2011), as the economic slowdown was sustained, part-time and temporary work increasingly became the *only* option for growing numbers of job market entrants. Thus, the number of male 'freeters' in the twenty to twenty-four age group alone increased from fewer than 200,000 in 1987 to close to 400,000 in 1997 (Odani 2001: 24). Overall, the number of persons under age thirty-five officially defined as 'freeter' had risen from less than one million in the late 1980s to over two million by the early 2000s (Kosugi 2008: 3–6; Yuzawa and Miyamoto 2008: 156, 157; also Genda 2005).

It was the coming together of these various forces outlined above, set against the intensifying collective socio-cultural anxiety discussed in the previous chapter, that really brought the interrogation of salaryman masculinity and all that it stood for to the surface in these post-bubble years. Specifically, the accelerated demographic trend of falling birth rates, coupled with population ageing and a shift towards a focus on gender at the government policy-making level, working in concert with the impact of the recession, were important foregrounding conditions to the growing public discourse.[19] The interrogation of the salaryman operated on two intersecting levels. One, the more widespread and visible, was the problematization of the salaryman's lifestyle and work habits, without specific reference to his masculinity (although masculinity often ended up being implicated through discussion of such issues as the lack of communication with his family). Much of the popular media coverage of the hardships faced by salarymen fell into this category, as did much of the academic literature pertaining to the salaryman during these years.[20] This wider media and academic treatment of the salaryman linked in with a growing visibility of critiques and interrogations of *masculinity* as a construct. While there had been some earlier antecedents where masculinity in itself was held up for scrutiny (e.g. Tanaka 1974),[21] it was largely from the 1990s that the voices seeking to tease out and unpack the term became pronounced and visible (Taga 2005). These critiques of masculinity ranged from discussion about masculinity in some mainstream popular media outlets, through personal accounts and reflective essays, to academic and/or activist literature seeking to 'deconstruct' Japanese masculinities. Of particular significance were the critiques of patriarchal institutions and ideological practices, from feminist scholars and grass-roots activists. While the history of such activism dates back to the prewar decades, the visibility and profile of campaigns for gender equality became especially pronounced from the 1970s (see Mackie 2003: 144–168). Indeed, the efforts of such activists and scholars contributed in a significant way to the promulgation of the Equal Employment Opportunity Law (*Danjo Koyô Kikai Kintô Hô*) in 1985, and the subsequent gender-related legislation and policy initiatives enacted through the 1990s (Mackie 2003: 179–193; also Roberts 2002: 61–87; Dales 2009: 27–31). Moreover, some of the serious academic critiques of masculinity as a construct in the 1990s came out of the writings of feminist academics (see Inoue *et al.* 1995; Shibuya 2001).

Through the 1990s, these various voices and strands seeking to interrogate masculinity and 'maleness' coalesced into a loose (yet distinct) social movement centred around men's studies/men's issues. The first 'men's group', *Menzu Ribu Kenkyû Kai* (Men's Liberation Research Association), was set up in Osaka in 1991, and similar groups were set up in other cities over the next few years (see Roberson and Suzuki 2003a: 11; Dasgupta 2009: 87–90).[22] While the issues and concerns of the groups sometimes varied according to specific local conditions, certain issues did cut across all the groups – the provision of a forum where men could talk about issues pertinent to their lives, such as relationships, work, and sexuality, and the raising of community awareness about masculinity. Underlying the thinking of most of these groups was the recognition that while men *did* benefit as a group from the patriarchal dividends of hegemonic masculinity, individual males could also be 'victims' of patriarchy and hegemonic masculinity. The fall-out from this 'burden of masculinity' manifested itself in the types of 'social problems' being publicized in the media – issues such as *karôshi*, suicide, domestic violence, dysfunctional family relationships, and bullying at schools and in the workplace. Many of these issues relating to the 'burden of masculinity' were also inextricably tied in with the underpinnings and features of hegemonic salaryman masculinity. It was in this sense that the 'deconstruction' and teasing out of masculinity – whether by the men's groups, or more generally in writings about masculinity – also invariably linked in with critiques of the discourse of salaryman masculinity. As brought out in the previous sections of this chapter, while critiques of the salaryman extend back to the early twentieth century, what was significant was the fact that the salaryman was now being critiqued as a *gendered* construct. It was the *man* aspect of salaryman that was now starting to be addressed and questioned directly (Inoue *et al.* 1995: 215–233; Nakamura 1996; Toyoda 1997: ch. 3). In addition, importantly, as previously highlighted, this questioning and reflection was intermeshed with all the social, cultural, economic, and political shifts that were occurring in Japan's watershed historical years of the 1990s and into the early 2000s.

Conclusion

It is at this historical juncture, against a backdrop of the shifts in expectations of hegemonic masculinity from the earlier pre-Lost Decade attributes to the newer post-Bubble neo-liberal expectations that the 'voices' of individual men I draw upon in the following chapters come in. As I have stressed previously, to fully appreciate the experiences of individuals at the 'micro' level we need to have some understanding of the socio-historical processes leading up to, and fore-grounding, those individual experiences and narratives. Accordingly, this chapter has set out the socio-historical backdrop against which men (and indeed, women) in the late 1990s and early 2000s were engaging and negotiating, in their day-to-day lives, with the shifting cross-currents of hegemonic masculinity. The chapter traced the shapings and craftings of salaryman masculinity, from its early articu-lations in the initial decades of industrialization and urban modernity, through the 'high point' of the discourse in the initial postwar decades, to the upheavals and shifts in the 1980s and during the recessionary 1990s. Underlying this dis-cussion of the genealogy and the historical trajectory of the salaryman has been the argument that the discourse of salaryman masculinity – as with discourses built around *any* form of masculinity – was *always* in a process of being shaped and re-shaped, crafted and re-crafted. At any one point in time, its shape and form was a product of engagements with the prevailing social, cultural, eco-nomic, and political conditions. This was the case whether we are talking about the emergent white-collar salaryman masculinity in 1920s urban Japan, or the *kigyō senshi* of the 1960s, or the seemingly crisis-besieged salaryman masculin-ity of the 1990s. Moreover, as pointed out earlier, the relationship between hege-monic masculinity and other masculinities is a dynamic, constantly shifting one. These other non-hegemonic masculinities (or aspects of them) may be appropri-ated into the dominant, hegemonic one, or may subvert or challenge it (with even a possibility of superseding it as a new hegemonic masculinity). As this chapter has shown, this has been the case with salaryman masculinity. It emerged out of earlier pre-existing discourses of masculinity, and continued to engage in a variety of ways with a host of different masculinities. Over the span of its historical trajectory, for instance, these various engagements have encom-passed absorbing and adapting aspects of the gender ideology of the pre-Meiji era, coexisting and intersecting with a variety of different masculinities (such as the soldier or farmer) in the decades leading up to the war, effectively becoming *the* hegemonic cultural ideal in the decades following the end of the war, being challenged and re-shaped by new globalized discourses of corporate masculinity (as embodied in figures like Carlos Ghosn) in the post-Bubble 1990s and early 2000s. While the contours and shapings of salaryman masculinity may be, his-torically *and* in the present, continually shifting and transforming in response to prevailing socio-cultural, economic, and political conditions, the question remains as to what extent the core assumptions that made this the cultural ideal shifted during the watershed years of the late 1990s/early 2000s – in particular, the belief that a man needs to work and support his family, in other words, to be the *daikokubashira*, the mainstay of the family. To get a sense of this, the fol-lowing chapters will explore the dynamics through which these core underpin-nings of salaryman masculinity are crafted and re-crafted, on a day-to-day basis.

3   Men's stories of becoming *otoko*

As signalled in the previous chapter, the focus of discussion over the next few chapters will shift to the 'micro' level of the individuals who were my informants. Specifically, what these chapters will attempt to do is to trace the crafting process of the 'gender project' (Connell 2002: 81), referred to in the introductory chapter, at the heart of which lies the individual male's negotiations with the expectations of hegemonic masculinity. While the requirements of this discourse are especially relevant to those men (such as newly inducted salarymen) who as socially 'responsible', adult *shakaijin* are in the process of entering into full-time employment, it would be wrong to assume that the expectations only apply to these men. The *reach* of these hegemonic ideals, as I have argued earlier, is far more extensive, encompassing men who at first glance may appear to be well outside the parameters of the hegemonic ideals. Moreover, as also highlighted previously, this is an engagement that occurs through the life-course trajectory, and begins early in an individual's life. In other words, long before an individual male becomes a *shakaijin* and has to contend with the expectations of salaryman masculinity, he has to engage with what constitute the requirements of the socio-cultural category of *masculinity* itself, and work out what 'being a male' means to him. Indeed, phrased in a slightly different way, we could say that hegemonic masculinity is situated within the wider framework of the ongoing gender project, referred to above, a gender project within which what is meant by terms like 'man' and 'male' (*otoko/dansei*), 'woman' and 'female' (*onna/josei*), 'masculine' (*otokorashii*), 'feminine' (*onnarashii*) are 'crafted'. Accordingly, this chapter will begin by exploring what the informants made of *masculinity* itself, what connotations being *male* had for them, in the context of the wider shifts at work at that particular historical moment in the late 1990s. This will then allow us to better situate their negotiations with the specific requirements of salaryman masculinity (e.g. work, marriage, fatherhood) discussed in subsequent chapters.

Being *otoko*

An appropriate entry point into the informants' own voices would be to start off with a sample of views as to their self-imaginings of 'masculinity' – what it was about themselves that they saw as making them male/a man (*otoko*). When I first posed this question to the informants during the initial focus group discussions, the reaction was one of confused hesitation – it struck me that none of them had really ever been asked to consider this before. Some of the initial responses displayed a deliberate glibness that seemed designed to hide feelings of embarrassment. Thus, the retort to this question from Kimura Kenji, a very articulate and self-confident young man who was my liaison contact in Northern Print, was a laughing statement that he was conscious of his 'masculinity' when he was 'having sex', especially the occasion when his partner became pregnant. In addition, the fact that he 'did not menstruate' (*seiri ga nai*) was another reminder of masculinity for him (Northern Print Focus Group (hereafter NPFG) Interview Transcript: 1). Masculinity, in his case, appeared to be framed primarily in biological terms. For Kajima Daisuke, a twenty-eight-year-old technical manager, to whom I will return in more detail in subsequent chapters, the realization of his own masculinity was reinforced when he got married. As he put it: 'Thinking back, it was when I got married and obtained a bride (*yome-san*) that I thought "Well, I'm a man"' (NPFG: 1).

Others defined masculinity by what it was *not* – attributes associated with femininity. Thus, for Inoue Toshifumi, a twenty-six-year-old technical shop-floor employee at Northern Print, his sense of being male was defined in relation to the (perceived) psycho-emotional differences between males and females – women, in his view, were more 'emotional (*kanjōteki*)' than men (NPFG: 2).

The focus group discussion with informants from Northern Energy also elicited a similar mixture of responses. One individual mentioned being 'stronger than females' as being a determinant of defining masculinity (Northern Energy Focus Group (hereafter NEFG) Interview Transcript: 1). Another member, echoing the observation by Kajima-san of Northern Print,[1] drew upon the image of the '*daikokubashira* [literally, "central pillar of the household"] ... working with all his strength to support a family' (NEFG: 1). Another informant, Murai Yukihiro, also saw masculinity defined by the need to be a *daikokubashira* figure, to 'financially and emotionally' support the family (NEFG: 2).

At one level, this sample of responses to my rather sudden way of opening the discussion seems to indicate the entrenched hold of hegemonic ideals surrounding masculinity (masculinity = strength, the need to be the *daikokubashira*). Yet, at the same time, the responses also seem to point to a certain distance between many of the informants and the very same ideals. This came through when I asked them to give me examples of public figures (such as popular culture icons) who they saw as embodying 'manliness' (*otokorashisa*). The name that came up in both groups was the actor Takakura Ken, the star of numerous films, particularly in the 1960s and 1970s (NEFG: 3, 4; NPFG: 5, 6). There is no denying that the characters portrayed by Takakura Ken embodied many of the hegemonic 'ideals' of masculinity; indeed as Standish points out, a kind of 'hypermasculinity' (Standish 2000: passim). Yet, not unlike the figure of *Sarariiman Kintarō* mentioned in previous chapters, the idealized masculinity portrayed by the movie characters played by Takakura Ken often borders on the parodic. The fact that my informants referred to a *caricature* as a metonym for masculinity seemed indicative of not just the pervasiveness of hegemonic ideals, but also the disjunctures and distance between the informants' everyday realities living and working in the context of late 1990s Japan, and the ideals they were presenting.

Becoming *otoko*

Arguably, to gain a deeper understanding of the complexity at stake in the engagements between individuals and the cultural ideals of hegemonic masculinity, we need to start by exploring the informants' own recollections of the 'gender project' – the 'crafting' process by which they became gendered, coming to recognize what the hegemonic expectations were of them as males (and conversely what the hegemonic expectations were for female siblings and peers). In order to achieve an appreciation of this process as seen by individual males, I asked the informants to reminisce about their childhoods – to talk about their families, about relationships with siblings, with playmates, about childhood dreams, about their experiences of 'coming into' masculinity. Their narratives reveal the richness and complexity at work in the process – the fact that 'coming into' masculinity is not just a simple process of learning to conform to the hegemonic discourse, but is fraught with contradictions, confusion, negotiations, and even (sometimes) subversions.

Shin'ya Naohiko, a twenty-two-year-old computer systems technician at the head office of Northern Energy, brought out some of this complexity while talking about his childhood. This informant came from a smaller coastal regional city, several hours by train from the prefectural capital where he presently lived. His earliest childhood memories were of his father being away for long stretches of time. His father was a fisherman on long-range ocean trawlers, and hence was away for periods of weeks or months. Thus, unlike those informants who came from more typically salaryman-type families where weekends (or at least Sundays) were often times given over to 'family service' (*kazoku sâbisu*) by the father, Shin'ya-san had no real recollections of the family doing something together as a unit, apart from times when they would visit his grandparents' home town. When Shin'ya-san was in primary school his father quit his seafaring life and established his own small business (*jieigyô*), a transport and removal company. In common with owner-operators of many small businesses, *both* his parents, in fact at times, all members of the family including himself, were involved in the running of the business. Indeed, he recalled no differences in even the physical labour his parents engaged in – both parents were equally likely to lift and move heavy boxes. Rather, in his recollection, the 'big [gender] difference in the household was based on who did the cooking' (Shin'ya, Round 1 Interview Transcript: 12).

In other respects though, Shin'ya-san recalled having conventional notions of gender inculcated early on within the family. For instance, he mentioned having memories of starting to cry as his parents left for work and leaving him at home, and being told that 'boys shouldn't cry, it's wrong to cry' (Round 1: 6). Although he noted that 'at the time it probably hadn't been such a shock' (6), thinking back now he could see the gender ideology at work in his upbringing. At the same time, he said he could understand his parents' desire to 'want a boy to grow up strong' (7), and maintained that he would probably follow the same course with his own son/s. This almost simultaneous validation and rejection of the dominant gender ideology might initially come across as baffling and contradictory. However, as highlighted earlier, it is *precisely* this type of ambiguity and contradiction that interweaves through the engagements between the individual and hegemonic masculinity.

Another instance when this complexity surfaced was in our discussions about his earliest memories of being 'a boy'. In common with several of the other informants, he remembered the first distinctions between boys and girls as dating back to his kindergarten years. However, as the following extract from his account indicates, Shin'ya-san seems to recognize the gender *policing* that was involved, what Connell, drawing upon Barrie Thorne's ethnographic study of primary schools, refers to as 'borderwork' (Connell 2002: 14; see also Thorne 1993: 64–88):

> It was kindergarten, so around five, four, five years, there was this realization of being male. Well, at kindergarten there was a distinction (*kubetsu*) made in the way of educating boys and girls. So, for instance, with, how do you say it ... is it the kindergarten clothes (*enji-fuku*) ... the kindergarten uniforms, boys wore blue, and girls wore pink. Even from that point, I think there was an understanding that 'boys are boys' (*otoko wa otoko nan da*).
>
> (Shin'ya, Round 1: 4)

As mentioned above, while many of the informants (as we will see) may have made passing references to similar practices, Shin'ya-san stood out in terms of his *recognition* (sometimes critical, sometimes approving) of these practices possessing a built-in gender ideology. As he continued with his account, this recognition of the dynamics at work continued to come across:

> well, another aspect that makes you realize [this distinction between] boys and girls is, in the lower grades of primary school they have health examinations [*shintai sokutei*, literally 'body measurements'] about twice a year, and although boys and girls did it together, by the middle grades of primary school, from around the fourth grade, they're separated into 'boys' and 'girls'. So in terms of perception, firstly, you're made aware that this is a difference in terms of the body.
>
> (Shin'ya, Round 1: 5)

He saw this inscription of gender through bodily practices as a form of regulation/discipline (*kanri*), something that became further accentuated as he progressed from primary school, through junior high school and onto high school:

they often call it 'disciplining' (*kanri*). And then, at the primary school level, as far as my image of what we'd wear, basically we'd wear track-suits, or those kinds of comfortable outfits to school. But once we got to grade five or six, you notice the girls starting to dress up.... Then once we got to junior high school, there were uniforms. The girls were made to wear skirts and the boys trousers. And by the time of around junior high, even the construction of the body (*shintai no tsukuri*) becomes completely different.

(Shin'ya, Round 1: 5)

He then went on to describe his experience in high school. He had gone to a technical high school (*kôgyô kôkô*), which although in theory coeducational, was in actual fact almost exclusively male. This experience further accentuated, in his mind, the supposed difference between work that men are able to do (*otoko ga dekiru shigoto*) and women are able to do (*onna ga dekiru shigoto*) (Shin'ya, Round 1: 5).[2] Significantly, this was an individual who had only completed high school before entering Northern Energy, and had almost certainly never heard of theorists like Foucault. Yet, the above account reveals a surprising level of sophistication in his analysis of these engendering practices through the disciplining of bodies (see Foucault 1979).

While not necessarily demonstrating the level of awareness shown by Shin'ya-san, other informants too were able to recall the complexities of the process through which they came into masculinity. Yoshida Shun'ichi, who had just entered Northern Energy a few months prior to our interview, was an only child in a family where the father was a carpenter (but significantly, as he was not self-employed, Yoshida-san referred to his father as a 'salaryman'), and the mother was a *sengyô shufu* ('full-time' housewife). In terms of realizations of his 'maleness', he mentioned being aware of differences between girls and boys quite early on, particularly of the image of 'boys are strong' (*otoko wa tsuyoi*) taking hold, despite the fact that at that stage, in kindergarten, 'since they're all just kids, there isn't much difference in strength' (Yoshida, Round 1: 3). Describing this 'coming into' masculinity, he made the following observation:

Is it, umm, a kind of unknowing 'mind control' [uses English term] (*shirazu, shirazu no maindo kontorôru*)? The environment's already like that. There's always [the expectation] of 'you're a boy, after all'. So right from the time of childhood, without realizing it everyone had formed [ideas about] what a man should be, what a woman should be.

(Yoshida, Round 1: 3)

Miura Tôru, a young twenty-year-old recruit, had also entered Northern Energy only a few months prior to our discussion. Like Shin'ya Naohiko, he came from a family where the father had quit regular paid employment when Miura-san was in the first year of junior high school, and had set up his own small business (a car-repair workshop) out of the family home. As with Shin'ya-san, all members of the family were involved to some degree in the business – his mother (who also worked part-time at a restaurant) would step in to help during busy end-of-month periods, and he and his sister would also help out when it was busy. Being brought up in such an environment meant that many of the spatial (work/home, outside/inside), temporal (work time/non-work time), and gender (male/female, masculine/feminine) boundaries that are thought to characterize the lifestyles of salaryman families were often transgressed. Rather, Miura-san's recollection of gender roles in his family pointed to a nonconformity to conventional expectations. For instance, when I asked him about who used to help with the washing-up after dinner, he laughed and said that his younger sister (who, in keeping with hegemonic gender expectations, would have been the one normally expected to help) did not do anything. 'Normally', he explained to me,

> my mother would do it, but sometimes, they [the dishes] would just be left lying around, and everyone would fall asleep. At those times, whoever'd find them first would just say 'it can't be helped' (*shikata nai na*) and do them!
>
> (Miura, Round 1: 4)

There seemed to be an almost tongue-in-cheek, playful engagement with the hegemonic gender expectations at work here, within his family. Moreover, when he was growing up, he never felt that his parents worried about his need to conform to expectations of hegemonic masculinity. As he put it, 'my parents didn't really care about those kind of things … they'd never say [things like] because you're a male you have to have a family (*katei o motsu*) or you have to go out [into the world]' (Miura, Round 1: 6). Indeed, according to him, his family seemed to have almost deliberately encouraged him *not to* subscribe to the cultural ideals of masculinity. For instance, unlike Shin'ya-san whose parents followed the 'boys should not cry' line, Miura-san was actually told to 'have a good cry and get it [what he was upset about] off your chest, then do whatever you have to do' (Miura, Round 1: 6).

Like Shin'ya-san, Miura-san's 'coming into' realizing the expectations of masculinity came more from institutions like school, his friends and peers, and popular culture. Whereas his parents may not have expected him to achieve certain standards just because he was a boy, he was told by teachers at school that 'since you're a male, some day you'll have to support a family and will have to work, so you need to get some kind of qualification now' (Miura, Round 1: 6). Indeed, as was the case with Shin'ya-san, his 'coming into' masculinity was also closely intertwined with regulatory bodily practices through institutions like schooling. When I asked him about his earliest recollections of 'being male', he mentioned that very early on, in kindergarten, the distinction between girls and boys was 'all mixed-up (*gucha-gucha*)'. However, he continued,

> in primary school, at the swimming pool, boys and girls were told to get changed separately. At that time, I think I realized that there are boys and there are girls.
>
> (Miura, Round 1: 4)

When I asked him if this distinct sense of difference between boys and girls strengthened as he progressed through junior high and high school, he agreed, and laughingly suggested that 'if that wasn't the case, you'd turn into a "weird person" (*ayashii hito*)' (Miura, Round 1: 6). What seems to underlie this statement is an acknowledgement of the need for the gender 'borderwork' I referred to earlier.

Ishida Naoki, another Northern Energy employee, mentioned a similar childhood experience triggering his awareness of the gendered body. This informant's father had died in his first year of junior high school, and he had been brought up by his mother. Although he had no siblings, he did have a female cousin who used to come over, and they would play together. He recalled first becoming really aware of his male gendered body around the fourth grade of primary school when having a bath together with this cousin. By the time they had entered junior high school, both he and the cousin felt embarrassed about this (Ishida, Round 1: 6).

Imai Shinji, another Northern Energy employee working in the customer relations section, also remembered the realization of masculinity coming through practices inscribing gender onto the body, particularly the way bodily changes (for example, the voice breaking at adolescence) are read as success or lack of success in maintaining a 'timetable' of masculinity. The following exchange between us brings out this inscribing of gender onto the body, and the associated anxieties:

I: Well, I suppose I first strongly became conscious (*tsuyoku ishiki shita*) of girls around junior high.

R: Was there, any, if you can remember, any particular incident?

I: Any incident? Well, it's not really an incident, but, umm, I was a bit late [in maturing] (*okureme-gachi*). You could say I was late, or, possibly my growth was slow, so my voice was like a girl's. Even now, my voice is a bit high though...

R: Is that so? [*his voice had not struck me as particularly out of the ordinary*]

I: Oh, do you think it's normal (*futsû*)? [*seems surprised and a bit relieved*]

R: Well, you know, lots of people's voices [are high]; I think perhaps I have a fairly high voice too!

I: Well, anyhow whatever the case, on the whole, I had a very high voice. The boys' voices started changing [breaking], probably from around the third year of junior high, and even the girls started to get shy [around boys]. Like, girls who'd been 'tomboyish' (*otokoppoi*) until then, well, they started to become more feminine (*onnappoku natta*). So you see them changing like that constantly. And you know how ... childish junior high school students are; as they become conscious of women's bodies (*onna no hito no karada*) they start going to those kind of sleazy places together, or [renting 'adult'] videos, it's an age when curiosity about those kind of things is strong. And seeing everyone around me like that, I started to think I should be like that too.

(Imai, Round 1: 4, 5)

The above exchange seems to signal an uneasy engagement – an anxiety, almost – with the expectations of masculinity on the part of those individuals like this informant whose bodies or minds do not quite match up to those expectations. It brings to mind Thorne's observation arising out of her ethnographic study of primary school children, that, whereas 'early-developing girls ... especially if they have large breasts are treated almost as if they are physically handicapped, early-developing boys reap social advantages' (Thorne 1993: 139).

A number of my informants recalled themselves as having been 'behind schedule' in terms of bodily maturation and 'coming into' masculinity. Shimizu Ayaki, a Northern Print employee, for instance, mentioned that he was '*okute*' (late maturing), and hence did not really become aware of his masculinity until the upper grades of primary school (Shimizu, Round 1: 3). Sometimes there was a mixture of early recognition at one level but notions of masculinity and femininity being blurred at another – Matsumoto Tadashi, the Northern Energy accountant who was my liaison person in the organization, recalled being 'interested in girls' as early as grade one of primary school, but at the same time also said that notions of male and female remained 'fuzzy (*aimai*) until around the fourth or fifth year of primary school' (Matsumoto, Round 1: 5).

Nevertheless, in the case of Imai Shinji, discussed above, the anxiety relating to not 'matching up' to the schedule of masculinity seemed to be particularly noticeable. His account is somewhat reminiscent of Connell's discussion in *The Men and the Boys* of one of her informants, Adam Singer, and the sense of 'spoiled masculinity' with reference to himself during his childhood and adolescence – looking down at his fat, 'wobbly' thighs while playing sport one day and feeling a sense of disgust at his body for not matching up to the hegemonic bodily ideal (Connell 2000: 92).

Unlike Shin'ya Naohiko and Miura Tôru, Imai-san came from a family background where the parents were in salaried employment – both his mother and father were teachers. Perhaps, partly as a result of the parents' occupation and the consequent influence on the home environment as he was growing up, there appeared to have been a considerable degree of expectation levelled at him to achieve the desired standards of masculinity. Indeed, as the more favoured of two male siblings, it appears that his parents had placed far more than just the standard expectations of hegemonic masculinity upon him. Integral to (what appeared to be) his parents' expectations of him were expectations directly related to how he should behave as a male; in other words, his embodiment of appropriate masculinity, physically, mentally, and intellectually – for example, being repeatedly told that as a boy he should not cry and should endure pain silently, despite his self-acknowledged proclivity towards being able to shed tears quite readily (Imai, Round 1: 6).

This need to live up to his parents' expectations of him *as a male* also extended to the constant pressure he felt to study hard, and excel at his studies, thereby ensuring his future academic and career pathways. However, according to him, this effort to live up to his parents' expectations had possibly been at the expense of a happy childhood and adolescence:

thinking back now, while I do think that it's been good for me, there were also lots of things I sacrificed (*gisei ni shimashita*). For example, in high school, while everyone was dating girls, I'd control myself (*gaman*) and keep studying. Or I'd want to go out and have fun with everyone, but instead of going would study....

Basically, my parents' teaching was if you persevere (*gaman*) and endure hardships (*kurô*) now, things will be easy later (*ato raku ni naru*). However, if you play around now, you're sure to have hardship later; they'd say that kind of thing.

(Imai, Round 1: 8, 9)

He now wished that he had 'stood up' to his parents and exerted his 'own will' (*jibun no ishi*) more (Imai, Round 1: 7), instead of following his parents' advice and going to a 'good university' (where he majored in law). In many senses his problematic engagement with the hegemonic expectations of masculinity dating back to his childhood and teenage years seemed to remain an issue for him in his engagements with salaryman masculinity at the time of our conversation.

Several other informants also mentioned gender expectations and expectations of responsibility on the part of parents (in addition to expectations of teachers or society in general) as being important in shaping their sense of being *otoko*. Yoshida Shun'ichi, the Northern Energy employee whose account of becoming aware of his masculinity was referred to earlier in this section, provided the following example illustrating the influence his parents (specifically his mother, a full-time homemaker) had on his masculinity:

for example, let's say, I'm eating. And, say, my mother seems busy in the kitchen, I say I'll go get some more rice myself. So that's what I do. But if I do that, my mother gets angry. She's says 'You're a male aren't you? It's [the kitchen] not a place men should normally go into'. [Things like] that make quite an impression, don't they? So if you think about that kind of [family] dynamic in relation to men and women in my family it's like, very, how should I say, men should work outside, women should cook ... and follow the man, or, I guess, that the wife should play a supportive role. It was that kind of family. So I think that's had something of an influence on me.

(Yoshida, Round 1: 4, 5)

Extended family members also played a role in the shaping of ideas about gender. Matsumoto Tadashi, my liaison at Northern Energy, mentioned that the expectations of masculinity on him came not so much from his parents, but from his grandfather, who would stress such points as not crying because he was a boy, and the need to exercise and be strong (Matsumoto, Round 1: 6, 7).

This informant came from a middle-class nuclear salaryman family, where both parents worked – his father worked in sales for a firm in the housing industry, and his mother, who had always worked, was also involved in sales.

However, while his mother may have been slightly unconventional in the sense that, by choosing a career outside the home even when her children were small, she was not subscribing to the full-time homemaker/mother 'ideal', in other respects his upbringing followed fairly conventional gender ideological lines. For instance, when I asked him if there had been any sense of difference between himself as male, and his younger sister as female, he talked about how, when they were growing up, while he was free to come home as late as he liked, his sister had a 'curfew' (*mongen*) imposed upon her movements (Matsumoto, Round 1: 4). Importantly Matsumoto-san recognized that this difference was linked to gender. He also mentioned that whereas his sister would help with housework, he hardly did anything. At the same time, he mentions starting to feel, from when he was in upper primary school, a sense that as the older male sibling (indeed, the eldest son, the *chônan*), he had a responsibility to 'properly look after' his younger sister (4, 5).

There were commonalities in the experiences of Matsumoto-san with Fujita Yûji who worked in the sales and marketing section of Northern Print. Fujita-san also came from a family where the father was an 'average salaryman (*futsû no sar-iiman*)' (Fujita, Round 1: 3). The father seemed typical of earlier generations of salarymen fathers (see Ishii-Kuntz 1993; also Hidaka 2010). He was strict, and apart from meals together on weekends, had limited interaction with the children. His mother, however, like Matsumoto Tadashi's, did not really fit the image of the typical salaryman's *sengyô shufu* (full-time housewife). She had returned to paid work when Fujita-san had been in primary school, and had continued working ever since. One year before our interview, the mother had established her own business – a trading company importing health-food products from China.

Yet, as with Matsumoto-san, the gender dynamics within his family when he was growing up seemed to operate according to conventional gender expectations. For instance, it was his elder sister, and not he, who helped with household chores like cooking and cleaning (Fujita, Round 1: 5). At the same time, he had the following to say with reference to expectations on him as a male child in the family:

> Well, it varies, but, well, when you become a junior high student, you think about things like your future course [in life] (*shinro*). At the time what I came to realize was that, if you were female, well, this may sound bad, but, as long as in the end you got married you could sit back and let the future take care of itself (*koshi-kake to ka demo daijôbu*). But if you're male you can't really do that. You've got to make sure you get a job, and then, you have to keep working to support your wife. I really felt this responsibility on me because I was male.
>
> (Fujita, Round 1: 6, 7)

This observation links back to the point highlighted previously, namely the importance of the *daikokubashira* imagery in constructing and sustaining 'idealized' masculinity. Fujita-san's words seem to reflect both the strength and pervasive grip of the hegemonic gender ideology, as well as the sense of *unease* – even in child-hood/early adolescence – with the ideological expectations of the discourse of the man as *daikokubashira*. As we shall see in later chapters, this concurrent conform-ity to, and contestation of, the expectations of hegemonic masculinity would con-tinue to inform and shape Fujita-san's life-path into adulthood.

Becoming sexual *otoko*

Another issue worth considering, alluded to in passing in some of the accounts discussed above, is the connection between this 'gender project' of masculinity and being 'crafted' into particular expectations of heterosexuality. Significantly, with one important exception which I discuss below, there appeared to be an assumption on the part of all the informants that cross-gender sexual attraction was integral to masculinity. Thus, most of the informants would make reference to developing crushes on female classmates, or becoming sexually attracted to girls from around junior high school (witness Imai-san's account outlined earlier). These accounts varied from Murayama Satoshi, a thirty-year-old North-ern Energy head office employee, who mentioned becoming fond of and feeling he 'had to protect' a female playmate in his first year of primary school (Murayama: 18), to Makimura Keisuke, a twenty-three-year-old architect/planner also with Northern Energy, who said he first realized his masculinity in grade two of primary school when he experienced his 'first love' (*hatsu-koi*) towards a 'cute girl in class' (Makimura, Round 1: 3), through to Kimura Kenji, my liaison contact at Northern Print, who blamed the sudden drop in his aca-demic performance when he got to the second year of high school, on his having 'learnt girls' (*onna oboeta*); in other words, the start of his sexual relations with the opposite sex (Kimura, Round 1: 8).

However, unlike what appears to be the case with patterns of 'coming into' masculinity in so much of the literature pertaining to Australia, the United Kingdom, or the United States (see, e.g. Walker 1988; Mac an Ghaill 1994; Martino 1999; Plummer 1999; Epstein 2001; Mills 2001), the construction of my informants' masculinity during childhood and adolescence did not appear to be pivoted around aggressively articulated homophobia. Indeed, the possibility of any form of sexual preference other than heterosexual was virtually absent from their (voiced) accounts. This was in striking contrast to the 'fear' of homosexu-ality that seemed to have been such a recurring source of anxiety for the inform-ants of writers like Mac an Ghaill (1994), Walker (1988), or Plummer (1999) in the construction of their masculinities. However, in the case of my informants, the situation was more a case of erasure through non-articulation. Thus, with the exception of a number of occasions when unvoiced cracks in the façade may have allowed for some ambiguity, the assumption on the part of my informants seemed to be of a mutual heterosexuality.[3]

The one case where this assumption of heterosexuality as a composite part of the 'coming into' masculinity fell apart was in the case of Arai Jun, a young public sector white-collar employee, who (although not publicly 'out' at work) defined his identity in terms of his same-sex attraction; in other words, he unambiguously referred to himself as 'gay'.[4] He came from a fairly typical salaryman family – his father was a bank employee, and his mother was a full-time housewife (although she had apparently worked part-time in the past). At the time of our interview, he was 'out' to his mother and younger sister, but not to his father, whom he described as conservative and unlikely to accept his son's alternative sexuality. When he was growing up, while his mother had encouraged him to help with housework (saying that men would have to be able to do such things in years to come), his father had placed great stress on what boys should and should not do. For instance, his father would say such things as 'a kitchen isn't a place for a man' (Arai, Interview: 2), or 'cooking is only for women' (3). Yet Arai-san found it hard to accept what he saw as his father's double standards when he was reprimanded for coming home too late when he was already a university student, something that (if his father was to be consistent) was conventionally regarded as a male prerogative (see, for instance, Matsumoto Tadashi's account, above).

Arai-san's first 'realization' of his masculinity emerged when he became fond of a female playmate in the group of four or five children he used to play with in kindergarten (Arai: 3). This did not, however, lead to a progression into *sexual* attraction towards girls (as seemed to be the case with other informants). He first developed a crush on a male classmate when he was in the sixth grade of primary school and then on an older *senpai* (senior) in the club he was involved with in junior high school. At the time he did not think it particularly problematic (Arai: 4). He 'explained' these feelings to himself by comparing them to the same-sex closeness stage in adolescent development he said he studied in junior high school, although he now realized that these feelings were perhaps more than just symptoms of 'normal' adolescent development.

It was around this time that the first notions of himself as 'gay' – in other words, a discourse of his whole masculine identity revolving around his sexuality – started to crystallize in his mind. Playing a part in this was a television programme he mentioned watching late one night. From his description, this late-night programme sounded to me like a sort of sensationalistic 'exposé' of the gay 'underbelly' of the Shinjuku Ni-chome gay bar area of Tokyo.[5] In his words:

> The programme, it was at night ... was [about] 'discovering gays'. The image formed from the media was that they [gay people] lead normal lives during the day, but come out furtively at night (*yoru da to koso koso koso koso shiteiru*). So [that made me wonder] if that was the case in Tokyo, was there anyone else like me in this city.
>
> (Arai: 4, 5)

However, although he had crushes on schoolmates and even started to think of himself as gay, he felt that he could not tell anyone about these things. As he put it, 'I didn't think of myself as strange (*hen*), but I felt that I couldn't tell any one, it was a "no-go zone" (*dame da*)' (5). As most of his fellow male classmates started talking about and then forming relationships with girls, he too started 'going steady' with a girl. They did not have sex though, and he said that he 'didn't even like holding hands' (5).

In high school, he came across the phone number of a local gay support group in *Hot Dog* (a popular teenage male magazine), and through them was introduced to his first gay contact – a person who apparently had a very positive influence on Arai-san's still formative self-image and self-esteem. At university he became quite heavily involved in exploring his sexuality, both through 'playing around (*asonda*)' on the gay scene, as well as through involvement in gay groups and activism (including participating in the city's Lesbian and Gay Pride Parade). He considered this year of 'playing around' as being 'a year of "experimenting" ... [and] extremely valuable' (7) in his life. Indeed, without having gone through these experiences, he felt that he would not have moved on to developing the more 'serious' facets of his sexuality. These included such things as his involvement in the support group for sexual minorities in which he participated, and the stable, monogamous relationship he had established with his current partner.

At the time of our discussion, Arai-san had graduated from university a few months earlier, and had made the transition to *shakaijin* life. I will return to his story in a later chapter, when I discuss how he negotiated the contradictions between his strong sense of *gay* masculinity and the hegemonic salaryman masculinity to which, as a *shakaijin*, he was expected to subscribe. What marked Arai-san out from the other informants was the fact that unlike them, he was far more *conscious* of the day-to-day engagements with the expectations of hegemonic masculinity. Thus, whereas for the other informants discussed above, their 'coming into' sexuality was presented as a relatively unproblematic element of the trajectory of their overall life-paths, Arai-san's reflections are valuable in that they serve to remind us of Connell's assertion that 'gender, even in its most elaborate, abstract or fantastic forms, is always an "accomplishment".... Gender is something actually *done*; and done in social life, not something that exists prior to social life' (Connell 2002: 55; emphasis added).

Conclusion

As the first of the five chapters drawing on individuals' narratives, this chapter has focused on the 'doing of gender' in the context of what I have called 'coming into' masculinity – the markers and practices through which the informants recalled their journeys into 'masculinity'. Their accounts in this chapter support the argument that there is no one assembly-line-like biologically predetermined trajectory of 'coming into' masculinity followed by all males. As their stories have brought out, while all of them did have to define their sense of being male vis-à-vis dominant social structures, institutions, ideologies, and discourses, each individual's experience was *his own* experience. In other words, the individuals had enough agency to carve out some sense of their own masculinity, albeit with reference to hegemonic expectations. For some individuals these engagements were relatively unproblematic (at least on a consciously articulated level). For others – for instance, Arai Jun, or even Shin'ya Naohiko – it was a process that appeared to involve interrogation, self-reflexivity, and strategic negotiations. For all of them, their 'coming into' masculinity was a rich, multifaceted process, part of the overall 'gender project' referred to earlier.

Chapter 4 will follow the informants during another extremely significant juncture in their lives – the weeks and months during which they were making the transition from pre-productive, pre-*shakaijin* student masculinity to productive (and reproductive) adult *shakaijin* salaryman masculinity, against the backdrop of the wider social, cultural, political, and economic shifts in process in 'Lost Decade' Japan.

4　Becoming *shakaijin*

'Craftings' into salaryman masculinity

The previous chapter explored the complexities of 'coming into' masculinity as boys and adolescents in informants' life-paths towards adulthood as fully fledged, socially responsible *shakaijin*. Over the next few chapters, the central concern shifts to the ways in which these individual informants, upon entry into the workforce, negotiated with the expectations of *shakaijin* salaryman masculinity, against the backdrop of the micro and macro cross-currents of the late 1990s/early 2000s workplace.

As David Plath noted in his Introduction to *Work and Lifecourse in Japan*, the 'essence of a career is that it is a predictable sequence of movements, a relay of roles set up to normalize the potentially turbulent flow of persons through an organization' (Plath 1983b: 3). Arguably, this 'predictability' has become considerably less so in the decades since Plath wrote these words. However, the underlying notion of a demarcated life-path along which the individual is expected to progress has continued to remain an important socio-cultural assumption, particularly in relation to hegemonic masculinity. Moreover, as signalled previously, an integral element of this process is the delineation of *markers* that perform varied (and sometimes contradictory) functions, including normalizing the 'potentially turbulent flow' (3) of traversing the organizational life-path. Importantly, such markers also serve a boundary-policing function, to rein in those in danger of transgressing the parameters set by the dominant ideology and discourse.

Within the context of the hegemonic expectations regarding masculinity, these 'markers' at various points of the individual male's life trajectory would include ceremonies marking the transition from one level of education to the next (for instance, high school graduation), entry into the workforce and *shakaijin* life, progression through various stages of his career, and subsequently retirement and 'honorary' *shakaijin* status. Not doing so, not undergoing the relevant 'markers' at the appropriate point in the life-path, still has implications of lack and immaturity – that somehow, the individual in question is not living up to the relevant *shakaijin* responsibilities, be they full-time work, marriage, parenthood, or even taking on the role of grandparent. While this has long been the case, it was of particular significance during (and since) the period I am focusing on in this book. As discussed earlier, it was really during these years, as male *freeter* numbers kept burgeoning, and as corporations relied increasingly on irregular and subcontracted labour, that the reality that not all young male graduates would be assured of stable, long-term employment that would take them from entry into the workforce through until retirement really started to take hold. Ironically, as increasing numbers of younger men found themselves unable (or unwilling) to gain entry into the orbit of hegemonic salaryman masculinity, these 'markers', for those who *did* gain access, took on additional weight and socio-cultural significance.

This chapter will highlight the first (and arguably the most significant) of these 'markers' of hegemonic masculinity – the new entrant's 'induction' into permanent work (and, simultaneously, into salaryman masculinity) in the liminal first weeks and months of his *shakaijin* life. Although, as stressed in earlier chapters, multiple masculinities coexist (and sometimes conflict) within the same individual through his life, the ambiguities, and conflicts and tensions resulting from the interplay of different discourses of masculinity are perhaps most apparent over this period. On the one hand, the new entrant is still influenced by discourses of adolescent/youth/student masculinity. This influence manifests itself in a variety of areas – in his fashions, his hairstyle, his verbal and body language, his time management, his daily schedule, his friendships, his sexual and emotional relationships, his interests and hobbies, indeed even his politics. At the same time, there is the expectation (even on the part of the individual) that he will 'progress' to the next stage of masculinity – that of *shakaijin* salaryman masculinity – and that the discourse hinging around *this* form of masculinity should now be the primary influence on all areas of his life. This, as flagged above, sometimes results in situations of ambiguity and instability as the new entrant attempts to negotiate these (seemingly) contradictory expectations of his masculinity.

This chapter will explore some of these issues with reference to my informants' experiences of making the transition from one set of expectations surrounding their masculinity to another, in the context of shifting faultlines of post-Bubble Japanese corporate culture. As in the previous chapter, I will draw upon the informants' voices as they reminisce about the initial weeks and months accompanying their entry into the workforce, and supplement these with discussions held with human resource managers, and with my own observation of the induction training for new staff at one of the organizations. Drawing upon these various sources will allow us to gain a sense of the complexity at stake in an individual male employee's engagements with the expectations of the hegemonic ideals of salaryman masculinity over the initial weeks and months of *shakaijin* life.

Miura Tôru's confusion

The complexity underlying a new *shakaijin*'s negotiations with the expectations of salaryman masculinity comes across vividly in the following account of one of my informants. Miura Tôru was a twenty-year-old informant who, as we saw in the previous chapter, had made the transition from student to *shakaijin* a few months prior to our discussions. Thus he was still in the process of negotiating his way through the uncertain, 'fuzzy' liminal zone of being a *shinnyū shaiin* (new entrant/employee), still learning the ropes at work, and still trying to sift out acceptable behaviour for a salaryman from 'un-salaryman' behaviour.

At our first meeting during the focus group discussion with Northern Energy informants, Miura had not said very much, perhaps due to the presence of more senior colleagues. He had, however, made reference to the adjustment he was trying to make from student life to his new *shakaijin* self. In his mind, the 'marker' separating the two stages to his life was the way he saw himself in relation to those around him. As a student he had enjoyed himself, partying and staying out all night without any real regard for the ramifications for himself, and for others. However, as a *shakaijin*, he now had to be conscious of the impact of his actions upon others, the 'inconvenience' (*meiwaku*) he could potentially cause others (Miura, NEFG: 6). For Miura-san, this 'responsibility' to others seemed to be at the core of his new identity as an adult *shakaijin*. Moreover, although prior to becoming a *shakaijin* he had been aware of the different set of expectations that would operate once he entered the workforce, it was only after actually making the transition that he could really start appreciating these differences. When we met, first during the focus group discussion, and subsequently at our first one-on-one conversation a few weeks later, Miura-san was still quite definitely in a liminal zone of negotiating his way from his earlier student masculinity towards 'perfecting' his new salaryman masculinity, *and* was very conscious of the slippery, unstable position he was in. Moreover, he was also aware of the need to *consciously* work towards perfecting his new masculinity over this period of transition. Talking about his first days and weeks as a company employee, he mentioned being

> fairly tense. Every day, every day! I didn't understand the work, and on top of that, still hadn't learned appropriate *shakaijin* conduct at all. ... I knew that as a *shakaijin* I was supposed to be able to deal effortlessly with 'common sense' matters (*jôshikitekina koto*), but I had no idea what constituted this 'common sense' ... how do I put it? It felt like I was spinning round in circles without going forward! (*karamawari shiteiru*)
>
> (Miura, NEFG: 7)

This often left him baffled and confused, and even resentful. However, given his status as a 'newcomer', this was not something he could express to his seniors (*senpai*) or colleagues very easily. On the other hand, my status as an unconnected (but nevertheless sympathetic) 'outsider' allowed some of this frustration and uncertainty to be voiced. This frustration and confusion was encapsulated in one particular incident that he related to me during our one-on-one meeting.

The incident itself did not strike me as being particularly noteworthy. However, the way in which he had constructed it in his mind, and the impact it appeared to have had on him, seemed to reflect the differing ways in which notions of 'public', 'private', 'friendship', and 'trust' were constructed within the parameters of pre-*shakaijn* masculinity and salaryman masculinity. Miura-san, more so than others, placed considerable importance on friendship, something that was possibly a residue from his student days. Within this framework from his pre-*shakaijin* life, the division between a private (and important) 'personal' world of friendship and a 'professional' public world was far more fluid and less watertight than what he was now encountering in the workplace. An example of this lingering influence of his pre-*shakaijin* priorities was the emphasis he still placed on maintaining contact with a circle of close friends from his student days. They had all promised to maintain contact and meet up regularly, even after entering the workforce and going their separate ways. At the time of our first interview, Miura-san still took this promise seriously, to the extent of driving the three hours or so to the prefectural capital straight after finishing work at the end of each week to meet up with these friends.

However, it was not so much his continued contact with his pre-*shakaijin* friends that caused trouble, but rather his transposing of 'acceptable' behaviour connected to friendship, from his pre-*shakaijin* life to his *shakaijin* life. The incident itself was relatively minor. Over the course of his first few months in the organization, Miura-san had made friends with an employee from a different section and had started corresponding with his new friend through the company's intranet system. One day someone overheard Miura-san and this friend talking about a message he had sent. This then apparently travelled back to his own section, and he was berated by a manager for sending personal emails instead of working. To Miura-san this was a groundless and unfair allegation, and he resented being reprimanded for what was quite a minor infraction. However, the biggest shock was the realization that *shakaijin* life was different to being a student, that the transparency and trust that had underpinned friendships as a student did not necessarily apply in his new environment, and that the expectations under which he now had to operate were quite different. This sense of disappointment comes through in his description of the incident:

> It came as a bit of a sudden shock.... I felt bad. It was like [the saying] 'ears against the wall, eyes at the screen door' (*kabe ni mimi ari, shôji ni me ari*)? It really brought home to me that you don't know who's watching and listening to what you say, where and when!... I felt really dejected. It made me realize that working in this company isn't all that straightforward, as you don't know what's being said behind your back.
>
> (Miura, Round 1: 19)

As pointed out above, the incident in itself was not really that significant. However, in Miura-san's mind it came to be construed as a 'watershed' that marked his shift from one set of expectations to operate by to another. In this respect, this particular incident, to him, may have been just as significant a marker of his transition from his student identity to his *shakaijin* salaryman identity as the more 'official' formal markers such as the company entrance ceremony he would have undergone when he entered Northern Energy. More-over, what his account also brings out is the fact that the tensions and disjunc-tures between the discourses framed around different masculinities may find expression through specific incidents and experiences that mark this period of transition.

'Rites of passage' into salaryman masculinity

Rather than being an isolated one-off incident, Miura-san's experience was situ-ated within a wider ideological framework. Working to consolidate the transition from one set of expectations to another are both wider social and cultural forces, as well as the more specific efforts of employers themselves. This was the case both at the moment in history Miura-san and I had the conversation, *and*, import-antly, continues to be the case into the present. Moreover, the efforts on the part of the organization to inculcate the values, conduct, behaviour, speech, and body – in other words, to inculcate the desired attributes of salaryman masculinity – are at their most intense over the first weeks and months of the employee's entry into the organization. As we shall see below, these are 'ideals' of salaryman masculinity that get inculcated and reinforced through the *body* of the new recruit, by means of repetitive embodied practices.

As many of the early ethnographic studies of the Japanese workplace high-lighted, this period of transition into salaryman masculinity commences with the employee's formal entry into the organization, marked by a formal entrance cer-emony (see Rohlen 1974: 35–40; Clark 1979: 158, 159; Beck and Beck 1994: 75–79). It ends (at least formally) when the new entrant has completed the induction training (which, depending on the firm and the type of work, may be anything from a few weeks to a couple of months), and takes up his post in the section in which he has been allocated. Indeed, in some organizations the formal entrance ceremony may be held after the employee has successfully completed the induction training, underscoring the significance of this period of transition as a probationary period through which the new recruit has to successfully navi-gate before being formally recognized as a 'real' *shakaijin*. Thus, this period is not dissimilar to a process of initiation, or a rite of passage, that the young men undergo, something that has perhaps been compounded by the absence, in postwar Japan, of institutions like compulsory military service, which in many countries (South Korea, for example) serve as a rite of passage (see Moon 2005). For the organization, this represents an opportunity to imbue the recruit with the ideology of the organization during this significant liminal period of transition in his life, and to craft out of this the desired 'corporate man'.

The sense of a peer group undergoing a rite of passage together is reinforced by the fact that the new recruits are often isolated from their families and friends (and other employees of the organization) for a period of days or weeks, usually at a separate training facility (*kenshû sentâ*), sometimes located in an isolated, difficult-to-access location. For instance, the facility I visited to observe the induction training I discuss below was located on top of a mountain on the outskirts of the city, compounding the sense of separation from the 'everyday' world. This process of the new recruit entering this isolated facility as a student and then re-emerging as a newly born *shakaijin* has resonances with novices being cloistered when taking vows for monkhood, or the 'boot camp' training of new military recruits. Indeed, as Frühstück and Ben-Ari in their discussion of the Japanese Self Defence Force (SDF) point out, many private organizations actually send new recruits to programmes organized by the SDF which allow civilians to experience military life first-hand. As they note, employers who send their new recruits to experience this training, 'testify that the SDF program facilitates the transition into professional life ... [and] are convinced that the program alerts young employees to the importance of rules and to the fact that the company is not an extension of school' (Frühstück and Ben-Ari 2002: 19; also Kondo 1990: 76–115). As far as the recruits themselves are concerned, the experience may provide an opportunity to start building networks in this next phase of their masculinity with others in the same cohort going through the same traumas and shifts accompanying the transition.

The discussion that follows maps the process by which corporations try to 'craft' out a new *shakaijin* masculinity, and the ways in which the new recruits negotiate with these processes of inscription. I start by drawing upon the discussions I conducted with members of the human resources section of Northern Energy, about the 'type' of employee the organization sought to recruit and mould. I then focus on the dynamics at work during an induction training for new employees I observed, following which I draw upon the informants' voices as they reflect upon their own personal experiences and memories of these initial rites of passage into salaryman masculinity, and how 'effective' they were in shaping them as salarymen.

'Crafting' *shakaijin*: conversations with human resources managers

While the focus of the discussion in this book is on the voices of the individual young men coming into the workforce in those years of flux and shifting expectations of corporate culture, the perspective, on the part of the organizations, about the *type* of employee they felt would successfully be able to negotiate these shifts is also worth reflecting on. More so than other sections within organizational structures, managers and staff working within human resources (*jinji*) deal, on the one hand, with the reality of the ways in which wider socio-cultural and economic shifts are reflected in the values and behaviour of new recruits, and on the other hand, are also the organizational face of 'crafting' the values and behaviour of new recruits to conform with the ideological expectations of the organization. Accordingly, this section draws upon discussions with human resources managers of one of the organizations, Northern Energy.

The discussion I had with these managers ranged over a variety of areas. The focus, however, was on the 'type' of employee the organization saw as 'desirable' (and conversely the 'type' *not* 'desirable'), and the process of selection and training new recruits. The responses to my queries about the selection process, the type of employees the organization wished to recruit, and the processes of training, yielded fairly predictable responses. I was filled in about the channels of recruitment. In past years, such as during the labour shortage of the 'Bubble Economy' years, visits would be made to high schools and universities throughout the prefecture. However, in the context of the lacklustre economic climate of the 1990s, with the concomitant 'Employment Ice Age', there was less of a need for an organization of Northern Energy's size and reputation to aggressively go out in search of potential employees. Thus, most of the new recruits were now being selected through references from local high schools, junior colleges, and universities. In keeping with the general pattern across private sector organizations, while there had been an overall reduction in the intake of new employees generally, the greatest reductions had occurred in the intake of female-recruits to fill ('OL'-type) clerical positions.

In response to my queries about the *type* of employee the organization looked for during the selection interviews, I was told that rather than looking for especially brilliant individuals, the important consideration was the potential recruit's 'humanity' (*ningenmi*) (Northern Energy Human Resources Discussion Notes, 1.12.98), which hopefully could be gauged by getting the candidate to talk 'normally' during the selection interview. More specifically, the type of new employee regarded as 'ideal' was someone who was 'normal' as a *shakaijin*, i.e. someone who did not convey an especially strong or striking impression, in terms of appearance and conduct. Of concern was whether the recruit would 'grow' adequately as a *shakaijin* after entering the company. In this respect the *kenshū* (the induction training) was, according to these human resources staff, an important stepping stone in crafting a *shakaijin* who would become a representative of the organization (and would think of him- or herself as such).

Yet, despite this rhetoric of seeking 'normal'-looking/behaving recruits, competing discourses surfaced from time to time, both during the formal discussion session, and (more so) during a subsequent more informal social gathering with the managers. For instance, juxtaposed against this 'ideal' of recruits who had the makings of the respectable salaryman-type *shakaijin* was the view that, given the rapidly changing socio-economic conditions, perhaps what Northern Energy needed to do was to hire new employees with more *uniqueness* and individual colour. Indeed, one of the managers asserted that it might be good to start taking in entrants who were slightly 'delinquent (*furyō*)' (Discussion Notes, 1.12.98), though he conceded that in reality this might be a little difficult to realize. Such views would suggest that, even for *management*, the reality vis-à-vis the hegemonic discourse (of gender, or of corporate ideology in general) may well be far more diffuse and fragmented than is often assumed (see Collinson and Hearn 1996c: 70–76).

'Crafting' *shakaijin*: an induction training session in progress

It was the opportunity to actually observe the process of 'crafting' and 'shaping' new *shakaijin* firsthand that really allowed me to gain a full understanding of its significance for all parties concerned. In April 1999, I observed the induction training (*kenshû*) for new Northern Energy employees. Northern Energy's intake that year was a mere eighty-six new entrants, a substantial drop from the 'Bubble Economy' boom years of a decade before, when the annual intake had numbered in the hundreds. Still, in the context of an economic slowdown which had hit this prefecture particularly hard, even this figure of eighty-six reflected the size and strength (and appeal) of Northern Energy compared with other employers.

As mentioned above, the training itself was held at a separate training facility (*kenshû sentâ*) located on top of a mountain on the outskirts of the main city in the prefecture, thus reinforcing a sense of incubation and cloistering. New recruits were sequestered together for a week, during which time their daily regime was regulated in accordance with a finely tuned programme of lectures, workshops, seminars, and off-site visits, from the wake-up call at 6:30 a.m. right through to 'lights-out' at 10:30 p.m.

I observed this training in progress on two consecutive days. On the first day, the training I observed was for high school and junior college graduates, whereas on the second occasion the session was specifically for university graduates and postgraduates. Of the two groups, the first, comprising around thirty individuals, was dominated by female recruits, largely junior college graduates, destined for clerical work in the various departments and sections throughout the organization. The remainder, about one-third, were males, who were high school graduates. By contrast, the second group, comprising the university/postgraduate recruits, was overwhelmingly male – of the thirty-five individuals at the session, only two were female. Significantly, this was despite the fact that Northern Energy, like many other large-scale private sector (not to mention public sector) organizations, adopted a public rhetoric of gender equality, and accordingly, was encouraging of female entry into the managerial track. The reality, however, as noted by various writers, including Brinton (1993), Ogasawara (1998), and Broadbent (2003), is a situation where, despite the enactment of the Equal Employment Opportunity Law in the 1980s, and subsequent strengthening legislations through the 1990s and into the 2000s, the elite, managerial fast-track (*sôgôshoku*) still continues to be dominated by men, whereas the general, clerical track (*ippanshoku*) is predominantly made up of female workers.[1]

What stood out was the difference between the two groups. This was a difference not just in content (as may have been expected), but also in format and style. The impression conveyed at the high school/junior college session was that it was largely a mechanical exercise, designed more for the sake of continuing an established precedent, rather than out of any kind of deep-seated desire to really 'mould' the new recruits. The format was that of a lecture, the contents of which had probably remained largely unchanged over the years. It was delivered by an elderly Northern Energy staff member, who was attached to the training facility, in a listless, unimpassioned manner. The contents were not unlike some of the 'pop management'-style texts found in bookstores throughout Japan, revolving around themes of what was and was not appropriate conduct/behaviour for a *shakaijin*. The point stressed was that these entrants were no longer students, and hence could not get away with things they could have done as students – the example provided was of instances of 'shameless' (*haji no nai*) behaviour engaged in by students (that is, by pre-*shakaijin* youth) such as sitting on the ground in front of convenience stores, or applying make-up in public places such as the subway![2] Indeed, a cornerstone of the instruction was the *responsibility* one had to society as a *shakaijin*, as reflected in the title of the session: *shakaijin toshite* ('as a *shakaijin*'). Accordingly, terms and phrases like *ningenteki ni seichō* ('growing/developing as a [proper] human'), *tokusei* ('moral quality/fibre'), and *shinrai* ('trust') kept cropping up throughout the session.

The session for university graduates and postgraduates was quite different, both in terms of gender composition, and with respect to the content and dynamics of the session. As mentioned above, with the exception of two individuals, the rest of the cohort was male. In addition, more so than with the high school/junior college graduate session, the impression of *kaisha no ningen* (literally, 'company person') in the making, as integral to this transition into *shakaijin* life, was far more explicit and visible. This came across, for instance, in such details as hairstyle and dress. Unlike the high school/junior college cohort, none of the members in the university/postgraduate group had dyed or tinted hair, and nor were hairstyles noticeably fashionable.[3] Virtually all were clad in grey or darkblue single-breasted suits, with white dress-shirts. All of them appeared to be wearing the lapel pin with the company insignia which they would have received at the time of the formal entrance ceremony. On the whole, despite the fact that in terms of age (on average) they would only have been a few years older than the high school/junior college cohort, they conveyed a distinct impression of being significantly older.

At the point when I entered the room, groups of six to eight individuals were engaged in some sort of decision-making role-play exercise, under the supervision of a very dynamic, professional-looking older female executive. I subsequently found out that she ran a management consultancy business providing new staff training and professional development workshops to organizations like Northern Energy. On that day, the task she had set the class appeared to be designed around themes of decision-making, information exchange, teamwork, and leadership. Watching (somewhat self-consciously from the back of the room) these future salarymen as they interacted with each other, the dynamism and confidence of the group stood out in stark contrast with the relative lack of enthusiasm of the high school/junior college cohort I had observed earlier.

This session was followed by one focused on the 'essentials' required of a *shakaijin*. The first part of the session, entitled *Shigoto no susumekata no kihon* ('The basics of working'), was devoted to the day-to-day mechanics of work and organizational culture. The second session focused on role-plays with different scenarios such as taking orders from a manager, interacting with co-workers, leaving the office to visit clients, and clearing the desk at the end of the work-day. What came across quite strongly was the message that it was not the know-ledge of the work itself that was of prime importance. Rather, it was the way the individual embodied and enacted the expected 'role' correctly, in interacting with co-workers, supervisors, management, juniors, and clients, that marked one's 'success' (or lack thereof) as a *shakaijin*. The training seminar itself emphasized the importance of these embodying and inscriptive practices. The members did not (as had been the case with the previous day's group) sit there passively and take notes while the lecturer spoke. Rather, they were made to bodily *act out*, through repetition and role-play scenarios, the 'ideals' of the organization. Thus, in the first section, which revolved around the 'rules' or 'eti-quette' of work practices, each of the members present was required to stand up and read aloud from a 'golden rules' type of list. This list covered such aspects of everyday work practices as: the need to report back to your supervisor on tasks you have been asked to do before he/she has to remind you; reporting any mistakes you make at work immediately; responding promptly and clearly when someone calls out your name, and going over to that person's side immediately to take a directive or request, or to respond to a question; making sure you strictly maintain the line between public and private with respect to time, money, and dealing with people; not gossiping about colleagues behind their backs; and not divulging work-related information outside of work ('Northern Energy' 1999: 3). In total, there were ten such headings, and every single new entrant present had to read through the list.

The second part of the session, as mentioned above, consisted of practising (essentially *bodily* memorizing) the rules and etiquette of workplace culture. The session started off with a demonstration of correct bowing techniques: depend-ing upon the degree of formality demanded by the situation, 30 or 45 degrees bending from the waist with the back held straight. This was followed by a run-through of a stock of standard greetings and polite expressions used in everyday situations with managers, seniors, and clients; expressions such as *itsumo osewa ni natte orimasu* (literally, 'I'm/We're always in receipt of your favours/kind-ness'), *omachi kudasai* ('Please wait a short while'), *omatase itashimashita* ('Sorry to have kept you waiting'), *makoto ni môshiwake arimasen* ('I'm extremely sorry'), and other such expressions. This drill was repeated a second time, following which the new employees were paired off, and made to read out the workplace rules from the pre-lunch session once again, and to practise the greetings and expressions that the instructor had just covered, in an appropriately loud voice, and with the correct degree of enthusiasm.

These drills were followed by role-play exercises that further accentuated this physical performance of workplace practices. The paired-off employees were given a script on which to base role-plays of simulated workplace scenarios. These scenarios included: coming into the office first thing in the morning; taking instructions from your manager/supervisor; reporting back to her or him; leaving the office to visit a client and leaving instructions with the clerical assistant/s (the 'OL/s') to pass on messages; announcing your temporary stepping-out of the office to your immediate supervisor/senior (*senpai*); returning to the office and announcing your return; checking with the clerical assistant if the instructions left had been carried out; and even tidying up and completing unfinished work before finishing for the day.

Each specific role-play exercise was not, in itself, particularly demanding. Rather, what was perhaps more challenging was memorizing and then enacting them *through* the body – bowing to the correct degree, using the appropriate tone of voice, and using the correct language and appropriate level of politeness (*keigo*). As each pair went through the role-play, the lecturer would interject when she felt that the individuals were not *physically enacting* their roles to a satisfactory level. For instance, at one point during a role-play based around the giving and receiving of documents in the office, she jumped in to stress, quite forcefully to the individual receiving the documents, that it is important to use *both hands* when receiving something from a senior. Indeed, throughout the various scenarios acted out the lecturer constantly gave advice and tips on a range of matters. Her advice ranged from tips about the proper protocol when interacting with your manager, to advice on appropriate workplace language, through to points about the correct way to tidy your desk before leaving the office. These embodied practices of correct *shakaijin* performance were not occurring in isolation. Rather, they were being enacted within a socio-cultural-scape in which employment manuals and books of the 'how-to' school of 'pop-management' literature had (and continue to have) a visible presence – for instance, most bookstores (and in particular large chains like Kinokuniya) devote considerable shelf space to this genre. As I have discussed in detail elsewhere (see, for instance, Dasgupta 2005a, 2010), such 'how-to' guides, along with other popular culture media such as magazines and *manga* targeting salarymen, play an important role in two respects. First, as Merry White noted with reference to the role of magazines in shaping youth culture trends in the 1990s, in a sophisticated, information-permeated society like Japan, such media play a vital role in disseminating information, and as a conduit of information (White 1993: 114–123). Second, and more directly related to the present discussion, popular culture texts (including the 'how-to'/self-improvement-style manuals and magazines and *manga* targeting salarymen) are important facilitators in the instruction and inscription of hegemonic ideals and expectations. This has long been the case – for instance, magazines like *Sarariiman* or *Kingu*, mentioned in Chapter 2, played an important shaping role in crafting the emergent discourse of salaryman masculinity in the 1920s and 1930s. In the 1990s and into the 2000s, however, such popular culture media took on a particular significance as they guided and instructed salarymen how to successfully negotiate expectations of corporate masculinity in the new, post-Bubble neo-liberal economic climate. Importantly, as I have discussed in detail elsewhere (Dasgupta 2005a: 102–115; also 2010), negotiating these shifts (and continuities) through the *body* figured prominently in many of these texts. Thus, the instruction as to correctly performing *shakaijin*-ness through the body that I was observing at the training session was the 'real-time' equivalent of the one-dimensional images of contemporary 'how-to' manuals and guides.

This emphasis on learning correct *shakaijin* conduct through the body came across right through the entire day's training. For instance, for their final task, the new recruits were again broken up into small groups and given topics, revolving around how they felt they could contribute to the organization, to brainstorm around. Each group had to discuss their allocated topic in relation to their work (*shigoto*), managers/supervisors and seniors (*jôshi/senpai*), customers (*okyakusama*), self (*jibun*), and the local community (*chiiki shakai*). The lecturer delegated one of these areas to each group, and they were all given three-quarters-of-an-hour to brainstorm around the topic. At the end of the forty-five minutes, the 'findings' for each group was posted up on the whiteboard, and a spokesperson from each of the groups was asked to come up to the front and explain the findings of her or his particular group to the room.

As soon as the spokesperson for the first group came up and began presenting on behalf of his group, the lecturer interrupted him, as his manner of presentation did not conform to the 'appropriate' format for work presentations. A 'proper' presentation, in the context of an organization, according to the lecturer, needed to follow the following sequence: opening greeting (*aisatsu*), stating your name and area of placement within the company (*shozoku*), the main body of the talk, mention of your name once again, and finally, an *aisatsu* of thanks to close the presentation. Once the desired format had been clarified, the spokes-persons for each of the five groups came forward and summarized the views of each of their groups. Questions were encouraged after each of the presentations, although in reality it was mostly the lecturer who asked the questions. Certain common themes appeared to cut across all the presentations and the ensuing discussions – the importance of 'teamwork', the recognition that as 'newcomers' to *shakaijin* life they had to maintain the correct protocol when interacting with managers and more senior employees (*senpai*), the importance of reporting (*hôkoku*) and seeking guidance (*sôdan*), and the fact that the very reputation of the company rested on the shoulders of each and every individual employee in the room. Indeed, the word that kept cropping up several times through the presentations was the term Northern Energy-*man*, along the lines of other occupational identity descriptions (probably harking back to English-language-derived terms such as 'businessman' or 'salesman') such as *ginkô-man* (banker), *hoteru-man* (hotel employee), *shôsha-man* (trading company employee), and of course the more generic *sarariiman* (salaryman). Needless to say, there is a strong gender ideology underlying these terms, with female executives performing those roles (e.g. of *shôsha-man*), becoming almost 'honorary males' by default.

At one level it would appear that over the course of a day the training had succeeded in crafting out of the pre-*shakaijin* mass of students the disciplined bodies and minds of future managers and executives of the organization. Yet, in reality, the dynamics at work tend to be a lot more complex than they might initially appear from the above discussion. This process of crafting the model Northern Energy-*man* (or for that matter the salary*man* of any organization) was not simply a case of the organization forcibly moulding the new recruits into subservient, disciplined automatons. There are inherent contradictions in the process and in the discourse/s surrounding the crafting of new *shakaijin*, something that comes out in the discussion in the following section, where I draw directly upon the informants' voices. As we will see, the memories of their entry into *shakaijin* masculinity recounted by the individuals themselves were a complex, richly nuanced interplay of compliance, resistance, agency, and appropriation.

'I learned ... I was no longer a student': memories of becoming *shakaijin*

Miura Tôru, the new Northern Energy employee, whose anxieties and confusion about the transition to *shakaijin* life were discussed earlier, provides an ideal entry into individual recollections of the induction training. Unlike many of the other informants, for whom the passage of time may have somewhat blurred the exact details, Miura-san, having only very recently undergone the new staff training, was able to provide me with a rich description of the experience. He talked, for instanc, about the finely calibrated schedule he and his fellow entrants underwent each day, while being sequestered in the Northern Energy training facility discussed above. Significantly, Miura-san saw the strengthening of bonds of friendship and solidarity among the new entrants as one of the (unintended) consequences of this period of enforced sequestering. These bonds, as we will see, were retained in the memories of many of the informants as the most valuable legacy of the training experience. Miura-san also described some of the specific instructions they received each day during this period. A lot of this, as brought out in my account of the training session in the previous section, revolved around

> proper conduct (*manâ*) within the company ... [things like] greetings (*aisatsu*), learning how to apologize properly when you make a mistake, also how to answer the telephone ... we spent a whole day having lessons on using the phone.
>
> (Miura, Round 1: 11)

In his view this instruction on how to talk properly (as a *shakaijin*) on the telephone was the most useful thing gained out of the *kenshû*:

> Honestly, if that [instructions on telephone etiquette] hadn't been a part of the training, I wouldn't have been able to [work as a *shakaijin*] from day one! You see, I didn't have the basics (*kiso*). Because, until then, I'd really only spoken to friends or my parents [on the phone]. So if you're talking about customers or business counterparts, I had no idea of the correct way of talking (*kotoba-zukai*) to them ... [expressions] such as 'would you mind waiting a short while' (*shôshô omachi kudasai*) ... honorific language

(*keigo*), the difference between everyday speech and *keigo* is the most difficult thing, after all.

(Miura, Round 1: 13, 14)

Satô Hiroshi, although a few years older, had also entered Northern Energy the same year, and had been subject to a similar training regime, revolving around etiquette (*manâ*) for a *shakaijin*, which included such things as 'the proper way of interacting with customers,... bowing and the proper way of expressing gratitude (*orei no shikata*) ... and also things like how to exchange business cards' (Satô, Round 1: 15). This informant also mentioned the concept of the Northern Energy-*man* (mentioned in the previous section) being talked about in discussions and lectures during the induction. According to him, one of the strongest memories he retained from the training were lectures and discussion sessions around themes such as 'living as a *shakaijin*' and 'how I want to live as a Northern Energy-*man* from now on' (Satô, Round 1: 14).

This notion of the Northern Energy-*man* also cropped up in my discussions with twenty-six-year-old Imai Shinji, whose sometimes difficult engagement with expectations of masculinity was discussed in Chapter 3. Imai-san worked in the customer relations section of the organization, and had been with the organization for four years. Yet he still remembered the details of the training he had undergone when he entered the company, and was able to provide me with a rich account of the experience. A significant part of the training revolved around what he called '*kokorogamae*' (literally 'preparing your heart') as a *shakaijin*, and more specifically as a 'Northern Energy-man' (Imai, Round 1: 26). When I asked him what this *kokorogame* had actually involved, he mentioned the inculcation of practices the others had also talked about, such as the proper way of exchanging business cards and answering the telephone, as well as

> things like being taught to be punctual, in order to lead a 'proper' (*tadashii*) *shakaijin* lifestyle. After all, those who are not careful about time, get into trouble ... [and] of course ... matters like work habits ... such as informing [the office] where you are. For instance, things like, making sure you say 'I'm stepping out of the office' (*gaishutsu shite kuru*) to someone close-by. And ... greetings and things, like bowing to forty-five degrees.... Sometimes, for instance, you'd get shouted at to put more fight into you. Also we were formed into groups (*han*), and each group was given a topic, which we had a discussion around. Umm, and also, we listened to talks by managers (*jôshi*), or ... the President (*shachô*) and Vice-President (*fuku-shachô*). Apart from that, specialists came and gave talks about what we needed to be like as *shakaijin*.[4]

(Imai, Round 1: 26)

Another Northern Energy employee, Makimura Keisuke, who worked as a planner (he was an architect by training) in the general administrative division, provided me with the following account of his *kenshû* experience a year prior to the interview:

The contents were pretty much like what's written in a textbook. Things like greetings, and answering the telephone, also the correct way to interact with people, it really was a 'textbook-like *kenshû*'. Speaking about what I acquired from it, I wonder what it was. ...? It went for ten days, so I guess a 'sense of time' (*jikan no kankaku*). The *kenshû* followed the same time schedule as when you're working, [so] start at 8:40, have lunch, until just after 5:00. So by following this schedule I was able to develop a bit of a sense [of time].

(Makimura, Round 1: 13)

He felt that the biggest change for him in the transition from student to *shakaijin* was the 'reduction of stimuli' (*shigeki*) and 'decrease in amount of [free] time' (Makimura, Round 1: 12). In contrast to his relatively easygoing life as a student, he now had to deal with various expectations:

Wake up on time in the morning, put on a suit, and come to work ... at university you could be quite 'flexible' [*uses the English word*] in choosing your classes. I've started to lose that [relaxed] feeling. I've started to live a regular life [*jikan dôri no seikatsu*].

(Makimura, Round 1: 12)

Taoka Kiyoshi, who had also been part of the same intake as Makimura-san, felt that for him, being taught the difference between 'conduct as a student' and 'business conduct' had been important:

being able to learn the difference between 'business manners' (*bijinesu manâ*) and 'student manners' (*gakusei manâ*) was a great lesson ... things like answering the telephone ... [instructions in] 'the way to dress', or else the way to talk, also things like talking properly (*kotoba-zukai*), also learning about the company, what the different areas within the company are.

(Taoka, Round 1: 12)

What cuts across the accounts of all five of these informants is the emphasis on how to embody and perform *shakaijin*-'ness correctly through the *disciplining* of body and mind down to minute details. This also came across in the account of Matsuzaka Kôhei, a twenty-year-old Northern Energy Accounts employee who had undergone the induction *kenshû* two years prior to our interview. Like Makimura-san, Matsuzaka-san juxtaposed the 'discipline' and 'regularity' of *shakaijin* life against the irregularity (or perhaps, freedom) of student life:

over those ten days [of the *kenshû*], you had to get up at the right time in the morning, and go to sleep at a set time. So you had to do things like that properly for ten days. Also the various things about proper etiquette for a *shakaijin*. In this regard, during high school I had been involved in [sports] club activities (*bukatsu*) so I was familiar with it [already]. We were taught things like with junior-senior (*senpai-kôhai*) ... would you say the 'proper way to talk' (*kotoba-zukai*)? ... basically ... how to talk properly.

(Matsuzaka, Round 1:19)

One of the interesting issues to emerge from this account is the cross-over between the disciplinary practices of sports teams and clubs, and similar regulatory and disciplinary practices in the *shakaijin* crafting process. This is something that Makimura Keisuke, the informant discussed earlier, also brought out in his account. In his student days he had played American grid-iron football, the training for which had apparently been rigorous. In fact, he felt that compared with the harsh training regime he had to endure in the sports team, the *kenshû* he underwent when entering Northern Energy was 'easy' (*amai*). Prior to undergoing the Northen Energy *kenshû*, he had expected it to be 'a lot stricter' (Makimura, Round 1:14). However, it turned out to be no different to 'following a textbook (*kyôkasho dôri*)' (14). In his view, spending a week at his sports club training camp had been far more rigorous than the *shakaijin* induction. The accounts of many of the informants made reference to practices, such as voice-training drills (which I discuss below), with resonances with the disciplinary training regimes of sports clubs. However, what makes Makimura-san's account especially significant is the actual recognition by him of the continuities between his sports club experience, and his training for *shakaijin* life.[5]

The *physicality* aspect of these disciplinary practices came through in many of the accounts of informants from both organizations, particularly those destined for technical placements, whose training was often for a longer period. For instance, Yoshida Shun'ichi, who had recently entered Northern Energy, talked about his *kenshû* which had extended over three months. Over this period he and his fellow recruits were accommodated in the training facility four to a room with little privacy (Yoshida, Round 1: 14). The training he underwent was a lot more rigorous than that for those destined for desk jobs, and included such things as becoming familiar with the basic specialist knowledge involved, learning about various kinds of equipment and operating systems involved, and even simulated exercises 'in the field' which involved such tasks as learning to climb poles of heights of fifteen metres, something that 'at first was frightening' (15). However, even though this recruit would probably continue to be employed in a technical capacity, he still had to undergo the same training to 'study the real basics of being a *shakaijin*' (15) as his 'white-collar' peers. Perhaps due to the extended period of training he underwent, more so than some of the others, Yoshida-san felt that he had been transformed quite significantly through the training – in his own words: 'I lost the feeling of being a student (*gakusei kibun ga nuketa*) ... over those three months, I guess what I learnt the most was that I was no longer a student' (16).

Many of the informants from the other organization, Northern Print, also drew attention to the ways in which the training had been reinforced through physically embodied practices. Shimizu Ayaki was a twenty-six-year-old computer systems/technical support officer at Northern Print, who had been with the organization for about eighteen months at the time of our discussion. Recalling his induction training he commented that he and his fellow inductees had undergone 'voice practice drills (*hassei renshû*) and the correct way of greeting' (Shimizu, Round 1: 10). Shimizu-san was not the only Northern Print employee to make reference to these 'voice drills' (*hassei renshû*), during which new entrants had to articulate loud greetings in a forceful manner, and respond vigorously to questions/directives from seniors, in a style reminiscent of a military 'boot camp'. Kajima Daisuke, a twenty-eight-year-old manager (*kachô*) in a technical area of Northern Print, recalled similar practices from his induction training when he had entered the organization:

> You see in the case of our company (*uchi no kaisha*), they're really fussy about, or rather put a lot of effort into greetings. So, we were made to do drills (*kunren*) where we had to practise greetings at the top of our voices in various places – inside the company, up on the roof-top of the company, out in the street...
>
> (Kajima, Round 1: 8)

While elements of this thinking extend across most organizations, the less sophisticated, aggressive military-style training and discipline, such as the voice practice drills referred to in the above account or the harsh physical regime at the 'Ethics School' described by Kondo (1990), seems to be more common among smaller and medium-sized firms. Thus, with respect to my informants, whereas informants from both organizations talked about the disciplinary practices accompanying *shakaijin* training, informants from Northern Print seemed to recall an almost military-like fervour with which these practices were inculcated.

Shakaijin contestations

When reminiscing about their first weeks and months in the organizations, many informants expressed reservations about the usefulness of the induction training in transforming them from 'irresponsible' students into 'responsible' *shakaijin*. For instance, Shimizu-san, referred to above, mentioned that prior to entering Northern Print, he had held a glamorous misconception about working life, where he thought that 'a wonderful [work] environment would be ready and waiting into which I'd ease in effortlessly' (Shimizu: 8). The reality, however, as we saw above, was somewhat different, with him having to undergo a military-style induction training. However, despite the intensity of the training regime, and the efforts put in by the organization, he was dubious about the success of the project. He commented that 'no one, including myself and my peers, was transformed overnight from student life into a *shakaijin*. It was just for appearance (*katachi dake*)' (11).

Shin'ya Naohiko, the Northern Energy computer systems operator, whose memories of his boyhood were discussed in Chapter 3, reflected quite deeply on the training he had undergone when he had first entered the organization. Since, as a systems engineer, his placement was in a technical area, he had undergone both the general training aimed at all new entrants, and a more specialized technical training. Reflecting on both types of training he had the following to say:

> For the [induction] *kenshû* ... we had training for different areas – for instance *kenshû* with themes like 'As a *shakaijin*' (*shakaijin toshite*), 'What's a *shakaijin*?', or 'What's a Salaryman?' (*sarariiman to wa nani ka?*) through to specialist training related to engineers and system engineers. Speaking for myself, I hated those 'What's a *shakaijin*' type of *kenshû*. The contents were really simplistic things that wouldn't be much use elsewhere ... for instance, things like telling you about work practices ... like planning a schedule and then writing it down on paper. I realize that these kinds of work habits are important, but [in reality] when you're really busy you just don't have the time to faithfully write down [the details of] your schedule one-by-one. And someone who knows this [reality] tries to teach us [such practices]! Somehow, I feel, no matter how wonderful [the *kenshû*] might be ... there are too many contradictions (*mujun*) between the aims (*shui*) and the contents (*naiyô*).
>
> (Shin'ya, Round 1: 21)

He felt that there was too much of this type of (what he regarded as) ultimately useless training for new entrants, which in the final analysis was little more than 'an ideal drawn on a picture' (Shin'ya, Round 1: 22). As this comment indicates, he seemed aware of the 'real' underlying corporate agenda – to craft 'company persons' (*kaisha ningen*) through this [kind of] 'personnel training' (21).

This awareness, even cynicism, in relation to the organization's efforts to shape specific types of behaviour, values, and bodily conduct extended to other informants too. For instance, Kimura Kenji from Northern Print, who worked in the sales and marketing section of that company, did not mince words when asked to talk about his early training. According to him, the year he entered Northern Print an election was on the horizon. As a firm involved in the printing industry, this meant that things were very busy at Northern Print due to the pressure of deadlines for the printing of posters and other election materials. Consequently, when Kimura-san first entered the organization, he found himself dispatched to help with the election work before undergoing the regular training sessions:

> We started the regular *kenshû*, by first [practising] greetings, then being made to memorize the corporate motto (*kaisha no shakun*) and corporate mission statement (*rinen*). Then ... we were broken up into groups and each group had to write down the slogan and the mission statement and make a presentation. Then some 'old geezer' (*jijii*) from Tokyo came to instruct us in the same old stuff like greetings and things all over again ... basically telling us things like 'It's going to be really tough!' ... That consultant came

for three days, and, apart from that the regular stuff like the morning greetings went on for two ... no, three weeks, and within that, we had things like presentations about understanding the company motto (*shakun no rikai*) or understanding accounts (*keiri no rikai*) in each of the weeks, and that was it.

(Kimura, Round 1: 12)

When asked what he thought had been the most useful thing he had gained out of the experience, his response was an unequivocal 'there's nothing (*nai desu*)'. Indeed, he confessed that due to his inherently cynical nature (or, as he expressed it, lack of 'purity'), he could see through the 'real intention (*kontan*)' (13).

While Kimura-san's response may come across as excessively cynical and 'world-weary', similar, albeit less colourful sentiments were echoed by other Northern Print informants too. Like the view expressed by Nakamura Tetsuya, a twenty-six-year-old employee who worked in an area dealing with customers' orders, many of the respondents remained sceptical of the extent to which they had been 'transformed' into a *shakaijin*, and, like him, often saw the only positive fallout from the experience being the acquisition of new friends. Nakamura-san summed up the voices of many when he talked about the experience being completely '*ippôteki*' (unidirectional) (Nakamura, Round 1: 9). Perhaps the strongest indication of the reservations many of the informants held about the induction training practices of the organizations was the view expressed by Kajima Daisuke, the Northern Print manager (*kachô*) whose recollections of the 'voice training' exercises he had undergone were presented above. When I asked him whether he thought such repetitive training practices were beneficial, his response was that he did not really think there was a need for such 'old-fashioned' (*mukashi-kusai*) practices to teach what he referred to as 'greetings that make you feel good' (Kajima, Round 1: 9). Significantly, unlike Kimura Kenji, who displayed an overall attitude of smug cynicism, Kajima-san was largely supportive of the policies of Northern Print management. Indeed, his appointment as manager at a relatively young age was perhaps evidence of the dividends of this support, and he struck me as someone destined for senior management within a couple of years. Yet, his assessment of the 'uselessness' of aspects of the induction process was really not unlike the views of Kimura Kenji, or Shin'ya Naohiko of Northern Energy.

Reading some of the above accounts of the ways in which the employees themselves 'read' the *shakaijin* moulding process (and its intentions), it may be tempting to come to two equally simplistic conclusions. On the one hand, there is the danger of reading the dynamics at work as a simple case of the organizations imposing and imprinting the hegemonic ideologies onto the passive bodies of these individual males as they make the transition from pre-*shakaijin* to *shakaijin* masculinity. Alternatively, particularly if we take into account the views of informants like Kimura Kenji, Shin'ya Naohiko, or Shimizu Ayaki, there is an equal danger of extrapolating from some of the cynical views expressed, and reading resistance into every little criticism levelled or disparaging comment made by the informants at the process (and the organizations).

However, in reality, the engagement between the individual (and his masculinity) and the discourse of salaryman masculinity he is moving into is far more nuanced and complex than a simple situation of either 'resistance' or 'compliance'. Resistance and passivity coexist (or rather intersect and interact) in what may sometimes appear to be a bewildering and confusing interweaving of responses in the same individual. This emerged in the account of Inoue Toshifumi, a Northern Print informant who reflected quite deeply on many of the issues we talked about. He felt that the *kenshû* (or, aspects of it) *had* been useful – in particular being taught 'how to come up with concrete plans (*gutaisaku*) that could be put into action' (Inoue, Round 1: 10). This, he felt, was something he had definitely taken on board and he used it whenever he needed to make specific work-related plans. Yet, at the same time, a little further on in our discussion, somewhat contradictorily, he mentioned that there was nothing useful about the experience, and the process had not generated any feeling of being a *shakaijin* or *kaisha no ningen* (company person). Rather, if anything it just left him feeling that he 'had been duped (*yarareta*)' (10). What his contradictory responses bring out are the shifting or simultaneously interweaving strands at play – a mixture of what could be seen as resistance (his feelings of being 'duped', his reluctance to consider himself to have become a *kaisha no ningen*), as well as conformity and appropriation of elements of the induction experience for his own interests (his utilization of specific teachings of the *shakaijin* crafting project).

Neither contestation nor conformity: unanticipated fallout of becoming *shakaijin*

Significantly, what came out of many of the conversations was the fact that the induction training, while not necessarily creating the kind of *kaisha no ningen* the companies may have set out to achieve, did, sometimes almost accidentally, generate a sense of identification with the organization through the networks and bonds created among fellow new entrants. This importance placed on the friendships and connections that emerged as an unanticipated side effect of the induction training came out in the accounts of a number of individuals. Makimura Keisuke of Northern Energy, who as a student used to play American grid-iron, made the following observation with reference to the friendships formed:

> Yes, I suppose the bonds [created] with my peers were the most important thing. Drinking and talking together at night was far more of an education! [*laughs*] ... There were clever guys who came from good universities, others who played different types of sport, guys who'd been abroad; listening to them talking was far more interesting.

> (Makimura, Round 1: 14)

Yoshida Shun'ichi of Northern Energy, whose extended *kenshû* experience was touched upon earlier, went even further in highlighting the significance of these friendships:

> Before entering the company I hadn't thought I'd be able to find such close friends, the kind of friends you can talk to about anything. So, with my peers ... because we lived together for three months, [the friendships] are an asset for life (*isshô no zaisan*). So quite apart from the work, this was my greatest lesson, or rather, what I acquired the most over [those] three months.
>
> (Yoshida, Round 1: 16)

As he stressed, it was not as though he had not had close friendships as a student. Rather, he had not expected that he would form such friendships once he started working. Prior to joining Northern Energy, his 'image of [working in] a company had been one where everyone just said "goodbye" [and went their separate ways] at the end of the working day' (Yoshida, Round 1: 16).

The significance of the unanticipated friendships formed during the induction training in relation to the overall process of moulding *shakaijin* was best reflected in the words of Taoka Kiyoshi of Northern Energy who had only recently become a *shakaijin*. According to him, the *kenshû*, rather than necessarily *directly* making him think of himself 'as a *kaisha no ningen*', had created a strong 'sense of camaraderie with peers (*dôki no nakama ishiki*)', and in that sense may have *indirectly* made him into a *kaisha no ningen* (Taoka, Round 1: 13). This points to an aspect of salaryman masculinity which I will be exploring at some length in Chapter 7 – the ambivalent position of homosocial bonds within organizational culture, which have both played an important role in sustaining and reinforcing salaryman masculinity, *and* have also contained within them the seeds for disrupting some of the core underpinnings of the discourse.

Conclusion

Whereas the concern of the previous chapter was the ways in which my informants were crafted into *masculinity* itself during their childhood and adolescence, this chapter has been concerned with the processes at work in crafting them into a specific form of *corporate* masculinity (that associated with the salaryman), at the point in their lives when they were making the transition from their pre-*shakaijin* selves to adult, *shakaijin*. This, as I have stressed throughout this book, was at a moment in Japan's history when what being a salaryman entails was itself undergoing considerable reassessment, with continuities with the past juxtaposed against the newer post-Bubble expectations. Consequently this chapter has tried to capture what the new entrants coming into Northern Energy and Northern Print during these years experienced, and importantly, how they articulated and framed these experiences. Their voices conveyed a sense of the intermeshing discourses they engaged with over these weeks and months of their lives. In particular, their accounts give tangible form to the ideological 'crafting' efforts on the part of organizations to mould new entrants into the kinds of employees who would conform to the hegemonic expectations of the employers. This ideological inculcation, as we saw from the discussion of Northern Energy's induction training, takes place through a variety of methods, such as lectures, seminars, group exercises, and drills, with an emphasis on moulding the 'ideal' (male) employee, not just in terms of his thinking, but also in terms of the way he *bodily* manifests the desired attributes of salaryman masculinity. In theory, the outcome of this period of induction training would be the re-shaping of the new entrant into someone both subscribing to, and visibly embodying, the ideals of salaryman masculinity.

The reality, however, as this chapter has revealed, is far more complex and nuanced. This complexity emerged in the discussions with my informants recalling their own induction training experiences when they became *shakaijin*. As the voices of informants like Miura Tôru, Kimura Kenji, Imai Shinji, Shin'ya Naohiko, and others revealed, the process they underwent of being crafted into *shakaijin* salaryman masculinity was characterized by the simultaneous existence of dynamics of conformity, co-option, appropriation, playful engagement, marginalization, refutation, resistance, and perhaps even subversion. Moreover, this complexity, vis-à-vis the hegemonic expectations of salaryman masculinity, also came out, somewhat surprisingly, in my discussions with the human resources managers from Northern Energy, underscoring a reality that management too (particularly at a time of shifts in corporate culture), rather than being some kind of monolithic bloc, is also characterized by individual positions and engagements.

5 Working with salaryman masculinity

The previous chapter discussed the crucial weeks and months following a new recruit's entry into organizational culture and his induction into the requirements of salaryman masculinity at a time when the juxtaposition of earlier assumptions about salaryman masculinity and the emerging post-Bubble assumptions was particularly pronounced. This chapter will continue to explore these ongoing individual negotiations and engagements with the expectations of salaryman masculinity, during these historically significant years. The focus of this chapter is the link between the idea and reality of 'work' in relation to defining salaryman masculinity. Specifically, I explore the ways in which my informants framed this link between work and masculinity on a day-to-day basis. This question of the 'meaning of work' for individual employees is crucial in fully appreciating workplace and organizational culture at any point in time. However, this question takes on even greater weight when we consider that the period I focus on in this book marked the watershed between (what today comes across as) a nostalgic 'golden age' of near-full employment of the pre-1990s 'Japan Inc.' era and the post-1990s era of permanent work becoming increasingly elusive for large swathes of young Japanese men (and women). For instance, as noted in earlier chapters, by the early to mid-2000s, over two million Japanese under the age of thirty-five were engaged in part-time or temporary work (Yuzawa and Miyamoto 2008: 156, 157). Ironically, this narrowing of access to permanent employment actually worked to accentuate its societal appeal (see Taga 2011b: 190–193). Thus, the young men whose narratives I draw upon were positioned at a historical moment of cross-currents, not only with respect to the discourse of the salaryman, but also in relation to the very idea of 'work' in itself, and its relationship with notions of masculinity.

The chapter starts off by setting out the conceptual framework of the work/masculinity nexus. I then bring in the voices of my informants in order to explore such themes as the importance of work in defining their sense of masculinity, the types of work they associate with masculinity, or the lack of it, their imagining of the discourse of the salaryman in the context of the work–masculinity nexus, and the lived experience at the individual level with the work–masculinity nexus.

Men and work

Right from the emergence of the field as a definable area of academic inquiry in the 1980s/1990s, the relationship with work was one of the prime concerns of many men's/masculinity (and more broadly, gender) studies scholars.[1] For instance, David Collinson, in his early-1990s discussion of intersecting masculinities at a manufacturing shop-floor in the United Kingdom, made the following observation with respect to the ways in which the concept of 'real', productive work was deployed to reinforce a sense of masculinity:

> Workers protect their dignity and elevate their identity over others by investing in specific highly masculine discursive practices of: sexuality; family breadwinner; production; the 'practical'; 'common-sense'; being a working man.
>
> (Collinson 1992: 98)

Similarly, middle-class masculinities can be just as dependent on work for a sense of identity and definition. As Michael Roper in his study of the first postwar generation of professional managers in Britain notes, given the traditional equation of 'hard' masculinity with physical labour, the white-collar managers he interacted with

> described a constant struggle to quell suspicions that they were unmanly or 'soft' ... they graded management hierarchies according to the level of aggression required to perform at each level ... and ranked different industries according to how masculine they were ... [However] despite the common tendency for men to endorse the cult of toughness in these ways, they often felt that they had failed to assert a sufficiently 'hard' masculinity. Qualities which they experienced as feminine kept resurfacing, hampering the will to power. Management was a constant struggle to keep fear at bay and hide sensitivity to others.
>
> (Roper 1994: 107)

Thus, regardless of whether we are talking about shop-floor workers, managers, or entrepreneurs, the common denominator of 'work' intersects with the respective discourses of masculinity.

With reference to Japan, as highlighted in Chapter 2, the concept of 'productive', salaried, non-household work was axiomatic to the discourse of salaryman masculinity over the pre-recessionary, 'Japan Inc.' decades. Some of the early works looking at the salaryman in the 1960s and 1970s (e.g. Plath 1964; Vogel 1971; Rohlen 1974), as well as later works like Beck and Beck's (1994) study of managers in the 1980s, drew attention to the centrality of work in the lives of men, even though they were not scrutinizing men as *men*. Subsequent works, such as Anne Allison's ethnographic study of 1980s corporate masculinity (Allison 1994), or Ishii-Kuntz's (1993) discussion of the importance of work in defining men's identities as husbands and fathers (a theme I explore in the next chapter), did foreground the interlinkages between work and *masculinity*.[2] As Allison noted in her discussion:

> although a larger proportion of women than ever before are now working in salaried jobs outside the home, work is still considered, ideologically and culturally, an activity that is more important for men and that identifies the male more than it does the female. A woman may work, but her social status and place in society is not defined primarily as a worker. When a man works, by contrast, it is to his work that he commits most of his energy, time, and loyalties, and it is as worker that his place in society is assigned.
>
> (Allison 1994: 91)

This connection between work and masculinity is also foregrounded in many works looking at the post-Bubble years (e.g. Dasgupta 2009; Tanaka 2009: 74–89; Gagné 2010; Hidaka 2010). Indeed, as I have suggested earlier, the fact that permanent, white-collar work became increasingly elusive for new entrants to the job market from the 1990s actually accentuated its importance as an underpinning of (hegemonic) masculinity. This is reflected, for instance, in the difficulty which single males in non-permanent work have in attracting marriage partners – for increasing numbers of *freeter*, and contract workers as they enter their thirties and even forties, not having access to the dividends of permanent, stable employment has meant not being able to live up to the *daikokubashira* expectations required of a husband and father (Miyamoto 2008: 87–92; also Allison 2009: 98, 99; Taga 2011b: 190–193). On the one hand, this may appear counter-intuitive, especially given the decreasing emphasis placed by younger people in public opinion surveys in recent decades on maintaining gender role distinctions (Tanaka 2009: 76, 77; also Taga 2011c: 20, 21). However, as both Tanaka and Taga point out, while social acceptance of women working after marriage may have expanded out to a point where it is approaching the cultural norm, the same surveys continue to show strong support for the idea of the husband being the primary breadwinner. Indeed, one could argue that public discourse on men who during the 'Lost Decade' (and subsequent) years were not able to gain entry into the discursive territory of socially validated full-time permanent work, or were evicted from that territory through unemployment, actually accentuated the importance of work in defining socially privileged hegemonic masculinity (see, for instance, Gill 2003; Mugikura 2006; also Dasgupta 2011; Taga 2011b: 190–193).

The meaning of 'work'

My informants were situated at that historical moment when these cross-currents in relation to both the reality, and imaginings, of 'work' were particularly visible. On the one hand, having found (seemingly) stable, permanent employment they had avoided a future of unstable, contract-based and/or

casual work that was starting to become the reality for many in their generation. On the other hand, these individuals were transitioning into salaryman
masculinity at a juncture when many of the underpinnings of the work defining
masculinity discourse were starting to unravel. Consequently, it would be
useful at this point to bring in their voices through which to untangle some of
the interweavings between work and (specifically, salaryman) masculinity. An
appropriate entry would be their responses during the initial focus group interviews about how they regarded work in their lives, and specifically in relation
to their sense of being male:

> I'd say I have an image of what you'd call a '*daikokubashira*' [literally,
> 'central pillar of a house', but more loosely 'breadwinner'], working dili-
> gently to support a family.
>
> (NEFG: 1, 2)

> Of course I think work's important, but I think men, in contrast to women,
> need to support, financially as well as mentally, their families, or else
> women. Of course I think there are areas where men are given support by
> women, but I personally think men should be the mainstay.
>
> (NEFG: 2)

> At the point I joined this organization … I expected to continue in this job
> for life; and thought I'd get married, and after a child was born, on the salary
> I receive, would support a family (*kazoku o yashinau*); that was my think-
> ing. And, since now I'm in that state [of being married and having a family],
> I [still] think that. But, generally I haven't really reflected on it 'as a male'.
>
> (NEFG Head Office: 2)

This sense of work being essential in an intrinsic, almost biological way gets
reflected in individual narratives too. For instance, Murayama Satoshi, a thirty-
year-old Northern Energy Head Office employee working in the administration
section, made the following comments on the prospect of being unemployed:

> just thinking about a situation when I may not have a job is scary!
> … [*in response to my question 'why?'*] It's frightening … [it's like you
> become] an animal that can't hunt/find its food (*esa o totte korenai dōbutsu
> ni natte*). Because an animal which can't get its own food, at that point,
> probably, within the animal kingdom that signifies death.
>
> (Murayama: 45)

Later in the same discussion, Murayama-san expressed his disapproval of unemployed men 'who hang around (*pura-pura shite*) the labour exchange and get an
allowance, and use that to live or go off and do things like play *pachinko*' (64).
This led me to again ask him what he would do if, in his forties or fifties, he was
suddenly laid off. The ensuing exchange between us is worth reproducing, as it

conveys the importance of the concept of *work*, any kind of work, being crucial to this informant's self-worth as a man:

MURAYAMA (M): If I'm laid off, umm, ah, you mean if I'm told not to come in [to work] from tomorrow?

ROMIT (R): Yes.

M: In that case, I'd think that my own ability is really poor, and would get quite depressed. [*laughs*] Things like I must be a completely useless person … why when there's also 'A-san', 'B-san', 'C-san' …

R: [So you'd want to ask] Why me …?

M: I'd think it was because I'm disliked, the line's being drawn at me, and at such times, I think I'd worry about why there was this disparity.

R: In other words, would that mean, that it's not just [losing] the job, but … your whole sense of being itself receives a shock?

M: You know, I, well, even if there were a drop in income, if I could find another job, the shock would be softened considerably. Any kind of job I could go into.… For instance, in the worst case scenario, I'd even want to live by making *rāmen* [noodles] in a stall, pulling a hand-cart …

(Murayama: 64, 65)

Ogasawara Takurô, another Northern Energy employee, best summed up this connection between work and masculinity when he told me that the time he 'most felt my "masculinity" (*otokorashisa … ga ichiban kanjiru*)' was when he had successfully accomplished a piece of work (Ogasawara, Round 2: 2). Elsewhere, he underscored his feelings of empowerment after successfully completing a particularly challenging work project: 'Once I was able to finish it, naturally, … I was able to gain confidence in myself. I achieved the ability to say to myself that "No way am I going to lose"' (5). While this statement does not specifically mention *masculinity*, given other statements he had made about the significance of work to masculinity, it would be hard not to see the underlying extension of his sense of achievement to his own *masculine* self-esteem. Indeed, what perhaps best summed up the centrality of work to masculinity in his esteem was his explicit condemnation of the type of man he disliked: 'someone who doesn't work and, … doesn't give importance to [looking after] his household (*uchi o taisetsu ni shinai*)' (12). This statement reflected the sentiments of many of the informants regarding the 'fundamental' qualification for *shakaijin* masculinity – being the *daikokubashira*, supporting and looking after the family, despite what the on-the-ground reality might be.

'Manly' and 'unmanly' work

Feeding into this intertwining of work and masculinity discussed above is the fact that the category of work itself is constructed through a gendered prism. As Rosemary Pringle notes: 'Not only are jobs defined according to a clear gender dichotomy, but the gendering of jobs has been important to the construction of gender identity' (Pringle 1993: 130). In this sense, 'being a man' is shaped as much by the type of work engaged in as it shapes (and genders) a particular type of work. Thus, in order to better understand my informants' engagements with the expectations of salaryman masculinity it would be useful to get a sense of where they situated the kind of work associated with salaryman masculinity within the scale of 'manly' and 'unmanly' occupations.

One of the themes raised was their personal imaginings of 'manly' (*otoko-rashii*) and 'unmanly' (*otokorashikunai*) lines of work. While the specific occupations listed varied across individuals, there was a common strand that appeared to link attributes such as the (perceived) degree of physical strength required for the job and/or technical skill. Several of the informants mentioned policemen as exemplars of 'masculine' work. Some informants listed occupational categories connected to construction and building such as labourer/construction worker (*dokata*), artisan (*shokunin*)/carpenter (*daiku*), or construction engineer (*doboku*). Other occupations that came up included fishermen, truck drivers, pilots, and professional athletes.[3]

The range of *otokorashii* occupations provided often had a bearing on occupations to which the informants had been attracted in childhood or adolescence. Thus, Fujita Yûji, an employee in Northern Print's sales office, who had offered car and motorbike racing as his choice of *otokorashii* work, had himself dabbled in motorbike racing and up until university had wanted to make his career in either professional racing or automobile design. He justified his choice in the following terms:

> Quite often, it's the apparent glamour that's seen. But I know the underlying serious (*jimina*) aspects [of the sport] ... only a person who's exceptionally tough mentally can survive.
>
> (Fujita, Round 1: 11)

For others, the association of particular occupations with masculinity was a combination of both childhood/adolescent attraction to culturally privileged attributes of masculinity *and* the individual's own perception that he did not quite measure up to these cultural ideals. Ishida Naoki, a twenty-one-year-old Northern Energy Accounts employee, touched on this issue during our conversation. Talking about occupations and kinds of work to which he had been attracted in the past, or continued to find attractive, he commented that as physical activity was not his 'strong point', he had been 'attracted by things like sport, where you can earn an income through physical activity' (Ishida, Round 1: 10). As a child he had been attracted to *Ultraman*, a popular children's super-hero popular culture icon, and had wanted to become a 'monster (*kaijû*)' (11). As he grew older, he continued to idealize physical strength and sporting skill; as he reflected: 'I'm attracted to what's missing [in me]' (10). His response to my question about occupations he associated with 'manliness' reflected this anxiety about his perceived lack of physical prowess and strength:

Let's see ... of course it would be in sports-related areas, since they'd require using the body ... I guess it's when the body's being used and it's related to physical attributes of the body (*nikutaitekina tokuchō*) that things like *otokorashisa* or the good things about being male come out.

[*in relation to my question asking him if he could think of more general kind of occupations that he associated with masculinity*] It's a bit different from *otokorashii*, but there're things that men are possibly geared towards more. For instance ... people like construction workers (*dokata*) working as labourers, things like that since they're jobs that require strength (*chikara*) and endurance (*tairyoku*).

(Ishida, Round 1: 11)

What seems to come through in many of these associations of 'manly' lines of work is the notion of the body being engaged in *physical* labour. Moreover, these were occupations that could (in the view of the informants) only be carried out by the *male* body. Takahashi Yoshio of Northern Print brought out this assumption of certain types of work being specific to the male body in his reflections on *otokorashii* work:

well quite definitely it would probably be physical work, wouldn't it?... In that sense, things like construction-related [work] ... things like line-work-related stuff (*genba kankei*) ... I guess, women wouldn't be able to do it.

(Takahashi, Round 1: 6)

Conversely, informants were also able to come up with occupations they associated with a lack of masculinity – *otokorashikunai shokugyō*, literally 'un-masculine/manly' occupations. For many of the informants these were often areas that they associated with women and stereotypically 'feminine' lines of work – what one informant, Imai Shinji, referred to as 'occupations requiring delicacy' (Imai, Round 1: 14). Thus, by implication, these occupations were considered to be lines of work not suited to men, reflecting Christine Williams' assertion, in her introduction to a collection of papers on men working in areas considered to be 'women's work', that 'the man who crosses over into a female-dominated occupation upsets ... gender assumptions embedded in the work ... he is suspected of not being a "real man"' (Williams 1993: 3). The list of such *otokorashikunai* occupations mentioned encompassed areas such as nursing, childcare workers, beauticians, florist, bakery/cake shop salespersons (*kêki-ya*),[4] and flight attendants.[5] However, in contrast to the listing of *otokorashii* (manly) work, where the informants generally seemed to be quite clear in their minds about occupations that matched ideals of 'manliness', the responses to *otoko-rashikunai* (unmasculine) work seemed to be less certain, revealing a greater degree of ambiguity and contradiction. Indeed, there were a number of informants who told me that they could not think of any occupation that was not masculine, or was not suited to men. Others came up with responses that brought out the contradictions in the gendering of categories of work. Thus, for instance,

Matsumoto Tadashi of Northern Energy, who mentioned nursing as one of the occupations he associated with a lack of masculinity, also acknowledged the contradiction in his position by distinguishing between *kangofu*, the female-specific term traditionally used for the term 'nurse', and *kangoshi*, the gender-neutral term which takes into account the growing visibility of male nurses in recent years (Matsumoto, Round 1: 9).

The contradictions in demarcating which type of work is or is not suited to men came out nicely in Hamada Shigeru's response. Hamada-san was the son of the President of Northern Energy, and at the time of our interview was being rotated through different sections of the organization, quite clearly as part of the grooming process to take over from his father down the track. When we met, he was working on the shop-floor (*genba*). Like many others, he had mentioned the physical work done by male employees on the shop-floor of the press as an example of *otokorashii* work (Hamada, Round 1: 9). When I asked him about work not suited to males, he responded with 'work not suited to myself' (10). When I asked him for specific examples, he mentioned 'jobs where you have to do the same kind of repetitive work day-in-day-out' (10). He then elaborated:

> Well, you know, if you go to large factories you have assembly-line work (*nagare-sagyô*), don't you? Seeing work like that, I, well, couldn't even consider it – this doing exactly the same thing every minute!
>
> (Hamada, Round 1: 10)

Ironically, repetitive assembly-line work is not really that different to the type of mechanistic, repetitive work Hamada-san was engaged in on the print shop-floor, a type of work that he associated with 'manliness'. This reflects the point I raised above about the complex dynamics involved in the ways in which gender ideologies both shape how occupational categories are constructed and are also shaped by those categories. Thus, reading into Hamada-san's imagining of *otokorashii* and *otokorashikunai* work, we could say that assembly-line work was associated with 'unmanliness' *because* of the fact that in the popular imagination, women constitute a significant proportion of such workers (see, for instance, Roberts 1994). Conversely, work on the shop-floor was associated with 'manliness', not due to the nature of the work itself, but rather due to the numerical dominance of men.

Another example of the ambiguity in informants' imaginings of the gendered construction of occupational categories was provided by Fujita Yûji, the Northern Energy salesman who had spoken about sports professionals exemplifying masculinity. In response to my question about 'unmasculine' occupations, Fujita-san mentioned the '*hosuto*' or 'host' – a male escort, whose job servicing female clients, in many respects, mirrors the female bar hostess servicing male clients (see Takeyama 2010). When I expressed some surprise, mentioning their (hetero-) sexual appeal (*josei ni moteru*) as underlying their masculinity, Fujita-san countered that 'it is precisely that kind of thing [i.e. the use of their sexual appeal] that probably explains the view that it [being a *hosuto*] doesn't have *otokorashisa*' (Fujita, Round 1: 11). This poses questions about what is often considered to lie at the very core of hegemonic masculinity – heterosexual virility. Yet, ironically, using Fujita-san's reasoning, this very heterosexual prowess explained the male escort's *lack* of masculinity. This resonates with Akiko Takeyama's observation in her discussion of male hosts that, despite their seeming sexual virility and appeal, the fact that they are the object of *female* desire disrupts the active male/passive female binary underpinning ideologies of gender and sexuality (Takeyama 2010: 240, 241).

'*Peko-Peko Shita Hito*': the salaryman viewed through informants' voices

The question that needs to be explored, then, is where, in the view of my informants, did the salaryman fit on this scale of 'manly' and 'unmanly' occupations? After all, despite its highly visible presence on the socio-cultural landscape, the kind of white-collar desk work usually associated with being a salaryman is a far cry from the exemplars of 'manly' occupations, such as policemen and construction workers, mentioned by my informants. Moreover, one would expect that the shifts in expectations of corporate masculinity towards a more aggressive, individualistic style, particularly pronounced at the time of these conversations, would bring in an added element of complexity to this seeming disconnect between the informants' everyday reality, and the idealized imaginings of 'manly' work discussed above. This is reflected in the following account by Ogasawara Takurô, the Northern Energy informant who had told me that he 'most felt his "masculinity"' when he had successfully accomplished a piece of work (Ogasawara, Round 2: 2). Ogasawara-san had struck me as an 'ideal' representative of salaryman masculinity. At our very first meeting he had come across as bright, articulate, outgoing, and sure of himself, but at the same time considerate of others around him, diligent in his attitude towards work and the organization, and 'safely respectable' in his general views regarding such issues as gender roles, organizational culture, and society at large. Indicative of this quiet confidence in his own ability was, for instance, the certainty (relative to other informants) with which he said that he expected to be in a management position by the time he was thirty-five (Ogasawara, Round 2: 9). He was also quite certain that he would stay with Northern Energy until his retirement. Yet, despite this apparent confidence, he also displayed a certain ambivalence about himself as a white-collar worker. He talked, for instance, with nostalgic admiration about the casual work he had done in his student days delivering newspapers:

> I'm a white-collar salaryman, right? But still,… I really think people sweating away doing actual physical work have it really tough, and I have strong feelings of gratitude towards them.
>
> (Ogasawara, Round 2: 3)

If this kind of tough, physical work conjured up images of 'manliness', what were the associations with the figure of the salaryman? Makimura Keisuke, the former grid-iron player who had trained as an architect at university and was now employed as a planner in the general affairs section of Northern Energy, provided a caricature of the 'typical' (*tenkeitekina*) salaryman that could have been straight out of some tongue-in-cheek popular culture representation. His view of the 'typical' salaryman was someone who

> [g]ets up early in the morning, puts on a suit and tie, reads the newspaper while eating breakfast ... this, of course is an image. And, well, carrying a briefcase he goes into a multi-storeyed building, sits down at a desk, faces a computer, and works.... Then, around six in the evening, he finishes [work], has a quick 'one-for-the-road' drink, and returns home with something for the family (*omiyage*).
>
> (Makimura, Round 1: 11)

Yoshida Shun'ichi, a twenty-year-old technician with Northern Energy who had entered the workforce just six months prior to our interview, had the following to say about his image of the 'typical' salaryman:

> It's pretty much like what appears on TV. A salaryman ... he's short ... and, wears a suit, every day squeezes himself onto a jam-packed train and goes to work. [He] doesn't really do that much work ... puts in just enough effort, then goes and lets off steam at an *izakaya*, and then, goes home and retreats back into himself.
>
> (Yoshida, Round 1: 11)

Matsuzaka Kôhei, another twenty-year-old Northern Energy employee from the Accounts section, said that his image was of 'someone who works from morning till night, and seems to come home just to sleep' (Matsuzaka, Round 1: 15). Arai Jun, a public sector employee involved with Customer Service, saw the 'typical' salaryman as a 'a cringing, obsequious person (*peko-peko shita hito*)', the kind of person who 'makes a hobby of his work' (Arai: 13).

These three informants were relatively new to *shakaijin* life, and hence their holding such excessively caricaturized views of the salaryman was understandable. However, even those informants who had made the transition to *shakaijin* life a number of years prior to our discussions often held not dissimilar images. Satô Hiroshi, who at the time of the first interview had been with Northern Energy for three years, also presented a caricature of a person 'usually wearing a suit and tie ... [who] leaves home early in the morning, and works hard until late at night' (Satô, Round 1: 12). Moreover, this was a person who was constantly plagued by the 'difficult dilemma of balancing the demands of home and work' (12). Nohara Nori, who had also been with Northern Energy for three years, drew upon similar stereotypes: '[someone who] wears a suit and tie, commutes by train, works until late at night, returns home also by train, goes straight to bed' (Nohara, Round 1: 13). Nakamura Tetsuya, a Northern Print employee who at the time of our interview was in the eighth year of his career with the organization, saw the 'typical' salaryman as someone 'meticulous (*kichômen*), who follows rules ... is very stiff' (Nakamura, Round 1: 6). In terms of appearance, he also held an image of a bespectacled, suit-clad figure with a 'seven-three (*shichi-san*)' haircut (along the lines of the JTB-man in Chapter 1), commuting to work in a 'jam-packed train'. Significantly, Nakamura-san also felt that such a 'typical' salaryman was 'valuable' (*kichô*) in terms of the economy and society (6). Takahashi Yoshio, who was into the fourth year of his employment at Northern Print, presented me with similar characteristics, but added that, in his mind, this 'typical' figure was married and 'supported a family' (Takahashi, Round 1: 7).

Thus, what the above accounts suggest is the *lack* of 'manliness' associated with the discourse built up around the salaryman. One Northern Energy informant put it quite bluntly:

> My thinking's changed now. But before I started working ... I had something of what you'd call a fixed idea ... of a suit-wearing [person] merely doing the same things everyday, definitely not an *otokorashii* image.
>
> (Yoshida, Round 1: 11)

Individual negotiations with the salaryman stereotype

Despite these often caustic views of the 'typical' salaryman, the informants also had a very real sense of having to engage with the same attributes of the caricature in their everyday lives. This is reflected in their responses to the question I posed about where they positioned themselves in relation to the stereotype presented.

With some informants, what came across was a reluctance to admit that the salaryman label applied to them. Yoshida Shun'ichi of Northern Energy was an example of this. For instance, when he presented me with his image of the 'typical' salaryman, he had stressed that, 'with regard to what you'd call salary-men, I felt particularly defiant (*hankôteki*)' (Yoshida, Round 1: 11). Perhaps, due to the non-white-collar/desk-work nature of his work at Northern Energy, this sense of 'resistance' to defining himself as a salaryman seemed particularly pronounced:

> In fact, that's [the non-desk-work aspect] also an attractive aspect of this job. You don't get the feeling that you're just an average salaryman. Well, in fact, although the work does involve working on a computer in the office, there's also labour, physical labour (*nikutai rôdô*), so it's a really broad-ranging job. That's why I don't feel like I'm a salaryman, compared with the image.
>
> (Yoshida, Round 1: 12)

However, at the same time, for many of the informants, there was also a degree of resignation – that no matter how much one might endeavour to do so, it was ultimately futile to try to prevent slipping into the 'markers' of the 'typical' salaryman. Thus, when I asked Makimura Keisuke, the Northern Energy planner who had provided me with a caricature of a 'typical' salaryman which could have been straight out of an advertisement for energy drinks, if he saw himself falling within the parameters of the description he had provided, he mentioned that he had 'started to think so a little, of late' (Makimura, Round 1: 12). Specifically, it was particular day-to-day practices of salaryman life that brought about this self-perception:

> Umm, well, such things as waking up in the morning, putting on a suit, and coming to the office. Making sure you arrive at the set time.... It feels like my lifestyle has become a punctual and regular one.
>
> (Makimura, Round 1: 12)

To me, this self-appraisal came as something of a surprise. Among the Northern Energy informants, Makimura-san had struck me as quite *atypical* of a salaryman. If anything, his appearance and the views he expressed seemed to signal to others that as an architect he was different to the run-of-the-mill, pen-pushing salaryman. For instance, my interview notes made reference to his 'unconventional' (by salaryman standards) appearance and deportment – coloured (as opposed to the standard white) dress-shirt, hair that was visibly tinted, and fashionable rimless glasses.

Matsuzaka Kôhei, whose description of the 'typical' salaryman as a stubborn, suit-clad, forty-year-old who only came home to sleep was referred to above, thought that although at the moment he did not consider himself to be like this caricature, 'I'll probably end up like that someday, even though I don't want to' (Matsuzaka, Round 1: 16). Takahashi Yoshio, who, as mentioned above, worked in a technical capacity on the shop-floor of the Northern Print plant, also did not think that his present life conformed to his image of the 'typical' salaryman. However, he felt that if he continued on in his present job and got married, he would end up becoming like the caricature he presented me with (Takahashi, Round 1: 7).

Nohara Nori of Northern Energy, who had mentioned an association of the salaryman image with a lack of self-motivation and merely going along with the flow of things, said that of late he had started to question the increasingly salaryman-like pattern of his own life – 'going to work as a matter of course in the morning, then, working until late, grabbing some food, and going straight to bed' (Nohara, Round 1: 13). In fact, Nohara-san's job was quite a non-white-collar one; yet he, like Takahashi Yoshio of Northern Print who also worked in a non-white-collar capacity, saw no contradiction in using the label 'salaryman' when talking about himself. Arai Jun, who had described his image of the 'typical' salaryman as a deferential, fawning workaholic, already saw himself fitting this stereotype sometimes, particularly when he was 'doing work that involved dealing with customers (*sekkyaku no shigoto*)' (Arai: 15). Nakamura Tetsuya, who had thought that white-collar office work was not *otokorashii*, saw himself fitting into the salaryman mould at times when he could not 'retort back to a supervisor, [or] refuse an allotted task' (Nakamura, Round 1: 7).

Another situation when Nakamura-san felt his 'salaryman-ness' surface was when he was 'pouring drinks (*sake o tsugu*)' for a superior (7), an action that not only reinforces junior–senior status hierarchies, but may also be seen as analogous to the tea-serving role associated with the female OL (see Ogasawara 1998). Like Ishida Naoki of Northern Energy, this informant's sense of ambivalence with regard to his assessment of his own masculinity, as well as his position within the organization, was quite palpable. For instance, earlier in the interview, when we were discussing what kinds of physical and emotional characteristics in a person he regarded as *otokorashii*, he told me that he thought of himself as *otokorashikunai* (not masculine) because he 'was not assertive enough when talking' (Nakamura, Round 1: 5). Moreover, when I jokingly suggested that given that he had been with Northern Print for a number of years, in all likelihood *he* was the one who had drinks poured for him by his juniors (*kôhai*), his (also joking) response was: 'this doesn't happen very often, unfortunately' (7). Nor did he think this was likely to be the case in the future. Rather, if anything, he mentioned feeling uneasy about the whole dynamics involved, including aspects of himself when he was operating in this kind of salaryman 'mode'. Seeing himself in such situations gave him a sense of 'seeing my future', one where, ten or twenty years down the track, he would be 'overworked (*koki-tsukaware yaku*), and grovelling to the boss (*jôshi ni heko-heko shiteiru*)' (7).

Even with informants who appeared to be more 'integrated' and struck me as being on the track to becoming exemplars of salaryman masculinity, there were times when this kind of ambivalence or contradiction came through. Thus, Murayama Satoshi, the Northern Energy employee who had likened being unemployed to being an animal unable to hunt for its food, also discussed what had been lost by the wayside since becoming a *shakaijin*:

> What's been lost after becoming a *shakaijin*?... Well, step-by-step, both in a positive sense and a negative sense, you end up getting fixed in your views, so conversely ... lots of things are lost ... because that set way of thinking's become entrenched, I think my ability to be creative (*hassô-ryoku*) has become really weak.
>
> (Murayama: 57)

This sense of regret at what may have been lost in the process of becoming a respectable salaryman was perhaps best summed up in his statement: 'I dislike this me that's stopped worrying about things' (58).

Statements such as the above seem to reflect the complexities weaving in and out of the day-to-day engagements between my informants and the discourse of salaryman masculinity that to varying degrees formed their reference point. In order to better bring out these complex and sometimes contradictory dynamics, I draw upon the narratives of two specific individuals over the remainder of this chapter. Both were my designated liaison persons in their respective organizations. Consequently, my interaction with them was more frequent than was the case with the other informants. Thus, through my interactions, I was able to get a sense of what Roper, with reference to his own informants, described as 'the pleasures and discontents of masculinity in their work' (Roper 1994: 215).

Matsumoto Tadashi – the 'good' salaryman

Matsumoto Tadashi, who worked in the Accounts section of Northern Energy, became my liaison contact for Northern Energy quite early on in the interview process. He brought to our dealings an impressive attention to detail. For instance, for each round of the interviews, he would provide me with a carefully organized schedule of dates and times, and was in regular touch with me about confirmations and last-minute changes. In terms of personality and appearance, he seemed to embody many of the 'ideals' of hegemonic salaryman masculinity; not unlike a younger, slightly more stylish version of salaryman caricatures like the 'JTB-Man' mentioned in Chapter 1. My notes, for instance, mentioned that 'overall, [he] gives the impression of being conservative, in a nice, wholesome way' (Matsumoto, Round 2 Notes). He was of average height and build, pleasant looking without being exceptionally good looking, wearing glasses and with a neat, conventional hairstyle. At all our meetings he dressed in a 'respectable' salaryman fashion – understated ties and white dress-shirt, for instance. His personality, too, projected a similar sense of dependability and responsibility. Indeed, the word 'responsibility' (*sekinin*) was one that often cropped up in our conversations, and he admitted that he probably felt this sense of responsibility more than many of his peers:

> I suppose, right from the outset I've tended to feel quite a strong sense of responsibility towards my job. If anything, I'm probably one who ends up taking too much on my shoulders.
>
> (Matsumoto, Round 2: 2)

Matsumoto-san's sense of 'responsibility', almost a sense of obligation, was also echoed in his approach and attitude to his employer, and the people around him. For instance, my query about how he had changed since becoming a *shakaijin* led to the following exchange:

MATSUMOTO (M): That's a tough question, isn't it? Yes, I think I've probably changed ... well firstly, ... I feel that inevitably I've been putting more stress on work responsibilities. Also, ... I feel that ... other [i.e. non-work] relationships have, of course, been becoming restricted.

ROMIT (R): So, [relationships] within the company have increased and ...

M: Yeah. And relationships [with people] outside the company (*shagai to no tsukiai*) have been decreasing. Well, I guess, you adapt to the environment, don't you?

R: But, somewhere [within yourself] do you sometimes think you regret it? That you're losing friendships from the past...?

M: Yes, I suppose there's a certain amount [of regret] ... But, I suppose, well, I still do meet them [non-work friends] when I can. However, certainly, since entering this company, compared with when I first entered, definitely, my work responsibilities (*shigoto no sekinin*) have increased, and accordingly I'm allocated a greater workload. So I sometimes feel I'm losing my freedom.

(Matsumoto, Round 1: 10)

In keeping with his keen sense of 'responsibility', Matsumoto-san also conveyed a sense of personally embodying the organization, the notion of the 'Northern Energy-*man*' discussed in the previous chapter. For example, he mentioned that, compared with many of his colleagues he had 'a stronger sense that his place in society was that of a part of the company (*kaisha no ichi-in*), even when away from work' (Matsumoto, Round 2: 21). Indeed, he confessed that even outside of work he was conscious of his behaviour reflecting negatively upon the organization (21).

This sense of his work and the organization providing an important reference point came through in our discussions about his projected life-path, something I got all the informants to reflect upon. I started off by asking Matsumoto-san, who was then in his late twenties, to present me with a picture of himself ten years down the track, in his late thirties:

ROMIT (R): What do you think you'll be like in ten years' time with regard to work, [and] in terms of family?

MATSUMOTO (M): In terms of work, chances are, probably, I would have made it to some extent into middle management-type (*chûkan kanriteki*) [jobs] like section manager (*kachô*)...

R: Out of interest, do you think you'll be in the same company?

M: [*without any hesitation*] Yes, I think so. Basically, there's no reason to quit. Thinking about the ways things are now...

R: I see.

M: I'll be in this company and would have made it to a reasonable level of management. And ideally, I'd like to continue doing accounts-related work, and well, am aiming to become a specialist [in that work], so I'll probably be doing that.

(Matsumoto, Round 2: 8)

He then went on to talk about how he saw himself as a husband and father (a topic I will return to in Chapter 6) but leading a single *tanshin-funin* life away from his family for a couple of years, due to job transfers.[6] Moving further on down his life-path, he once again stressed the likelihood of his remaining with

Northern Energy over the course of his career, and saw himself, twenty years or so down the track, as a *buchô*, or departmental manager. As he put it, talking about the way he saw himself in his fifties:

> Well, to tell the truth, if conditions go favourably for our company … as long as I do my best, and since I'll definitely continue on that premise, basically I don't think there'll be any major changes in terms of where I work.
>
> (Matsumoto, Round 2: 10)

He then, in response to my question about whether he thought he would attain the rank of *buchô* by his late fifties, stated confidently that 'that's how I imagine myself' (Round 2: 10). His quiet confidence (and I stress quiet; as mentioned earlier he was extremely unassuming and modest), both in his own future career success, and in his continued association with the same organization, made him, in many regards, come across as an 'exemplar' of salaryman masculinity (see Connell 2000: 70–85).

Yet, for all his apparent closeness to exemplifying the ideals of salaryman masculinity, there were faultlines and disjunctures vis-à-vis the hegemonic ideal of which he seemed not unaware. This comes across in the following introspective comment, in relation to his image of himself after retirement:

> Well I suppose, at the end of the day, work still takes up a fairly large part of my thinking. I've started to realize this of late. When we talk about things like this, I realize that there isn't much besides work [in my life].
>
> (Matsumoto, Round 2: 11)

Moreover, despite his (apparent) closeness to the salaryman 'ideal', his negotiations with the expectations of salaryman masculinity had not necessarily been any less complicated than, for instance, informants like Miura Tôru, discussed in the previous chapter. As I discuss in more detail in Chapter 7, when exploring the *senpai/kôhai* dynamics, Matsumoto-san had been at the receiving end of some unsavoury victimization and bullying from a senior colleague when he had first become a *shakaijin*, which, as he put it, 'resulted in a lot of pressure, stress' (Matsumoto, Round 1: 18). This confession indicated that the complexity underlying individual negotiations with salaryman masculinity, what Roper refers to as 'the pleasures and discontents of masculinity in … work' (1994: 215), can be as relevant for an (apparently) 'exemplary' individual like Matsumoto-san as for someone like Kimura Kenji of Northern Print, who, as I discuss below, deliberately defined himself in opposition to many of the ideals of salaryman masculinity.

Kimura Kenji: the 'recalcitrant' salaryman

Kimura Kenji, whose rather caustic observations about the employee training process we encountered in the previous chapter, worked in the sales section of

Northern Print, and was my liaison person in that organization. However, he was quite different to Matsumoto-san, his counterpart at Northern Energy. In contrast to the latter's meticulous, organized style, Kimura Kenji sometimes struck me as chaos and disorganization personified. Given that he worked in sales and was out on sales rounds for much of the day, it was often virtually impossible to get through to him, unlike Matsumoto-san who diligently returned every call. Also in contrast to Matsumoto-san's carefully planned and neatly typed interview schedules, the schedules Kimura-san came up with were invariably hurried, handwritten jobs, passed on to me a few days before the interviews were due to commence. However, despite all this, I found his style rather refreshing, and the truth was that in the end, he always came through and the interviews would progress smoothly.

Even in terms of appearance, in contrast to Matsumoto-san's neat, respectable, understated 'typical' salarymanlike appearance, Kimura-san projected a decidedly unsalarymanlike impression. For instance, his hair reached below his collar, and the glasses he wore were reminiscent of a style more likely to be favoured by a fashion designer or someone working in advertising or the music industry (an area with which, as I discuss below, he did in fact have close ties) than a respectable sales executive. In all our meetings I never once saw him wear a white dress-shirt. In fact, through his appearance, he seemed to be deliberately trying not to fit into the parameters of salaryman masculinity.

This trait was reinforced by his personality and his behaviour during our interactions and interviews. He was very articulate and did not mince words, nor shy away from expressing an opinion, something that could (and apparently did) result in negative reactions from co-workers and managers. At the same time, his way with words, as well as his outgoing, 'street-smart' demeanour, suited his work in sales, which required dealing with a wide range of individuals and organizations. Consequently, I got the sense that he was able to get away with much of his unsalarymanlike behaviour precisely because he was effective at his job, and quite clearly an asset to the organization in terms of bringing in sales orders from customers. In fact, he admitted this himself during our interview. Talking about his disenchantment with certain work practices and policies insisted upon by management, such as the need to go away to refresher/professional development workshops on weekends, he mentioned that although all his colleagues in the Sales section felt the same way, only he and one other person publicly expressed their dissatisfaction (Kimura, Round 1: 13). However, he acknowledged that 'had my [sales] figures not been that good' (14), it may have been more difficult to be so vocal. Quite clearly, as I discuss in more detail below, Kimura-san seemed to bask in appearing as nonconformist as possible within the allowable limits of acceptable bodily and behavioural nonconformity.

As mentioned in passing above, Kimura-san had connections with the music and entertainment world; throughout his university years he had been heavily involved in this scene, working at various *freeter* jobs including as a bartender and disc jockey at nightclubs. Even after joining Northern Print, he had continued his involvement with the music scene – organizing music events on weekends, for instance. The first time we met, he presented me with both his 'official' Northern Print *meishi* (business card) *and* one for his alter-identity (with his nickname 'K-man' rather than his actual name printed), almost as a means of stressing his difference from the 'average' salaryman. This emphasis on marking himself out came across when he was recounting to me his reasons for joining Northern Print:

> Well, you know generally around the time just before you graduate from university, you look for employment (*shûshoku katsudô*) don't you? But, in my case, I didn't engage in a formal process of looking for a career. At the time I was asked by [someone] from the 'night-sector' (*yoru no hô*) if I wouldn't consider joining the 'night'[entertainment sector] ... at that time I thought about the future, you know after working for about four years, you have some idea about the ins-and-outs of the 'night' [world/sector], don't you? So consequently, at that point although I thought that 'maybe someday I'd like to give it a shot' – even now [I think that] – I gave up [on the thought of making a regular career in the 'night-world'], and thought I'd learn about [work in] a 'normal company' (*futsû no kaisha*), so I took the [entrance test for and] joined this company [Northern Print].
>
> (Kimura, Round 1: 9)

This sense of having become a salaryman almost by a quirk of fate seemed to be quite influential in the way Kimura-san related to himself, his colleagues and managers, and to his future within the organization. He had very little in the way of a sense of loyalty to the organization, and, unlike Matsumoto Tadashi, did not see his future as tied to his employer. Admittedly, this was generally the case with many of the Northern Print informants, and reflected the pattern of higher job mobility and lower 'loyalty' in the small and medium-sized firm sector (see, for instance, Roberson 1998: 122–131). However, with Kimura-san I got a sense that although, like many of the other Northern Print informants, dissatisfaction with the working conditions or the low salary did underlie his attitude, there was also an almost egotistical sense that he was far better than an organization like Northern Print deserved. This found expression through a sort of 'devil-may-care' breezy defiance towards his superiors and the organization in general, as well as in his everyday negotiations with specific work practices and expectations. The following exchange regarding his work schedule on an 'average work-day' (*goku futsû no heijitsu*) (Kimura, Round 1: 15) brings this out quite well:

KIMURA (K): Generally, the usual workday is from eight in the morning until 5:30, but in sales we're told to come in at 7.30.

ROMIT (R): I see.

K: Anyhow, I'm a 'regular' at running late every morning, arriving at 7.40 ... between [7:] 45 and 50, coming in late by twenty minutes, on late days, around thirty minutes...

R: Was that the case right from the beginning?

K: It was like that right from when I was a fresher (*shinnyû shain*).

R: Really?

K: That wasn't looked upon too favourably (*ki ni kuwanakatta*).

R: umm, so didn't you get told off?

K: I sure did! I'd get scolded and scolded! And for about the next day I'd go [on time] but, I'm pretty incorrigible (*mikka bôzu*). They [the superiors] ended up giving up on me! [*laughs*]

...

K: I keep saying that going in early just to clean [i.e. prepare for the day] isn't my work, so...

...

K: Well anyway, during the day [I'm] usually on outside [sales] rounds (*soto mawari*). Then, when I get back [to the office] there's desk work to be done. When, on the rare occasion when there's nothing to do, I'm able to finish up and go home early around 6.30 [in the evening]. Apart from that, usually around 7.30 or 8. If it gets a bit busy, 10, 11 o'clock.

R: Is that right? I see.

K: At such times, I rest during the day, you know...

R: Yes, I guess with sales, because you have to meet so many different people, you need to have a rest to get re-charged, right?

K: Yeah, I do things like say I'm going over to a customer's place and instead slack off (*sabori shimasu* [*sic*])

R: Um, so how do you 'slack off'? Things like going to a coffee-shop?

K: Sometimes I go to a coffee-shop, sometimes go home and take a nap!... well, this may be a bit extreme, but sometimes I go for a whole week without doing any work at all!

(Kimura, Round 1: 15, 16)

At one level, exchanges such as the above may open up the possibility of reading 'resistance' and/or 'subversion' into these acts of insubordination and avoidance. However, while recognizing that such responses form part of the complex inter-play of engagements between the individual and the hegemonic expectations of masculinity, it is also important not to read *too much* resistance into (relatively) random acts of insubordination or noncompliance. Indeed, as Dorinne Kondo notes in relation to (seemingly) easily identifiable acts of resistance, 'people can be caught in contradictions ... they simultaneously resist and produce, challenge and appropriate meanings ... inevitably participate to some degree in their own oppressions, buying into hegemonic ideologies even as they struggle against those ideologies' (Kondo 1994: 187, 188).

Kimura-san himself recognized this – the fact that people end up becoming agents of their own compliance to the hegemonic discourses – albeit more in relation to others in the organization than himself. Talking about how he saw his future in the company, he stressed that he was 'really not thinking about the future at all. You don't know what's going to happen, when' (Kimura, Round 1: 14). We then went on to have the following exchange:

K: I've really got nothing in particular to make me stick to this company.

R: I see. So, with respect to this company you don't have any particular sense of something like what you'd call 'loyalty' (*aichaku*)?

K: No I don't.

R: How about other people ... is it generally the same kind of feeling?

K: No, I don't think so. I can't speak for the people inside (*naka no ningen*) [i.e. shop-floor employees], but with sales that's not the case. Well, I guess I just had a kid too, but for those further up [in terms of age and seniority], they've got kids, and have taken out home loans, so they're pretty much resigned to it.

(Kimura, Round 1: 15)

Elsewhere, there were echoes of this sense of (what *appears to be*) 'resistance' to the expectations of salaryman masculinity. For instance, by the time of the second interview, he had gone from not being sure whether or not he would remain with Northern Print into the future, to being '90 per cent sure' that ten years down the track he 'would not be here' (Round 2: 4). With regard to how 'representative' he felt he was of Northern Print, unlike Matsumoto Tadashi (and many of the other Northern Energy informants) he was quite blunt in stating that even in situations where his behaviour in public might reflect negatively on his employer, 'the thought never crosses my mind' (13).

What seems to come across here, once again, is a sense of Kimura-san's conscious marking of himself as *not* being the same as everyone else (or at least his colleagues), of refusing to buy into the expectations built around the hegemonic discourse, and consequently not being affected by the expectations of salaryman masculinity. Thus, when early on in the first interview I had asked him about the changes he felt he had undergone since becoming a *shakaijin*, his reply was an unqualified 'nothing's changed' (Kimura, Round 1: 11). Nor did he think he had 'lost anything' (11) since entering the workforce. His response at the end of the same interview to my query about what had been his most positive experience since entering the organization was also a blunt, unequivocal, 'nothing (*nai*)!' (17). Yet, at the same time, my question about what he felt had been the most *negative* experience since entering the company brought forth the following response:

K: The worst aspect ... wonder if it would be the most negative thing? Probably, having to go over to see a customer ... go to see a customer who's some irritating old 'geezer' (*hara* [*ga*] *tatsu oyaji*), and have to acquiesce to him.

R: So, having to humble yourself to a client, but at the same time...

K: Yup. Except in my case, even while I'm 'lowering my head'[while bowing] I let my dislike [of the person] show quite clearly on my face!

(Kimura, Round 1: 17)

This extended to the management of his own organization too. With the exception of the president of the company whom he admitted admiring, and the manager of his own section, he considered everyone else to be 'inept' (Kimura, Round 1: 20). Indeed, when I followed up this statement by asking if there was anyone he 'respected as a person', he responded with, 'the person I respect as a human being is myself' (20).

Such a statement would have been unthinkable from Matsumoto-san. Hence, at one level it would be tempting to locate the two at opposite ends of the spectrum to corporate masculinity. One reading of their narratives would be to locate Matsumoto-san as an embodiment of the sober, respectable pre-1990s, 'Japan Inc.' style of salaryman masculinity, and Kimura-san as signifying an emergent, more individualistic, post-Bubble corporate masculinity. Yet despite the striking differences in the personalities and circumstances of Matsumoto-san and Kimura-san, both of their narratives bring out the ways in which *individual* salarymen were negotiating with the cross-currents surrounding expectations of work, masculinity, and by extension, being a salaryman during these watershed years of the late 1990s.

Conclusion

This chapter, while continuing to employ the voices of my informants, has shifted the focus of the discussion from the informants' memories of becoming male and then becoming salarymen to their accounts of everyday engagements with salaryman masculinity. This discussion was located within the informants' own framework of how they looked at the concept of work itself, where they located the discourse of white-collar salaryman masculinity in terms of socio-cultural notions of 'masculine' and 'unmasculine' areas of work, and how they negotiated with their own, sometimes ambivalent, positionings. Their accounts of all of these issues point to a contradiction in the ways in which hegemonic masculinities are constructed – the reality that, at the end of the day, the culturally pervasive/powerful hegemonic masculinity *may not* always be the culturally 'idealized' one. Yet, as I argue in this book, it was (and, to a degree, continues to be) the discourse of masculinity surrounding the salaryman and not the builder or the carpenter that occupied a hegemonic position in postwar Japan. While at first glance this paradox may appear puzzling, it does in fact make sense if we return to the unpacking of notions of 'hegemony' and 'hegemonic masculinity' discussed in Chapter 1. As – drawing upon Demetriou's theorization of masculinity as a 'hybrid bloc' (Demetriou 2001) – I argued in that chapter, what may initially appear to be a weakening, even destruction, of hegemonic masculinity may in fact translate to a strengthening of its hold, through the incorporation of aspects of previously less socio-culturally privileged masculinities. My informants' idealization of (physically) 'manly' occupations, or the appeal of popular culture icons like Salaryman Kintarô incorporating attributes of working-class masculinity into the discourse of salaryman masculinity, or indeed the narrowing of the gates of access to salaryman masculinity through the 1990s and 2000s, are, I argue, manifestations of this paradox.

6 Working with heterosexuality

Sexuality, marriage, fatherhood, and salaryman masculinity

The previous chapter explored negotiations with the demands of work in relation to informants' sense of masculinity, at a time when the contours of hegemonic masculinity were shifting rapidly. However, work, integral as it may be to hegemonic masculinity, is not the only determinant of it. Intersecting with work are other considerations that are just as significant in an individual's engagements with the expectations of hegemonic masculinity. Arguably, of particular significance is the notion of the male as the *provider*, as the primary breadwinner upon whom the whole family unit depends for sustenance. Thus, with reference to postwar Japan, merely becoming a *shakaijin* and earning a regular income was not enough. Rather, the individual's ability to conform to a specific public and visible discourse of (hetero-) sexuality – one signified by the public 'markers' of marriage and (to a lesser extent) becoming a father – had (and continues to have) a bearing on his 'success' at salaryman masculinity. It is through publicly acquiescing to these culturally privileged 'markers', that he could demonstrate his successful transition from one stage of masculinity (unproductive, non-adult, pre-*shakaijin*/student) to the next (productive, mature, *shakaijin* salaryman). Indeed, as Lunsing points out, 'in order to become *ichininmae no shakaijin* [a fully adult social being] one has to marry ... men who do not take upon themselves the responsibility of supporting a household are not considered fully mature and thus can not be given responsibility for the most independent or powerful types of work' (Lunsing 2001: 74, 75). Moreover, as I suggested in the previous chapter, the post-Bubble structural changes to the employment sector have, if anything, worked to accentuate the desirability of attributes of hegemonic salaryman masculinity (such as the stability offered by full-time, permanent work) while simultaneously narrowing the entry to these dividends for growing numbers of young men.

This chapter will focus on the intersections of a particular discourse of (hetero-) sexuality, at the core of which lie the institutions of marriage and fatherhood, with salaryman masculinity, at that historic moment when many of the assumptions surrounding these very intersections appeared to be unravelling. The first part of this chapter sets up a conceptual framework for this discussion. The second part moves on to focus on the ways in which my informants negotiated with the expectations of salaryman masculinity revolving around the public expression of sexuality.

Organizational masculinity and sexuality

The significance of heterosexuality to hegemonic masculinity has been recognized and commented upon by a number of writers. Connell, for example, points out that 'the most important feature of contemporary hegemonic masculinity is that it is heterosexual, being closely connected to the institution of marriage; and a key form of subordinated masculinity is homosexual' (Connell 1987: 186). Pyle Frank also highlights a similar point, noting the dominance of heterosexual hegemonic masculinity within the political economy (Frank 1987: 160, 161; see also, Hanke 1992; Kimmel 1994; Connell 1995; Bird 1996; Beynon 2002). Likewise, the intersections between sexuality, hegemonic masculinity, and *organizational culture* have also been examined in the works of numerous authors, both from the perspective of gender studies as well as in the area of management and organizational studies.[1] These works have alerted us to the reality that although organizational culture may appear 'to be a sexless, rational realm' (Hall 1989: 125), sexuality is in fact a pervasive (but unacknowledged) aspect of organizations (see Acker 1990; Ackroyd and Thompson 1999: 121–143).

This pervasive sexuality, at least at the level of public discourse, was, until very recent years, 'relentlessly heterosexual' (Pringle 1989:164; see also Rich 1980). Moreover, rather than any kind of heterosexuality, it was the *signifying* of a particular discourse of heterosexuality through markers such as marriage, parenthood, and home ownership that was particularly privileged. For male employees, traditionally, 'proving' this heterosexuality in public was thus closely linked to hegemonic masculinity. Further, while displays of unregulated heterosexuality (for instance, promiscuous (hetero-) sexual behaviour) may fortify an individual's claim to hegemonic masculinity (see, e.g. Collinson 1988:190–192; McDowell 1995: 85, 86), this was true up to a point. Beyond a certain age and/or a certain level of seniority, however, *regulated* heterosexuality through marriage (and subsequently fatherhood) became an important condition for access to the dividends of hegemonic masculinity. This comes across powerfully in Michael Roper's study of postwar British executives, in which he notes that 'marriage was frequently an informal prerequisite for promotion' (Roper 1994: 84). Similarly, Collinson's work on shop-floor workers also highlights the importance of being a married, family breadwinner in relation to working-class masculinity (Collinson and Collinson 1989; see also Collinson 1992). Thus, regardless of whether we are talking about white-collar managers or blue-collar line workers, *regulated* heterosexuality seems integral to the day-to-day dynamics of corporate industrial capitalism. Arguably, since the publication of Roper's and Collinson's works, the situation has shifted somewhat, at least in some Euro-American and/or multinational organizational contexts. As flagship multinational corporations such as IBM move to incorporate sexual diversity as an aspect of corporate policy, one could argue that the concerns raised in Roper's or Collinson's works are less relevant. However, the reality, even in the most 'progressive' corporate organization, continues to be one where upper management is still heavily dominated by heterosexual married (or once-married) *men*.[2]

Sexuality, marriage, and salaryman masculinity

By way of a lead-in to discussing some of the above issues in the specific context of salaryman masculinity, I draw upon a 1992 Japanese film directed by Naka-jima Takehiro, *Okoge* ('Fag Hag').[3] The film centres around the two main male characters: Tochi, a middle-aged married salaryman, and Goh, his younger male lover. Tochi makes constant reference to the pressures of having to maintain the *appearance* of married heterosexuality in his workplace. In one scene, for instance, he is shown forcing himself to laugh along with everyone at a homo-phobic comment made by a colleague. The relationship between Tochi and Goh is discovered by the former's wife, who offers her husband the choice of either giving up his boyfriend or being 'outed' at work. Needless to say, Tochi's rela-tionship with Goh does not survive. However, neither, in the end, does his mar-riage and his salaryman identity. In a telling scene towards the end of the film he chooses to publicly 'come out' in quite a spectacular fashion in front of col-leagues, thereby effectively opting out of salaryman masculinity. The setting for this is an occasion which is perhaps as significant in a salaryman's life-path as any, and which signifies in a very public manner his inclusion in this discourse of masculinity – a wedding. Moreover, it is the wedding of one of Tochi's junior colleagues, and he has been asked to officiate as the *nakôdo*, the symbolic matchmaker or go-between, for the couple. The role of *nakôdo*, as Walter Edwards notes, although largely symbolic, is an extremely important one; he 'must be a married man ... one who has already demonstrated his ability to lead a stable married life. He is likely to be considerably older ... and should be socially prominent and respected as well' (Edwards 1989: 15).

The scene in the film has Tochi arriving at the ceremony, not with his wife, but with a male partner who is dressed (not very convincingly) as a woman in a formal kimono and hairstyle befitting the wife of a *nakôdo*. Tochi formally intro-duces his 'wife', announces his resignation from the company, and performs a parodied children's song (with concealed sexual references) much to the horror of all present. As Sandra Buckley comments in relation to this scene: 'this "coming out" at a company-sponsored wedding ceremony, in front of his wife, her family and his boss marks Tochi's decision to refuse to continue to perform the roles of *sarariiman* ... and household head/husband' (Buckley 2000: 241).

Okoge, in particular this specific scene, brings into sharp relief the intersec-tions of marriage, household, heterosexual performance, and company which over the postwar decades underpinned the discourse of *shakaijin* salaryman mas-culinity. Becoming a *shakaijin* involves more than merely entering into paid work upon completion of education. Rather, for both men and women, linked into the status of becoming *shakaijin* has been the notion of becoming '*ichinin-mae no shakaijin* [a fully adult social being]' through marriage (Lunsing 2001: 74). The implicit assumption, as Lunsing notes, is that a person is not fully adult unless married with the accompanying social responsibilities. Historically, for a man, this 'social responsibility' involved being the *daikokubashira* support and provider, and for a woman, it entailed being a wife and mother, sustaining and nurturing the household from within. This, as highlighted in earlier chapters, is despite a reality over the postwar decades (and, to an extent, over the prewar era too) of women *always* having played a significant role within the paid employment sector (not to mention the generally unpaid, household/family business sector).

Thus, for both men and women, marriage long signified acquiescence to widely held socio-cultural notions of '*jôshiki*' (common sense, what is considered normal, natural) (see Lunsing 2001). It also signalled conforming to the expectations of good citizenship – embodied, for instance, in the salaryman/professional housewife pairing. Conversely, *not* getting married had (and arguably, continues to have) implications of being '*hanninmae*,… half of a person … not independent individuals but like children waiting to grow up, no matter what their age is' (Lunsing 2001: 75). Indeed, not getting married beyond a certain age could be seen as noncompliance to, or even active rebuttal of, the responsibilities of good citizenship. This was evident in the media discourse in the late 1990s/early 2000s following sociologist Yamada Masahiro's application of the label 'Parasite Single' to unmarried young people living at home, and supposedly sponging off their parents without contributing anything in return (Yamada 1999). While the term itself is gender-neutral, it was largely applied to single women. The implication in much of the media commentary at the time was that these 'parasite singles', by not getting married and starting families, were avoiding their social responsibilities, thus contributing to Japan's demographic crisis (and consequently, its social and economic decline).[4]

Thus, while marriage and becoming *ichininmae* have long carried both tangible and intangible dividends, remaining single can often have negative social and career repercussions. This comes through, for instance, in research by Murata Yôhei on middle-aged single men – his informants mentioned such things as being passed over for promotions, or being expected not to complain about workloads that were heavier than those of their married colleagues (Murata 2000). Even where there may be no negative consequences per se, single men still have to negotiate with expectations of heterosexuality, particularly assumptions centred around marriage and taking on the role of provider. For instance, in an April 2000 issue, the periodical *Queer Japan* featured a collection of essays, interviews, and survey data entitled *Hentai-suru Sarariiman* ('Queering the Salaryman'), focusing around sexuality and work. Many of the survey respondents talked about experiencing and dealing with 'marriage pressures (*kekkon atsuryoku*)' in the workplace – having to put up with comments like 'men who don't marry aren't *ichininmae*', or 'a man's happiness lies with supporting a wife and kids', or even 'men who don't have a family to support can't be trusted' (*Queer Japan* 2000: 67–103).

What the above points to, then, is a specific model of regulated heterosexuality revolving around being the family provider that gets privileged, and can act almost like a default setting for men above a certain age. Nevertheless, despite the grip of this hegemonic ideal (of the married husband/father provider) there has always been a disjuncture between it and the reality on the ground; a situation further exacerbated in the context of the socio-cultural and economic shifts of the 1990s and 2000s. This gap between ideal and reality is reflected, for instance, in both the increasing age of marriage for men and women, as well as the growing proportion of single, 'never-married' persons within the population. The average marriage age had been rising over several decades, and by 2007 had reached 30.1 for men and 28.3 for women, placing Japan in the same league as Scandinavian countries (Yuzawa and Miyamoto 2008: 100). At the same time, the proportion of never-married persons in the thirty to thirty-four age cohort (arguably the peak years for marriage and starting a family) had increased from 14.3 per cent for men and 7.7 percent for women in 1975, to 47.7 per cent for men and 32.6 per cent for women by 2005 (Shimoda 2008).

Significantly, the backdrop to these statistics was not necessarily a socio-cultural refutation of the *institution* of marriage. If anything, as the voices of my informants in this chapter will bear out, attitudes towards the importance of marriage itself have not shifted significantly – surveys point to a continued desire among younger people (close to 90 per cent) to get married and have a family (Yuzawa and Miyamoto 2008: 102; also Allison 2009: 98, 99; Tanaka 2009: 146, 147; Taga 2011b: 192, 193). However, what *did* change quite markedly from the 1990s was the growth in the temporary/casual *freeter* sector of the economy – as noted previously, by the mid-2000s over two million Japanese under the age of thirty-five were engaged in part-time or temporary work (MHLW 2005). Moreover, whereas initially *freeter* were largely in their late teens or twenties, as the economic slowdown continued beyond the mid-1990s, many continued working in the non-permanent sector into their thirties and even forties (Allison 2009: 98, 99). For male *freeter*, in particular, not having access to stable, permanent employment made it that much more difficult to live up to the expectations of a *daikokubashira* provider, thereby making them less attractive as potential marriage partners – as Ronald and Alexy highlight, behind the seemingly high proportion of unmarried men in the thirty to thirty-four age category, is a clear distinction between those in regular employment (41 per cent unmarried) and those in the non-regular sector (70 per cent) (Ronald and Alexy 2011: 16; also Taga 2011b: 192, 194; 2011c: 24).

What the above suggests is that from the mid- to late 1990s, while the discursive ideal may have remained entrenched, the ability to attain that ideal was becoming far more difficult for growing numbers of younger men. Thus, although they may not have been aware of it themselves (at least at the time), the men with whom I was interacting were negotiating with these socio-culturally sanctioned ideals of (hetero-) sexuality at an important historical moment. The remainder of this chapter will focus on the ways in which, as individuals, they negotiated with these expectations of salaryman masculinity at a time when many of the assumptions underpinning these expectations *appeared* to be unravelling.

'It just seems the natural thing': imaginings of marriage in informants' lives

Due to its significance as an underpinning of salaryman masculinity, marriage was one of the key questions I covered with both single and married informants. Of the various issues covered, marriage was one of the easier ones in terms of eliciting immediate, concrete responses, possibly due to the immediacy of the topic. Many informants were around (or approaching) what is considered to be the culturally appropriate 'marriageable age' (*tekireiki*) for men. A few were already married, others had concrete plans to do so in the immediate future, and the remainder (even if they did not currently have a girlfriend) saw themselves married in the short- to medium-term future. Perhaps reflecting the pervasive socio-cultural hold of marriage as an institution, not one informant mentioned an intention to never marry (though one or two may have questioned their own *ability* to attract marriage partners). Moreover, there seemed to be an implicit assumption of my concurrence with their views regarding marriage. Given that I seemed – in my behaviour, speech, attitudes, familiarity with reference points they identified with – basically like them, there was an unspoken assumption that I too must consider marriage to be *atarimae* (natural).

The meaning of marriage

An appropriate entry to the informants' voices would be the responses provided when asked about the meaning of marriage in their lives, irrespective of actual marital status. At twenty, Miura Tôru, the Northern Energy employee, whose transition difficulties into *shakaijin* life were discussed in Chapter 4, had barely entered adulthood. Yet he had clear ideas about what marriage meant to him. Ideally, he stressed, he wanted to get married 'before 25' (Miura, Round 2: 10). Marriage to him represented 'not being alone' (20). Expanding on this notion of the need to be a part of a coupled pairing in order to become *ichininmae*, he argued that: 'it's natural to want someone, someone to talk to (*hanashi-aite*)' (21). When I then asked him why he saw getting married as a necessary condition for companionship, given that it was possible to be with someone without necessarily getting married, he responded:

> Somehow, it just seems the natural thing (*atarimae*). Maybe that's because, possibly, I've grown up seeing everyone else [do so]. Possibly, you want to do the same things as everyone else, don't you?
>
> (Miura Round 2: 11)

At the time of our conversation, this informant did not have a girlfriend and hence did not have a specific person in mind when making these observations. Yet, for precisely this reason, the strength of the discourse that sees getting married as *jôshiki* (common sense) (Lunsing 2001) resonates in his words.

This notion of marriage as an antidote to the loneliness of being single was echoed in the words of a number of other individuals. Takahashi Yoshio, a twenty-three-year-old Northern Print technical shop-floor employee, wanted to get married before the age of thirty. To him, getting married represented a solution to the loneliness of 'living alone' (Takahashi Round 2: 7). In his view, the loneliness of being single extended to 'even … food not tasting good (*gohan … mo oishiku nai*)' (7) when living on one's own. Ogasawara Takurô, the Northern Energy employee whose reflections on work and its significance in his life were discussed at length in the previous chapter, also mentioned wanting to be married by the time he turned thirty. His main reason for wanting to get married was because he 'desired peace of mind (*yasuragi*)' (Ogasawara, Round 2:14). Satô Hiroshi was another Northern Energy employee who wanted to see himself married by the age of thirty; ideally, between twenty-seven and thirty (at the time he was twenty-three). Marriage, in his view, was 'part of the course nature takes (*shizen no nagare*)' (Satô, Round 2: 8). Children born through marriage were 'one of the main reasons for living (*jinsei no ikigai*)' (8), something that he had never questioned. Indeed, as he put it, the 'major role for marriage was to raise children to be responsible adults (*ichininmae*)' (8). Kobayashi Kazushi, another Northern Energy employee in his mid-twenties, also linked marriage to something that was akin to a natural part of the life cycle; to him it was 'something that one does' (Kobayashi Round 2: 10).

Another association with marriage that cropped up in discussions was marriage as a conduit to adulthood – a means of channelling the 'wildness' of youth. Thus, for Saiki Yasuo, a twenty-three-year-old technician in Northern Print who wanted to see himself married within his twenties, marriage signified 'settling down (*ochitsuku*)' (Saiki, Round 2: 8). He described his present lifestyle as one where he was 'wandering aimlessly' (8). This consisted of 'playing hard' (1), specifically 'drinking, picking up girls' (2). In his view, this was a condition that only marriage could rectify. He reflected on this notion of 'settling down':

> I suppose, the first thing would be supporting a family properly, … strange as it may sound … living a normal life (*futsû ni seikatsu shite*), having children, raising them properly, that's how I interpret 'settling down'.
>
> (Saiki, Round 2: 9)

Significantly, with the exception of Takahashi Yoshio of Northern Print and Kobayashi Kazushi of Northern Energy, not only were all of these informants unmarried, but also, at the time of the interview, none were involved in steady relationships. Yet, despite this, they all seemed to have very specific ideas about marriage.

However, one unmarried informant did express a fairly 'open', even questioning attitude to this notion of marriage being a necessary marker of *ichininmae* adult status. Unlike most of the other informants who put thirty as the age by which they saw themselves married, Ishida Naoki, the twenty-one-year-old Northern Energy employee whose perception of his own shortcomings with regard to 'ideals' of masculinity was touched upon in an earlier chapter, thought he would still be single ten years down the track. As he put it, 'I'll probably still be living a carefree single life' (Ishida, Round 2: 5). He thought that the late thirties would be an appropriate age to get married, but if by then he 'had not met the right person, remaining single wouldn't really be a problem' (9). At the time he did not have a girlfriend, and had been single for around six or seven years (10). The reason for marriage, as far as he was concerned, was 'wanting to be with someone for the rest of your life … that's the major premise' (13). However, he had no real problems with continuing a relationship without a formal marriage; as he put it, 'marriage, well, I think it's just one type of structure (*hitotsu no katachi*)' (13).

Marriage and workplace status

With regards to marriage and its connection to work, the initial reaction of many of the informants was to deny any connection. Saiki Yasuo's was a fairly typical response. On the one hand, he denied any connection between being married and the way one is regarded in the context of the workplace – his exact words were 'there's no connection (*kankei nai*)' (10) – but at the same time, almost inadvertently, he brought out this connection:

> The company looks at things like the way you work, your work [performance], so there's no connection with being married or not married. As a result of getting married there might be 'pluses' on your work, or 'minuses'.
>
> (Saiki, Round 2: 10)

The 'pluses' of getting married, according to this informant, included 'a change in attitude in some people' (Saiki, Round 2: 10) due to now needing to 'work hard for the sake of the family' (10). On the other hand, the 'minuses' from getting married would be situations where family responsibilities, such as child-rearing, result in your 'mind and body getting tired' (11), thereby impacting negatively upon your work. This, he stressed, would never happen to him; no matter how involved he got with his children; he was 'confident it would not interfere with work' (11).

Unlike Saiki Yasuo, Ogasawara Takurô of Northern Energy did explicitly recognize the connection between a person's marital status and the way he was regarded at work. As he explained, 'I think that within the context of a Japanese organization, after a certain age [being married] makes the biggest difference as to whether or not you're able to gain society's trust' (Ogasawara, Round 2: 15). Indeed, he was quite honest about his own prejudices in this matter, stating that although 'in my head I know that it shouldn't be a consideration in evaluating people, yet, to tell you the truth, if I see someone unmarried at forty or forty-five, I end up thinking "I wonder if there isn't something wrong with him?"' (16). This sentiment was also echoed by Satô Hiroshi who noted that regardless of what the company's official line might be, 'I myself do take it [i.e. marital status] into account a little. I suppose, I'm concerned with what others think' (Satô, Round 2: 9).

This connection between work and marriage, and more generally the relationship between marriage and societal validation, was made particularly visible in the conversations with recently married informants as they reflected upon the ways in which colleagues had responded to their change in marital status. Fujita Yûji was a twenty-seven-year-old Northern Print employee who worked in sales and marketing. At the time of our discussion, he had been married for four years. Moreover, before marriage – somewhat unusually in the context of Japan – he and his partner had cohabited together for a number of years; they had been involved with each other for eight years before deciding to get married (Fujita, Round 2: 8). Fujita-san admitted that their decision to get married after so many years of already living together had an element of wanting to make the relationship 'official', particularly as he was from Kyûshû, a part of Japan that, he mentioned, is quite traditional in social attitudes. As he put it:

> For example ... even if you're living together, when you're not married, well, [people are] taken by surprise ... if you say things along the lines of '[we're] living together', [they] get taken aback. But if you're married and say 'we're married', that's where it [the curiosity] ends.
>
> (Fujita, Round 2: 10)

As he admitted, however, this was not the only consideration. There was also an element of 'it was the right time ... as we'd already been together for five or six years' (Fujita, Round 2: 9). In one sense, marriage, to him, was 'just a piece of paper, and signing on it wasn't going to change my life' (10). However, as he discovered, marriage 'turned out to be of far greater significance than I had thought' (10). This 'great significance', hinged on the 'responsibility' he now had towards immediate family, relatives, and friends as the husband in the husband–wife pairing (*fûfu*). He did not, however, feel that there was any strong connection between (his, or in general) marital status and being 'trusted' at work. Despite the existence of a dominant societal image of the 'responsible' married man, in reality, 'it doesn't always follow one hundred per cent, that just because you get married and become a parent you develop a sense of responsibility' (Fujita, Round 2: 13).

Kajima Daisuke was another married Northern Print employee. However, unlike Fujita-san who worked in Sales and Marketing, Kajima-san worked in the actual printing press. He represented an interesting combination of several diverse masculinities within himself. On the one hand, he seemed to be the prefect embodiment of hegemonic masculinity – not only was he respectably married (and on the track to fatherhood), he was also, although only twenty-eight years old, already a *kachô* (section manager). Yet, on the other hand, he also had a darker history of getting involved in fights and into trouble with the police, and years of hard drinking, leading to a weakened liver and being ordered by the doctor to stop drinking (Kajima, Round 2: 14).[5] At the time of our interview he had been married for over a year. Prior to getting married he and his partner had dated for around one year, but the decision to get married was made only six months into their relationship. One of the considerations behind his decision to get married after a (relatively) short period of time was the sudden death of his father, and the 'desire to comfort' (Kajima, Round 2: 16) his mother, something compounded by people around him urging him to get married with comments like 'hurry up and give your mother some peace of mind' (16). Although marriage, according to Kajima-san, had not resulted in any kind of significant change within himself, he felt that it would eventually lead to him 'to some extent, seeking greater stability' (17). Kajima-san did acknowledge the relationship between a man's marital status and his standing in the workplace. While he himself did not think a person being married or single was relevant to his work, he was aware that others in the workplace might regard things differently. As he put it:

> I think management takes the view that your performance and your sense of responsibility (*sekinin-kan*) gets stronger when you get married. I was told that myself, when I got married – something along the lines that I'd become a proper adult (*ichininmae*).
>
> (Kajima, Round 2: 20)

Murayama Satoshi, the thirty-year-old Northern Energy head office employee working in general administration whose reflections on the importance of work in his life were discussed in the previous chapter, had been married for just over a year. He had also very recently become the father of a baby girl. His comments on what getting married had meant to him reflected many of the wider assumptions underpinning marriage. Compared with other married informants, Murayama-san had married relatively late. His reason for getting married, as he put it, was:

> because it was something that was inevitable. You know, [becoming] a 'unit' (*yunitto*).... So since there was someone I really liked I got married, it was just a matter of course.
>
> (Murayama: 47)

In response to my question about why he felt the need to formalize, to make 'official' his relationship with his wife-to-be, instead of just cohabiting together, he made the following observations:

> I think I have a strong need to be validated by society. ... So, admittedly although we live in a world where things like having sex without being married don't constitute an illegal act (*ihô kôi*) or anything, but ... you know at some level I think that if you are able to marry and don't, it's almost like an antisocial act (*han-shakaiteki kôi*).
>
> (Murayama: 49)

His marriage represented an example of a classic 'salaryman' marriage, where a work colleague or superior becomes an intermediary (see Rohlen 1974: 235–242; Edwards 1989: 75, 76). He and his wife (who had been a bank teller prior to marriage) had been introduced through the auspices of a workplace superior (*jôshi*) – this person had apparently been a former colleague of the father of Murayama-san's wife. Thus, his marriage, in his view, was 'somewhere in-between' (Murayama: 50) the traditional arranged *o-miai* marriage and contemporary *ren'ai* ('love') marriage. He had not really anticipated getting married through such formal channels; however, in what came across as a stereotypically salaryman response he mentioned 'a lack of free time [to meet prospective partners]' (50) as the reason for allowing his marriage to be 'semi-arranged' in such a manner.

Like Kajima Daisuke of Northern Print, Murayama-san also perceived a change in the way people interacted with him as a consequence of his new married *ichininmae* status. The comment he made in relation to the issue captured beautifully both his own feelings and the importance of married heterosexual respectability to salaryman masculinity: 'Yes I got the feeling they [i.e. people's attitudes] changed. Could a mere ring on my finger make such a change? – that's what I felt!' (Murayama: 53). He then went on to illustrate with an example the extent to which the *appearance* of married sobriety is integral to salaryman masculinity:

> This is something I heard, not an experience I had myself, but I've heard that [men] working in banks are told to wear their wedding bands at work after they get married. It's like it's one way of creating an impression to gain trust, [by visually stating] 'I'm married, I've got a family to support'. I myself can really relate to that.[6]
>
> (Murayama: 53)

For Murayama-san himself, the dividends of marriage extended beyond strengthened respect and esteem at work. He related in no uncertain terms that getting married had 'taken a load off my shoulders' (Murayama: 47), since he was able to hand over to his wife the responsibility of looking after his diet, his clothing, and the management of the household. As he laughingly commented: 'I've been liberated from an irregular diet (*zusanna shokuseikatsu*)' (48). Moreover, he saw himself as having become more culturally 'refined' thanks to marriage; his wife had exposed him to 'a world I didn't know … like ballet … art, also theatre, the artistic side I didn't have has been able to come out' (48). Significantly, he mentioned that the negative consequence of marriage was similar to what had been sacrificed as a result of becoming a *shakaijin*, namely 'a loss of free time' (48) to pursue his own interests, or to meet friends.

Matsumoto Tadashi, the twenty-eight-year-old Northern Energy Accounts employee, and my liaison person in that organization, echoed some of Murayama Satoshi's sentiments regarding the link between marriage, respectability, and esteem at work. At the time of our discussions, Matsumoto-san was still single and living in the dormitory for single male employees. However, he was due to get married shortly after our second interview, and planned to leave the dormitory and move into company-subsidized housing for married employees (*shataku*). He provided the example of the single male employees' dormitory to illustrate the link between marriage and work culture. Technically, any unmarried male employee, regardless of age, could live there. In reality, though, since most residents got married and left the dormitory before the age of thirty, a single employee continuing to live there beyond his twenties would feel particularly conscious of his still unmarried status – an invisible and unarticulated pressure, not dissimilar to the kind of subtle marriage pressures felt (particularly in the past) by many female clerical employees (the 'OLs') beyond a certain age (see Ogasawara 1998: 58–60). As Matsumoto-san explained:

> In the end it's up to the individual, but I suppose there is [that kind of] a restriction (*seiyaku*) … well it's not just restricted to our company, but in Japan if you're still unmarried after a certain age, there's probably that kind of hidden pressure…. Also, I feel there's the aspect of being 'socially trusted' (*shakaitekina shinyô*) – in Japan it makes some difference depending on whether you have a family [to support] or not.
>
> (Matsumoto, Round 2: 18)

Being a father and *daikokubashira*: imaginings and realities

As pointed out above, rather than heterosexuality per se, it is the privileging of a specific discourse of heterosexuality within the framework of salaryman masculinity that we are concerned with. At its core lies the notion of the husband and father as a provider for a dependent family – the *daikokubashira* of the household. As outlined in Chapter 2, various socio-economic changes in the early postwar decades helped reinforce the ideological grip of this discourse. These included such socio-economic and cultural shifts as rapid urbanization as a consequence of rural–urban migration; the growth of suburbs leading to long commuting hours and the distancing of the home from the workplace; the emergence of a white-collar middle class; and a trend towards smaller nuclear families, which ironically further focused the role of women on motherhood and household management and the role of men on the productive *daikokubashira* breadwinner (see Uno 1993).

This clearly gender-segmented discourse of parenting began to come under pressure from the 1980s and 1990s, as one aspect of the overall interrogations of hegemonic expectations of gender roles referred to in Chapter 2. Underlying this shift in the discourse were the successive government campaigns and initiatives from the 1990s, namely to encourage mothers to remain in the workforce by providing support for childcare provision, and encouraging fathers to take on a more active role in child-rearing (see Roberts 2002; Dasgupta 2009: 86, 87; Taga 2011a; also Ishii-Kuntz 2003).[7] Moreover, younger men were coming of age in an era when, at least discursively, the idea of women and men being equally involved in child-rearing and household work was increasingly becoming the norm. For instance, as Taga notes, Office of Cabinet surveys indicate that support for a clearly demarcated gender role division in the household declined quite markedly over the 1980s and 1990s (Taga 2011c: 22, 23). However, despite this growing public validation of the need to move to new gender expectations, in reality, the notion of masculinity being defined by being a *daikokubashira* continued to remain entrenched. Indeed, as I previously noted, the post-Bubble economic conditions actually worked to accentuate the work/masculinity nexus, thereby strengthening the appeal of the *daikokubashira* ideal. First, despite surveys pointing to a greater *willingness* on the part of men to participate in housework and child-rearing, the reality on the ground did not necessarily change that much – by 2006, even in households where both partners worked, the husband's share of household labour still remained at around 10 per cent, up only slightly from just over 5 per cent in the mid-1980s (Yuzawa and Miyamoto 2008: 31). Furthermore, even this increase did not necessarily translate to a radical questioning of gender roles. As Yuzawa and Miyamoto note, men's 'housework' and 'child-rearing' tend to comprise less onerous activities like shopping or playing with children, than more demanding ones like cooking and cleaning, or changing diapers and feeding children (30, 31). Second, as I suggested in the previous chapter, as full-time permanent employment became increasingly less certain through the 1990s, those younger men who *were* successful in gaining full-time work were all the more conscious of the precariousness of their privileged positions. Hence, for such men, the pressures to perform in order to succeed (or even survive) in an increasingly competitive, unstable workplace translated through to more time and energy devoted to work in their lives, despite an expressed desire to the contrary – an early 2000s survey, for instance, noted that the proportion of male employees working in excess of sixty hours a week was greatest for men in their twenties and thirties (Fujimura 2006: 209).

My informants were situated at the crossroads of these shifting discourses in relation to fatherhood and the male as provider. On the one hand, they had come of age in a Japan where the notion of work being the sole preserve of men was becoming an anomaly – many of them had mothers who had worked during their childhood, and, as we will see, many were not averse to their partners or future partners continuing to work outside the home after marriage. At the same time they were equally shaped by the expectations of hegemonic masculinity, not least the notion of the husband as the *daikokubashira* primary breadwinner of the household. Perhaps the strength of this man as *daikokubashira* discourse can be gauged by a comment made by Kajima Daisuke, the twenty-eight-year-old Northern Print *kachô*, whose views on marriage were discussed in the preceding section. At the time of our discussion Kajima-san had been married for over a year, and he and his wife were considering starting a family. Talking about the significance of being the provider for a dependent family he commented:

> When you're single, if you lose your job or something, well, you only need to worry about your own survival. But when you have children, well then

the whole family has to survive together, don't they? Since you can't let your family starve by the wayside,... you can no longer think along lines like 'this job isn't interesting so I'll quit'.

(Kajima, Round 2: 17)

This type of sentiment was echoed by several other married informants, particularly those who had to deal with the responsibilities of fatherhood. Shin'ya Naohiko of Northern Energy, who had recently become the father of a baby girl, made the comment that fatherhood had made it 'that much harder to quit the company' (Shin'ya, Round 2: 6).

Matsumoto Tadashi: visions of an 'ideal' husband and father

Matsumoto Tadashi, the Northern Energy Accounts employee who was the liaison person for my research in that organization, was, as mentioned above, about to get married to his girlfriend of six years. Hence, his future as a husband and father was a topic that was particularly pertinent to him at the time of our discussion. He and his fiancée had been seeing each other for six years, a fairly long period of time for a couple to be involved in a relationship without getting married. However, the reason they had not previously 'settled down' was not so much due to any desire to flout socio-cultural conventions, but rather to their personal circumstances. Both of them had entered the workforce about four years previously, and they felt it best that they work for a few years to get established (Matsumoto, Round 2: 13, 14). As he explained, 'I thought that it wouldn't be until I was around 28 that I'd be sufficiently *ichininmae* to get married' (14). Once they decided that it was time to get married, though, the girlfriend had resigned from her job in anticipation of her new role as a salaryman's *sengyō shufu*. As he explained:

> to speak honestly, probably, since my income's stable we can maintain our lifestyle without [her] needing to work.... Also, to tell you the truth, when everyone else around you is like that [i.e. the wife stays at home], well, you end up going along with the flow, don't you? Everyone lives in the *shataku* (company housing). So with people from the same company all living in the same place, there's probably an element of being conscious of the opinions of everyone around you.... But once the children are born, straight after birth would be difficult, but once they're a bit more independent, I don't mind if she wants to work, I don't plan to place any restrictions.
>
> (Matsumoto, Round 2: 15)

Matsumoto-san's vision of himself as husband and father was one that seemed to be on track to replicate all the major markers of salaryman masculinity over his life-path. At the same time, while living up to all the older hegemonic ideals (male as primary provider, dedication to work, etc.) he also came across as wanting to incorporate some of the more recent ideals of masculinity – for instance, being more 'sensitive' and 'understanding' as a husband, and interested in the upbringing of the children. Thus, his consciousness of the need to conform to the gender expectations of a salaryman family was tempered by a desire to appear to be liberal or broadminded. He wanted to wait at least two years before he and his wife had children in order to enjoy life as a couple, something he felt would become difficult once the children were born.

Yet, in the end, his views on his future life as husband and father were still firmly within the parameters of the hegemonic ideals of salaryman masculinity. For instance, when talking about his wife working after marriage, what was significant was the *tone* that was adopted – a sense of 'allowing' his wife to work as a gesture to changing gender norms:

> To tell you the truth, we could probably get along fine on [just] my income, but, well, I think that if I make her stay at home all the time, she might get lonely or something. So, rather than that, I plan to get her to do some sort of part-time work (*arubaito*), and she herself says she'd like to do that, so I don't think it'll be like she'll be at home all the time.
>
> (Matsumoto, Round 2: 15)

He planned to 'allow' his wife to work until childbirth, after which she would probably devote herself to being a full-time housewife and mother, as 'looking at our company, well, there aren't many double income couples (*tomo-bataraki*)' (Matsumoto, Round 2: 15).

Similarly, his views on his future involvement with his children, and the way he imagined his future family life, also reflected the influence of the hegemonic discourse of salaryman masculinity. His imagining of this future family seemed almost a caricature of the standard two-children salaryman nuclear family – ideally he hoped that he and his wife would have one girl and one boy (Matsumoto, Round 2: 9). Elaborating on this vision of his 'ideal' family, he stated that he wanted to:

> build a normal (*futsû*) family – I know saying [the word] 'normal' might be a bit you know [old-fashioned] (*futsû to iu iikata wa are desu ne*) – also, do things like go somewhere together as a family, go on trips and things when there's time.
>
> (Matsumoto, Round 2: 8)

While he did approve of fathers being involved with the children, when it came to the *specifics* of this involvement he was vague. He wanted to be a father who 'respected the children's opinions' (Matsumoto, Round 2: 8), and 'as far as possible give them freedom and let them live as they want to' (9), but beyond that he was vague about the nitty-gritty details of what active involvement in the children's lives would actually involve. Indeed, there seemed to be a pre-empting of the inevitability, due to work commitments, of his non-involvement in child-rearing. Talking about his imagining of himself and his family ten years down the track, he said that although he would like to live together as a family,

> in the case of our company to an extent around the time the children are in junior high school, usually there's quite a bit of coming and going [i.e. transfers] to the regions and to the head office. So I can see myself as a *tanshin-funin* (living away from the family), in terms of my circumstances.
>
> (Matsumoto, Round 2: 9)

Twenty years or so down the track, by the time he was in his fifties, he saw his life as one where

> [The children] will be around high-school age, won't they? Although I might be able to spend some time with the family, almost certainly, I'll have gone to a regional area as a *tanshin-funin* working away from the children and all. Well, I suppose I'll be able to return home on weekends, but still, the amount of time we'll be able to spend together would have decreased ... I can picture my situation as being close to one that's dominated completely by work.
>
> (Matsumoto, Round 2: 10)

As he somewhat apologetically commented: 'the share occupied by work within my thinking is quite large. I've started to realize this recently. I guess talking about these things, I realize how little all else matters!' (Matsumoto, Round 2: 11). In this sense, Matsumoto-san came close to embodying – warts and all – the stereotype of a salaryman masculinity harking back to an almost nostalgic pre-'Lost Decade' era of (seemingly) uncomplex assumptions about gender roles.

Single informants and imaginings of daikokubashira

This notion of the husband/father being the mainstay and provider of the family was not limited to just the married informants, or informants like Matsumoto-san who were at the point of transition to husband/father status. In common with many of the younger informants, Minami Toshio, a nineteen-year-old Northern Energy employee working in Sales, was not averse to the idea of his future wife working after marriage; as he put it, it was 'probably best to keep working, as long as she [his future wife] wants to' (Minami: 8). However, when I asked him about his feelings were he to stay at home, with his wife being the primary income earner, his response was an explicit, 'I'd hate that ... if I'm not working while she is, somehow it's distasteful, it's like being defeated (*maket-eiru mitai*)' (8).

Saiki Yasuo, the twenty-three-year-old Northern Print employee who said he saw marriage as a means to '*ochitsuku* (settling down)' (Saiki, Round 2: 9), presented the following picture of himself, and the type of family he saw himself being the head of. He saw himself as getting married while in his twenties to the sort of woman he could 'feel comfortable with' and who was 'a responsible person' (9). In other words, his preference was for someone who would be a good household manager. He said that after marriage, he would 'prefer [the wife], given present circumstances, to be a full-time (*sengyô*) [housewife], but, should things get tough she might have to work' (5). He wanted either one or two children (4). If he and his wife ended up having two children, his preference was for one girl and one boy. Should they only have one child, however, the preference was for a boy (4). Yet despite these fairly clear ideas about what he expected of his future family, he seemed vague (indeed vaguer than most of the other informants) about how he saw himself as a father – his response to my question about what kind of father he wanted to be was a non-committal repeating of the question to himself. When I then rephrased the question to make it a little more specific, by asking him if he would like to be involved in child-rearing if he had children, his response was a slightly embarrassed (laughing) 'I wouldn't be able to' (9).

Ogasawara Takurô of Northern Energy also wanted to have two children, ideally boys, as he himself had grown up as the older of two male siblings. As mentioned in the previous chapter, when discussing his views on work and its connections to masculinity, Ogasawara-san had quite specific views of his future as husband and father. This may partly have been due to his ability to articulate his thoughts and feelings very clearly. It may also have had something to do with his own family circumstances when growing up. His father had died when Ogasawara-san was still in junior-high school, and his mother had brought up his younger brother and himself while working full-time in insurance sales. He clearly had great respect for his mother, who, he said, after the father's death, despite criticism from relatives, had remained determined and had brought up her two sons as a single-mother.

His father, however, seemed to be a different matter. From his description, his father (who had also been a salaryman) came across as a weak, indecisive alcohol-dependent man, unable to stick to a job. This criticism of his father came up, generally without any prompting from me, several times during our interview. Accordingly, Ogasawara-san appeared to define himself in opposition to the kind of man his father had been. For instance, he made it a point to stress that unlike his father he did not drink alcohol at all (Ogasawara, Round 2: 12). He also mentioned that 'the type of man I dislike is someone who doesn't work … someone who doesn't look after his family properly (*ie o taisetsu ni shinai*) … doesn't give a damn about going out drinking every day and having affairs' (12, 13).

Thus, his very clear ideas about his future rising through the hierarchy of Northern Energy, as alluded to in the previous chapter, seemed to be constructed against his recollection of his father, from whom he had 'had really nothing worth learning about work' (Ogasawara, Round 2: 2). Similarly, his views about how he saw himself down his life-path as a husband and father seemed to be constructed in reaction to his own father and also, despite his admiration for her, his mother. While he respected his mother's determination to be independent (of her in-laws) and work full-time to raise her children, he felt that there had also been a negative impact upon himself and his brother when they were growing up:

> Although we don't really talk about it openly, for both my brother and myself we really didn't have a mother at home – for me right through grades 1, 2, and 3 of junior high, and 1, 2, and 3 of high school, so six years, and for my brother an additional three years…, so nine years.
>
> (Ogasawara, Round 2: 11)

Consequently, according to him, 'as a reaction (*handô*) to [his] mother having to work so hard' (11), he did not want his own wife to work, even prior to child-birth. In terms of his future family, he mentioned that he did not want a situation where he himself might have a successful career and his wife might be 'a brilliant person' (17), but the children were neglected and ended up becoming 'wild delinquents' (17). Rather, the kind of family he wanted to work towards, one that was his 'most important dream (*ichi-ban no yume*) [was] … an "average family" (*heibonna katei*)', one where 'I'd be trusted completely by my wife, and loved completely by my children, so much so that sometimes I'd have to ask myself if this can be real!' (17). He outlined for me in some detail what, in his imagining, constituted such an 'average family':

> The wife who remains as a wife (*okusan wa okusan de*) and provides support to her husband, you know, when you come home there's a warm meal ready for you, and the bath's warm too, and the children say 'Welcome home dad', and 'You know such-and-such happened today', and you'd go 'Oh, is that so? Is that right?'
>
> (Ogasawara, Round 2: 17, 18)

When I then commented that this was not unlike the idealized representation of 'typical' family life (*kazoku no tenkei*), depicted in advertisements and television commercials, he agreed with me, but added the following comments:

> It is an 'archetype' (*tenkei*). But even if we call it a *tenkei*, I think [the reality is] that it's hard to find such families nowadays! You know, [in the situation today], parents are unaware that the daughter's off selling herself [for sex], the father's out drinking and doesn't come home. The wife, for her part, says whatever she likes, telling those around her things like 'I don't give a damn about my husband' … I detest that type of thing, I've grown up seeing these aspects that I hate…. But [by contrast] the family of one of my superiors at work (*jôshi*) is really, unique in being 'ordinary' (*heibon*). You hear things like the father being welcomed home with 'Father, you've had a long day' (*otôsan otsukare*) or 'Welcome back' (*okaerinasai*) in response to 'I'm back' (*tada ima*). I've been to their house several times, and seeing them, that's the kind of ideal I have.
>
> (Ogasawara, Round 2: 18)

Ishida Naoki, a twenty-one-year-old Northern Energy employee working in the Accounts office, brought out some of these issues when talking about the way the status and esteem of the father within the household has apparently been weakening:

> Well, you know, if we talk about the past … the father was a person to revere, someone you were told to respect as he supported [the family] … that's the kind of thinking there was from Meiji through Shôwa, not treating the father sloppily. But if you look [at the situation] now, for some reason, [the father is] looked upon lightly by the wife and kids.
>
> (Ishida, Round 2: 23)

This 'ridiculing' of the father could, according to him, be seen in such things as *manga* representations, and even in everyday situations in families he was acquainted with:

> You know, when the father comes back, say, from *tanshin funin* [living away from the family due to work], the wife and kids have all gone out, and when they come back greet the father with a casual, 'Oh, so you're back' kind of thing
> [*laughs*]
>
> (Ishida, Round 2: 23, 24)

Such a view is an example of the contradictions in individuals' positions to which I referred earlier. This was the same person who, as noted in the previous section, expressed some fairly 'open-minded', indeed non-standard, views regarding marriage. Similarly, his views regarding his idea of being a husband and father did not seem to sit too comfortably with the views outlined above. In response to my question about his wife working after marriage, he mentioned that this would not be a problem, even after childbirth. Indeed, he was possibly the only informant to actually come out and state that 'if needed I'd stay at home' (Ishida, Round 2: 14). He did, however, qualify this by saying that given the reality in Japan of women's income being lower than men's, it was unlikely that he would be able to 'completely hand over having to earn an income to the wife, and look after the house myself' (14). He was also keen to play an active role in future child-rearing, stressing that he did not want a typical salaryman family, where the father had little interaction with the children (15). Miura Tôru, the young Northern Energy employee who had only recently become a *shakai-jin*, also felt that there was no need for his (future) wife to stop working even after childbirth. He mentioned practices like fathers being entitled to childcare leave, giving the example of Germany, and pointing out that although there had been a few cases of men taking childcare leave in Japan, the practice had 'still not become entrenched' (Miura, Round 2: 13). As mentioned in the previous section, Miura-san wanted to get married young. One reason behind this was that he could then become a father early; as he put it: 'I feel that it's good to be a young "papa". When you're young you feel like playing [with your child]' (6). A view such as this seemed reflective of the new 'glamorization' of fatherhood, along the lines of the 'Sam Campaign' referred to earlier, that was becoming increasingly visible in public discourse through the 1990s and into the 2000s.

Daikokubashira *realities*

With the exception of Kajima Daisuke (and Matsumoto Tadashi, whose marriage was imminent), the responses discussed above are all from informants who were still single at the time. Thus, as was the case with the discussion of marriage in the previous section, their responses represented an 'ideal' or 'archetype' they held of the married, *daikokubashira* father/provider. The responses of the married informants, on the other hand, reveal a more complex and nuanced picture. These were individuals who had to negotiate the reality of being a husband and (in some cases) father on a day-to-day basis. Kajima Daisuke, although not a father, had obviously given some thought to the ways in which he saw fatherhood and the *daikokubashira* role shaping his future life-path. He stressed that he did not want to be like a 'typical' salaryman father, did not 'want to become domesticated ... tied down by kids and a wife' (Kajima, Round 2: 18). He equated this 'domesticated' salaryman model with a parallel reading of the married provider model, one in which, 'marriage = the end of life (*jinsei no owari*)' (18), something he saw reflected in the lives of his friends and in popular culture:

> 'Giving up on life' (*jinsei no akirame*) – you often hear it on TV and things, and also when friends get married they say things like 'Well it's all over'. But surely a big part of that is because the family's not free? For all of them [i.e. his friends], you get married, and after the children are born the wife doesn't work, so on just your own income, after taking into account [money needed for supporting] the wife and kids, there's nothing left over for enjoyment.
>
> (Kajima, Round 2: 19)

Kajima-san stressed his difference from this pattern. He always, for instance, made it a point to organize his social life around himself and his wife as a couple (Kajima, Round 2:19). Moreover, not only did he mention not wanting to be 'tied down [by wife and family]', he also made it clear that he had no desire to 'tie [his wife] down' (20). His wife was working full-time, and although he thought he would 'get her to quit at childbirth' (Kajima, Round 1: 5), once the child was old enough he wanted her to 'put the child in childcare and [return to] work' (Round 2: 7). He did not, he stressed, 'want her cloistered away at home' (7). Indeed, at various points in the interviews, he alluded to the importance of having a double income in order to maintain a comfortable lifestyle. This was something he attributed to the influence of his own parents, both of whom had worked full-time as public servants, and whose double income had helped sustain consumption and leisure activities:

Since our household was always a double income family (*tomobataraki*) ...
there was always enough money. So my mother, being who she was (*kâchan
wa kâchan de*), would go off and buy herself things she wanted, and my
father for his part, since he was fond of gambling, would always be off to
the races or *mahjong* or *pachinko*! I used to think 'they couldn't do this if
both of them weren't working'!

(Kajima, Round 2: 21)

The point that needs to be stressed is that, despite what may appear to be relatively 'progressive' views, Kajima-san was no 'poster boy' for gender equality.
As his observations at the start of this section about having to support a family,
and his comment above about '*getting* my wife to quit at childbirth' (Round 1: 5;
emphasis added) reflect, 'conventional' ideas of gender were just as much a part
of his engagements with discourses of fatherhood and masculinity. This was best
reflected in his response to my question about what role he saw himself taking in
future child-rearing. Talking about how he would raise sons, he said that he
'would not want to raise them to be too "strait-laced"' (Kajima, Round 2: 9).
Indeed, in keeping with his own and his younger brother's experiences as adolescents of getting involved in fights and even getting into trouble with the police, he
mentioned that he would not be averse to his son also being a bit delinquent and
running a bit wild (9). He explained the rationale in the following terms:

I think that if you become too over-protective and just try and get them to be
'goody-goodies' (*majime-majime*), you can be sure that when they become
adults and get jobs, they won't have any guts (*konjô*) and will become total
failures. So I think it's good to do things that get you into a bit of strife.

(Kajima, Round 2: 9, 10)

However, when it came to daughters, his response was quite different. When I
asked him for his thoughts on raising a daughter he was less sure, stumbling a bit
as he tried to think, before settling on: 'I suppose a normal kind of upbringing ...
along the usual lines' (Round 2: 9). A little further on, he mentioned that as 'I
didn't have any female siblings I wouldn't know what to do, so I guess, if it's a
girl, I'll leave [the upbringing] completely to my wife' (10).

While Kajima-san's ruminations about fatherhood may have been hypotheti-
cal, Murayama Satoshi of Northern Energy, as mentioned in the previous
section, was the father of a one-month-old baby girl. In many senses, the immediacy of the event meant that the reality of being a father had not really sunk in –
as he put it: 'To tell you the truth the realization (*jikkan*) is still weak ... it's like
having a toy, or a pet' (Murayama: 40). He had, however, fairly clear ideas about
what kind of father he wanted to be and how he saw himself in relation to his
wife and children through the remainder of his life-path – for instance, when
talking about the likelihood of being transferred, he stressed that 'no matter how
small a place it is, I'd like us all to live there as one family' (Murayama: 42),
rather than leading a separate life as a *tanshin funin*.

As discussed in the previous section, he placed considerable importance on the institution of marriage; he had, for instance, expressed some disapproval of individuals entering into (hetero-) sexual relationships without seeing marriage as being the final outcome. When discussing these issues, he stressed that this would apply to the way his daughter would be raised. Talking about the supposedly 'free-and-easy' attitudes towards sex, he added: 'Even with my daughter, in a "free" (*furii*) environment like this, if she becomes involved in such a relationship [i.e. disregarding marriage], I won't hesitate to tell her that it's a mistake' (Murayama: 49). His own marriage, as outlined in the previous section, was the result of a more senior work colleague stepping in and introducing Murayama-san to his future wife. Prior to marriage, his wife had worked as a bank teller, but had quit her job at the time of marriage. When I asked him if she planned on re-entering the workforce once their child/children had entered school, he mentioned that while he had no objection, his wife had expressed a desire not to work and to 'look after the household' (51). When I presented him with a scenario where he was not working and was dependent upon his wife's income (hence, the antithesis of the *daikokubashira*), he was quite explicit in stating that 'that would be unacceptable', using the analogy of a 'male animal not going out to hunt (*osu ga kari ni ikanai*)' (51). Perhaps the importance he placed on living up to the expectations of salaryman masculinity came out best in his response to my question at the end of the interview about the most and least appealing aspects of being a man. He felt that the best thing about being born as a male was 'having a family, and being able to support (literally, 'being able to feed' – *gohan o tabesaserete*) that family' (Murayama: 70). Conversely the worst thing was 'being unable to quit your job even if you want to' (71) due to the same responsibility of supporting a family.

Shin'ya Naohiko, the twenty-three-year-old Northern Energy systems engineer whose passion was ice hockey, had also recently become a father. In fact, as discussed above, both his marriage and his becoming a father had taken place almost inadvertently. Over the period of our acquaintance (just over one year) he had gone from a carefree young single without too many adult responsibilities and commitments, to the father of a newly born baby girl. When we first met he was living by himself in the single male employees' dormitory. At our second meeting, the first one-on-one interview, he mentioned having just started going out with a new girlfriend, but stressed that neither had any intentions of getting married, particularly as his girlfriend had just returned to full-time study (Shin'ya, Round 1: 28, 29). However, shortly after they had found out that she was pregnant, and decided to get married. All of this was unknown to me, so it came as quite a surprise to see him in this new incarnation of husband and father at our second interview.

His feelings about fatherhood and living up to the *daikokubashira* ideal were more complex than Murayama-san's, perhaps due to the suddenness with which he had had marriage and fatherhood thrust upon him. Like Murayama-san, his new status as a father had not quite sunk in. The realization was more the result of being told by those around him, rather than any sense of 'fatherly feeling' coming to the surface of its own accord. This was despite having attended pre-birth classes (Shin'ya, Round 2: 4). He reflected on the complex interplay of emotions he was going through:

> Well, there's some sort of realization (*jikkan*). Or rather, a real feeling of being a father came about through it being reinforced by people around me. Just chatting in the corridors at work and being congratulated by everyone I talk to, being told that time and again, I gradually started to feel a sense that I've become a father, being born within me. But the child still doesn't move, so somehow it still feels too early to feel any sense of social responsibility (*shakaitekina sekinin*).
>
> (Shin'ya, Round 2: 5)

Shin'ya-san expected this sense of responsibility as a father to strengthen as the child grew older and the responses demanded of him as a father became concrete – for instance, 'getting hurt or injuring other children at kindergarten and primary school' (Round 2: 5). At the moment though, fatherhood seemed to carry associations of disruption and chaos. He mentioned having to juggle his work commitments, his ice hockey coaching duties, as well as the housework and bathing the baby, since his wife was still too weak to see to such things. Comparing his present situation with the time prior to marriage and the birth of the baby, he reflected that:

> I guess my thinking's changed. Well I suppose the fact that I've ended up being married at 23, when I really thought I'd marry after 30…
>
> …I suppose, before my child was born, my thinking about [marriage and being a father] was quite naïve and simplistic. I guess now, looking at myself married at this age I've started to get a sense (*jikkan*) of the gravity of the matter. I'm not saying that it's causing me to suffer though.
>
> (Shin'ya, Round 2: 13)

He was also aware of the restrictions now placed upon his ability to fulfil many of the dreams he had recounted to me in the first interview. In that first interview, he had elaborated on two possible courses he saw his life-path taking in the future. One vision of himself – the way things actually turned out – was a future where he would be married with possibly one child, and still working at Northern Energy. The other path he presented me with was the more 'adventurous' vision. In this alternative imagining, he was no longer in Northern Energy, but was doing things like studying to become an interior architect, or designing the lighting for famous buildings (Shin'ya, Round 1: 35–38). Now, less than a year down the track, he realized that with a child to look after 'it is that much harder to quit the company' (Round 2: 6); a reflection that seemed to point to Jeff Hearn's comment that 'fatherhood can bring *both* power and powerlessness to men' (Hearn 1994: 54, *italics* in original). Shin'ya-san elaborated on how his new status as husband and father had shifted relationships at work:

I suppose, as a result of having a child to raise, I've started to place more importance on interpersonal relationships at work. On the other hand, I feel that the distance with which others used to regard me has shrunk as a result of me becoming a father. Now, because I've had a child, from the time I announced the birth of the child, it's like 'You're a father too aren't you. Just like us, a father!'

...While I was single I had a circle of unmarried friends [at work]. But I've moved out from [that category] and have been admitted into [the circle of] more senior colleagues who are fathers, have children. Also, I've found work being passed on to me more, I guess ... I get the feeling that my trust-worthiness at work has increased and things are moving in a favourable direction, that I'm trusted more.

(Shin'ya, Round 2: 16)

For Shin'ya-san, despite all the tumultuous changes his new status had wrought in his life, his future as a husband and father was a matter to which he appeared to have given considerable thought:

When we were told about the pregnancy, the immediate response was to talk about getting married. ... Well, we had to face the reality that we were dealing with a new life. This meant that we had to think about the future of this life, that we had to raise the child, and what we would have to do. And also, this was our child so not for a moment did we think of an abortion.... And, thinking about the future of the child, if that child didn't grow up in an environment with both a mother and a father, we felt that that would be a disadvantage.... We wanted the best environment, one where both a mother and a father were on hand, as they should be.

(Shin'ya, Round 2: 14)

He then went on to reflect upon what kinds of things he would teach his newborn daughter, what type of person he felt he would like to see her grow into. At the core of these expectations was what he called 'a sense of gratitude (*kansha suru kimochi*)' (Round 2: 14). Expanding upon this, he explained that he wanted her to realize that this 'gratitude' was 'towards the parents, towards people [in general]' (14). In addition,

within the family, I'd like her to grow up to become a kind, gentle child (*yasashii kodomo*) ... I guess I want to raise her to be a child who places importance on her family.

(Shin'ya, Round 2: 14)

As pointed out above, Shin'ya-san had just become the father of a baby *girl*, so his comments above were in relation to (his views on) bringing up girls. When I asked him about his thoughts on bringing up a son his response was that he would be a lot stricter. In other words, I think while teaching him, I think I might end up being a little violent, you know hitting him a bit, hitting him while teaching him, and stuff. I guess it's to teach him through pain (*itami o oboesasete*), so that he learns that he shouldn't inflict pain on others.

(Shin'ya, Round 2: 15)

Moreover, he felt that with a son there would be an element of comparison with himself. Part of this comparison with himself would entail drawing upon his own experiences of hardship and perseverance from his younger ice hockey years:

for a father the greatest pleasure is a son having the same interests, and being able to teach the son that [hobby/interest] as part of the upbringing.... I suppose, yes, if I have a son I'll probably end up forcing him [to learn ice hockey].

(Shin'ya, Round 2: 15)

What comes across in the accounts of both Kajima-san and Shin'ya-san is a clear distinction between expectations about raising sons (teaching them to be tough, to 'survive' in life) and raising daughters (teaching them to be 'nice' and 'caring'). Moreover, their comments are by no means particularly biased or out of the ordinary. Indeed, if anything, they would appear to be fairly representative of attitudes towards parenting in the wider community at the time. For instance, Itô Kimio draws attention to a survey carried out by the newspaper *Mainichi Shinbun* in the late 1980s in relation to community attitudes towards parenting. In response to a question about what kind of person they wished to raise their child to be, the most popular attributes for daughters were such responses as 'a gentle person' (*sunaona hito*), and 'a considerate person'. For sons, on the other hand, people wanted to see qualities such as 'not being dependent on others and able to act independently' (*hito ni taerazu, jibun de yaru hito*), and 'someone who is able carry out his responsibilities' (*jibun no sekinin o hatasu hito*) (Itô 1998: 27; see also Amano and Kimura 2003). Kajima-san and Shin'ya-san's reflections seem to articulate these views quite vividly.

The final informant whose voice regarding fatherhood and being a *daikokubashira* I want to bring out in this section is that of Kimura Kenji, the Northern Print sales employee who was my liaison contact for that organization. He was, as noted in previous chapters, a very articulate, bright, confident young man who was well aware of his capabilities and the contribution he was making to Northern Print's sales figures. This work performance allowed him, as discussed previously, a certain leeway in displaying quite atypical – indeed consciously resistant – ideas and conduct in relation to the expectations of salaryman masculinity. He was also someone who struck me as being supremely confident of, and comfortable in, his own heterosexual masculinity. This may have explained why his ideas and opinions regarding hegemonic expectations of gender sometimes came across as a curious mixture of questioning and gender blindness. For example, early on in our first interview when I asked him about his early recollections of gender differences between himself and his younger sister in the ways in which they were socialized, he flatly denied (indeed, dismissed) any such notion. Moreover, his response was in a tone that suggested it was too trivial a matter to warrant his consideration (Kimura, Round 1: 4). He also denied any recollection of ever being told to behave or not behave in a certain way because he was a boy (6); once again the tone he adopted was one of impatience or non-comprehension at being asked such a question. Yet, in other areas he displayed quite atypical (compared with many of the other informants) and 'progressive' views. For instance, he felt that because 'upper management was not broad minded enough' (19), gender equality in the workplace was being held back.

This combination of conventionality and wanting to 'thumb his nose' at the very same conventional expectations was also evident in his ideas about marriage and fatherhood. Like both Shin'ya Naohiko and Murayama Satoshi, Kimura-san had also, immediately prior to our first interview, become a father. Moreover, his decision to get married had also been a consequence of his girlfriend's unintended pregnancy. However, unlike Shin'ya-san and Murayama-san, he did not appear to place much weight on marriage and fatherhood as far as the impact upon himself was concerned. His retort to my question about why he got married was a blunt 'because [my girlfriend] got pregnant' (Kimura, Round 2: 9). When I asked him what marriage signified to him, he laughed, and admitted that he 'had never given it any thought' (9). There was absolutely no desire, according to him, to be recognized by society as 'respectable' or as *ichininmae*. Indeed, as he took some pains to stress, he did not think becoming a husband and father had changed him at all. As he put it:

> No it won't change, my life won't change because only I make my own decisions about my life. It's just a one-off event, my getting married and having a child and a family, it is just one event in life. So I think there's no way I'd want to say that I've become more conservative or anything.
>
> (Kimura, Round 1: 21)

In contrast to both Shin'ya-san and Murayama-san, who felt that marriage and fatherhood had strengthened their links to corporate masculinity, Kimura-san did not think anything had necessarily changed. As he stated:

> I wouldn't really be concerned about my family ... you know, if I get the sack from this company for some reason and I've got to keep feeding them, I've got total confidence in my own ability to earn a living.
>
> (Kimura, Round 1: 21)

He did, however, acknowledge that his status as husband and father had changed the way he was treated by those around him in the workplace, although this was not something that made much sense to him:

There's often [the perception that] if you get married, since things must be tough financially you'll be responsible (*shikkari suru*), or that [you'll become responsible] because you've got a wife in the background, but because these things don't relate to me at all…

…I don't pay any attention to them.

…But I think in this company, I get the feeling that people worry about such things.

…I'm sometimes told things like 'You've got married quite young, haven't you?', or 'You've already got a child', or 'You must have your act together'. I just listen to them, but think [to myself] when I hear [such things] that this is weird!

(Kimura, Round 2: 10)

Also in contrast to Shin'ya-san and Murayama-san, who talked in some detail about how they envisaged their future life-paths as fathers, Kimura-san hardly made any reference to fatherhood during our interviews. His response to my question about whether he had given any thought to what kind of family life he desired or what kind of father he wanted to be was a straight-out 'No [I haven't]' (Round 2: 10). When I persisted and asked him to think about it, he came up with: 'As long as I get on with them [the children] (*naka-yokereba ii*)' (10). The only other times he made a reference to his newborn child was in response to my question in the second interview about what brought him the greatest happiness (the response to which was 'my child who's just been born' (Round 2: 17)), and earlier when he was complaining about not being able to take any time off when the child was born, despite being entitled to three days' leave (13).

Looking at these various voices regarding marriage and fatherhood, we get a sense of the complex interplay and shifts between various discourses surrounding these gender institutions, structures and practices. On the one hand, there is the continuing importance placed on 'proving' masculinity through work – being the breadwinner, the outside provider, upon whom the whole family is dependent for sustenance. At the same time, there also appear to be shifts from past practices. For instance, unlike many of the salaryman fathers in Ishii-Kuntz's earlier (1993) study who tied a public expression of disinterest or non-involvement in child-rearing to their sense of masculinity, most of my informants (both married and single) articulated a discourse of active involvement by fathers as being a priority for themselves. This seemed to convey a sense of fatherhood somehow being 'cool', as reflected in the statement by Miura Tôru that 'being a young papa is good … [because] you want to play [with your child]' (Miura, Round 2: 6). However, the reality for most of the informants – including those like Shin'ya-san upon whom fatherhood had been thrust suddenly, but who seemed to *want* involvement in his children's upbringing – seemed to be still limited to the level of public statements supporting active involvement, without a real shift in the expectations of masculinity being tied to being a husband and primary breadwinner.

Playing with heterosexuality?

Twenty-five-year-old Arai Jun fitted the profile of a young salaryman perfectly. He came from a standard, middle-class, salaryman family. His father was a white-collar bank employee who had worked for the same organization over his entire career, and his mother was a full-time housewife (Arai: 1). Arai-san himself had followed a fairly typical path towards salaryman masculinity – going to university, and upon graduation, entering a public sector organization, where he was involved in white-collar work that also involved dealing with the public. He was in a steady, committed relationship with a partner to whom he was quite obviously very attached. However, because his partner worked in another city, they were usually only able to meet up on weekends (28). What set Arai Jun apart from my other informants, though, was the fact that his partner happened to be *male*.

As the informants' voices in relation to marriage and fatherhood reveal, mutual heterosexuality seemed to be an unstated assumption in our interaction (see Dasgupta 2005a: 58, 59). However, I was interested in exploring what happens when an individual in his negotiations with salaryman masculinity cannot, or does not wish to, conform to expectations of heterosexuality. How would he then negotiate with expectations such as marriage being a necessary precondition for becoming *ichininmae*? How would he see his future life-path as a salaryman in the context of his inability or refusal to conform to the expectations of heterosexuality? Although, as noted previously, the opportunity to raise such issues with my informants did not arise, through my involvement in a gender/sexuality study group I was introduced to Arai-san, who was happy to be interviewed. His account reinforced the complexity and richness of the strategies adopted by gay salarymen, discussed by Lunsing (2001) and in the *Queer Japan* (2000) issue on gay salarymen, referred to earlier in the chapter.

In many respects, Arai-san was representative of the shift that has become more pronounced over the past decade or two in the way non-heterosexual identity is framed, in that rather than being just the enactment of a sexual act that happens to be between members of the same sex, sexual orientation and its (self- and public-) acknowledgement is seen as being integral to identity and constant over the entire life-course (see, for example, McLelland 2001). Thus, he regarded 'coming out' and recognition of himself as 'gay' as a cornerstone of his masculinity. Unlike many older gay men, he had no intention of getting married to a woman for the sake of social convention (Arai: 24, 25). In his student days, he had been fairly active in a local gay support group, and had even marched in a local Lesbian and Gay Pride Parade. He had begun the process of 'coming out' to himself from around the time he was in junior high school (5), and in recent years he had started coming out to a variety of selected individuals, including his mother and younger sister, and a male colleague with whom he had undergone the new employee induction training (*kenshū*) when he first entered the work-force. Significantly, the reaction of this colleague to the revelation had been an unremarkable 'Oh, is that right?' (9) response.

However, his revelation to this colleague was an exception. In general, Arai-san – not unlike many of the respondents to the *Queer Japan* survey discussed earlier – made some effort to keep his (implicitly heterosexual) work identity and his (gay) private identity separate. Unlike most of my other informants, who probably would not have considered situations where they would need to withhold information about their non-work/social lives from work colleagues, Arai-san was acutely conscious of the necessity for this almost total separation between his two lives. At one level, he wished for a workplace environment where he could be open about his sexuality. For instance, in response to my query about what he regarded as an 'ideal' workplace situation he came up with 'quite simply ... [one] where I'm accepted as gay' (Arai: 23). However, he then stressed that 'in the end, this was an "ideal"', and that just as he did not worry about his colleagues' private lives, there was no need for people at work to be concerned with his own life (23). In short, he was conscious of the reality of the workplace culture within which he had to interact with his colleagues:

> Yes, it would be nice to be accepted [*laughs*], or rather, to be understood (*rikai shite hoshii*) ... But probably the thing is ... because it's a section with just five or six people, if I told them I'd have to keep working together with them, so I suppose [the fact that I can't tell them] can't be helped (*shikata ga nai*).
>
> (Arai: 23)

Like many of the other informants, work for Arai-san was a significant part of his identity. He presented me with his image of the 'typical' salaryman as a '*peko-peko shita hito*' (literally, someone who is constantly bowing and scraping to others) (Arai: 13), someone who 'works earnestly, whose hobby is work' (13). He said that he felt himself approaching this caricature when dealing with the public at work (15) – something rather at odds with the earlier image presented of the gay activist who had marched in the Lesbian and Gay Parade. Indeed, there appeared to be some contestation as he tried to reconcile his two 'identities'. At some level, there appeared to be a desire for validation or recognition of his right to salaryman masculinity precisely *because of* his sexuality. This came through on a number of occasions in the course of our discussion. For instance, at one point, when talking about the balance between his work and non-work identities, he reflected:

> You know, as I see it, I never ever think that being gay will somehow impact negatively on my work. I may have [a male] lover, but I'm working, and working with 'straight' people, so at work I treat it as just work, and realize that I have to interact with them [my heterosexual colleagues].... So you've got to interact with people as human beings, or else if you keep wondering is this person gay or not gay, it'll end up being too stressful.
>
> (Arai: 15, 16)

And, returning elsewhere in our discussion to a similar theme:

> At this stage, as far as work is concerned, I don't think me being gay or me being not gay has any bearing [on work]; I think of myself as normal. You know, everyone has or doesn't have partners (*koibito*). So I just think of myself as pretty much the same. Not really much as a gay [person].
>
> (Arai: 23)

At yet another point in our discussion when I asked him to reflect upon the significance of work in his life, he articulated his thoughts as follows:

> in the past work was [ranked] second (*ni-banme*). And, number one (*ichibanme*) was my lover. And with that, on the whole I used to think that was fine, but at present they [work and boyfriend] are about the same. In other words, it's like they're equally balanced on a scale (*onaji tenbin ni kakeru*) – work's work, and my lover's my lover.
>
> (Arai: 14)

In the context of engaging with these various facets of his identity, how did he negotiate with the implicit assumptions of heterosexuality in the workplace? As mentioned above, despite the importance of marriage as a determinant of *ichininmae* status, he had no intention of entering into a heterosexual marriage for the sake of social conformity. At twenty-five, he was still too young for questions about his marital status or future marriage plans to be an issue of concern. However, he was aware that a few years down the track this would start becoming an issue he would have to deal with. As he admitted: 'I have absolutely no intention of getting married, but when you're working, there's always the concern that some day there'll be comments [about being single] in the workplace' (Arai: 12). Although he was not entirely sure how he would do so, he stressed that he was 'thinking of ways to deal with it, so as not to be defeated [by such comments] (*makenai yô ni*)' (18). Either way, he mentioned that:

> In actual fact, given there are lots of gay people who remain single and work, if those people can do it so can I.
>
> (Arai: 17)

Although marriage itself had not yet figured prominently in his interactions with colleagues and managers, the question of his presumed heterosexuality was something he had to deal with on a day-to-day basis. His responses to such questions – for instance, questions about his girlfriend – was a mixture of irritation and defiance at what he saw as an intrusion on his privacy, and the kind of 'playful', flippant strategy which Lunsing refers to as '*gomakasu* … avoiding answering a question, ideally in such a sophisticated manner, that the questioner does not notice that one is evading the subject' (2001: 221). This mixture of irritation and strategic 'bluffing' comes out in the following reflection:

I get asked things like whether I have a girlfriend or not. Since it's too tedious, I just replace 'boyfriend' with 'girlfriend' (*kareshi o kanojo ni okikaete*) ... I want to think of my private time [life] separately [from work], so I feel [irritated] at having to speak about such things. But, when they ask it'll be strange if I say I don't [have a girlfriend]. So I say that [i.e. replace boyfriend with 'girlfriend'].[8]

(Arai: 16)

This combination of different emotions and strategies in negotiating with expectations of heterosexuality was also evident when Arai-san was talking about his responses when the topic of homosexuality came up in discussions among work colleagues. His workplace was close to the entertainment district of the city. Consequently, it was not unusual for individuals associated with this sector – employees of the restaurants, bars, nightclubs, massage parlours, and other services that constitute the *mizu shôbai*, 'water trade' (see Allison 1994) – to come into his workplace on business during office hours. This included individuals who appeared 'visibly gay', people he felt he had at some time 'seen around [the gay "scene"]' (Arai: 16). He described his way of dealing with the comments made by colleagues about such 'obvious' individuals:

if I'm told something like, 'That person's "that way", he's *okama* [derogatory/slang term for a homosexual male], did you know that?', I'll turn around and say 'Oh, is that so?' This may sound strange, but, observing that kind of situation is fascinating [for me] – it's interesting because it's not gay people having the conversation.

(Arai: 16)

There seems almost a sense of the tables being turned here, the gaze being reversed with the 'other' now doing the observing. However, how would he feel if the comments made were particularly derogatory, homophobic ones? His reaction would be one of 'getting angry (*hara* [*ga*] *tachimasu*)' (Arai: 17), but there was nothing he could really do about it apart from console himself by 'thinking that that's how low this person is' (17). The sense of frustration at not being able to openly counter or challenge such views lest he himself inadvertently 'reveal' himself is reminiscent of the scene in *Okoge* discussed earlier in the chapter, where the character playing the gay salaryman swallows his anger and forces himself to laugh along at homophobic jokes being made by a colleague.

However, it needs to be stressed that Arai-san should not be seen as some kind of cowering 'victim', constantly in fear of being exposed. In a different situation, he was just as likely to reveal himself to colleagues, but *strategically*. For instance, when talking about the ways he negotiated with expectations of his heterosexuality, he mentioned that although he tried to skirt around the issue, if someone were to ask him the question, 'are you gay?' directly (Arai: 16), he would admit it to that person. The reasoning he provided was that the fact that the person had actually asked of her or his own volition was an indication that

that individual had some inkling, and hence would be better able to deal with Arai-san, than someone who had absolutely no idea (16).

Conclusion

I believe Arai-san's voice is an appropriate way of bringing this chapter to a close. The focus of this chapter has been to draw attention to the ways in which certain specific (and often invisible) assumptions about sexuality continued to be integral to salaryman masculinity, the various post-Bubble socio-cultural fragmentations and shifts notwithstanding. In a nutshell, the informants' voices would suggest that the assumption of the salaryman needing to be 'productive' not just in relation to economic 'production', but also in relation to sexual 're-production' – that he will get married, and be the main provider for the family – seemed to remain entrenched in the years when the conversations occurred. However, as their narratives also reveal, the actual engagements between the 'ideal' and the day-to-day reality for many of the informants were far more complex and nuanced, often simultaneously incorporating elements of conscious (and internalized) compliance *and* conscious (and not-so-conscious) non-compliance and disengagement. Perhaps my reason for expanding upon Arai-san's account at such length is precisely that he was consciously aware of and able to articulate the strategies and negotiations at work in his engagements with the expectations of salaryman masculinity (particularly, in his instance, the expectation of performing heterosexuality). Although many of the other informants also responded to and negotiated with the expectations of salaryman masculinity in varying ways, many of them were not conscious of doing this in the way that Arai-san was. In the next chapter, I will return to the nexus between sexuality and corporate masculinity, but in a context where sexuality becomes sublimated into homosocial spaces of work and friendship.

7 Working with homosociality

The previous chapter explored the connection between salaryman masculinity and a publicly privileged discourse of regulated (hetero-) sexuality pivoted on the male employee as husband, father and sustainer of the family unit. Yet, while this discourse undeniably played (and continues to play) a role in the shaping of salaryman masculinity, coexisting with it have been other, less visible currents that are also influential in the engagements between individual male employees and the expectations of the discourse. Among these less apparent strands of corporate culture is the realm of friendship – particularly same-sex friendship – and its intersections with other expectations of corporate masculinity. On the one hand, the discourse of salaryman masculinity and its role as a cornerstone of Japanese industrial success through the decades of high economic growth was situated within a matrix of discourses privileging homosocial same-sex 'bonding' within the company and with (male) clients, often at the expense of cross-sex relationships such as the husband–wife relationship.[1] One such example would be the *senpai-kôhai* ('senior' and 'junior') hierarchy-based relationship. Similarly, group-based interaction such as company-centred occasions like *bônenkai* (end of year – literally, 'forget the year' – parties) or *shinnenkai* (new year parties), or work-related golf sessions with colleagues or clients, would also fall within the orbit of publicly sanctioned – indeed, sanctified – forms of same-sex interaction, that, particularly during the 'Japan Inc.' era, were often considered integral aspects of corporate and organizational culture. On the other hand, however, same-sex relationships may also possess the potential to disrupt established rules and assumptions of salaryman masculinity. For instance, the incident discussed in Chapter 4, where one of my informants – Miura Tôru of Northern Energy – was publicly reprimanded by his manager for his inability to distinguish between his pre-*shakaijin* notions of friendship and acceptable rules of conduct in the workplace, is a good example of the slippery nature of negotiating same-sex relationships. Thus, as with sexuality there is a constant tension. This tension is between the channelling of same-sex relationships into configurations accepted (and indeed, sanctioned) by official corporate ideology and the dominant discourse in the workplace, and the potential for 'unregulated' friendships to challenge and undermine these configurations. This chapter explores how some of these issues intersected with my informants' engagements with salaryman masculinity during the years of focus in this book – the post-Bubble late 1990s. As the informants' voices will highlight, these were years when, in common with the issues discussed in previous chapters, expectations about friendship and collegiality within the workplace were also especially subject to competing pulls. The first part of the chapter sets out the theoretical and conceptual framework within which the informants' narratives may be situated. The second part will then draw upon their actual 'voices' to explore the ways in which friendship and homosociality intersected with their engagements with the dominant expectations of salaryman masculinity.

Male friendship, homosociality, and corporate culture

Just as, until the 1980s/1990s, works dealing with men did not address the issue of masculinity, 'friendships' between males had rarely been analysed through the lens of gender and sexuality. For instance, although on one level male friendship and interaction is a highly visible strand in *Learning to Labour*, Paul Willis' renowned study of working-class youth in Britain, this interaction is discussed and commented upon without reference to a gender/sexuality framework (Willis 1977). This lack of critical gender research on friendship started to change from the 1980s, in part as a consequence of pioneering historical work by scholars working within the emerging field of lesbian and gay studies, whose research made visible strands of implicit homoerotic *possibilities* (rather than necessarily actual sexual relations) at work in many pre-twentieth-century male and female same-sex 'friendships' (see Katz 1976; Faderman 1981; Rotundo 1989; Duberman 1991; Vicinus 1991). The work of such scholars coming from the angle of uncovering a 'hidden' history of same-sex sexuality intersected with an emerging body of work examining male–male interaction, not specifically connected to lesbian and gay studies. These works ranged across historical studies of male friendship and interaction, ethnographic studies, both within and outside the Anglo-American socio-cultural framework, literary studies, and more empirical sociological analyses.[2] Many of them drew attention to the fluidity over time and space in the dynamics of same-sex interactions that fell within the category labelled 'friendship' (Nardi 1992b: 1–6).

Such research, drawing attention to the realm of friendship, was given greater theoretical rigour with the emergence from the late 1980s/early 1990s of the body of work which came to be known as queer studies and/or queer theory (see Jagose 1996). In particular, Eve Kosofsky Sedgwick's 1985 *Between Men: English Literature and Male Homosocial Desire* had – and continues to have – an impact on studies of male–male interaction and friendship, well outside of the author's original focus of literary studies. In this seminal work Sedgwick analysed selected pre-twentieth-century Anglo-American literary texts through the lens of what she terms 'homosocial *desire*' (italics added), a seemingly oxymoronic term incorporating the intersections and disjunctures between patriarchy, homophobia, male–male homosocial interaction, and desire, underpinning the emergence of Anglo-American patriarchal industrial-capitalist society. While

Sedgwick's engagement with this construct is multifaceted and theoretically complex, for our purposes, the notion of 'homosocial desire' – of bringing the possibility of desire into the homosocial – is of interest not so much in the context of the literary texts she examines, but rather for its deployment (not necessarily as intended by Sedgwick) with reference to male–male interaction in a variety of settings.[3] This includes one of the prime bastions of traditional male homosociality and heterosexual patriarchal privilege – the corporate organization.

As Jeff Hearn has pointed out, despite the pervasiveness and hegemony of a discourse of public heterosexuality, organizational masculinity is also structured around 'men's preference for men, men's company and men's spaces' (Hearn 2002: 46). Moreover, sublimated desire between men may well also be a built-in aspect of these relationships. This 'desire' aspect of organizational masculinity was, however, until quite recently generally overlooked or glossed over as 'male bonding'. Indeed, as Michael Roper points out, even writers who do use terms such as 'homosexual reproduction' (Kanter 1977) or 'male homosociability' (Morgan 1981; Witz and Savage 1996) do not adequately address the issue of sexuality and hidden desire between men when deploying these terms (Roper 1996: 212).

Roper himself uses Sedgwick's concept to draw attention to 'the fluidity of boundaries between friendship and desire in men's networks' (Roper 1996: 213) in the context of discussing the dynamics of same-sex interaction among faculty in a management college. In his view, 'homosocial desire' is an apt term to apply in the context as it 'captures rather than erases the ambiguities between the "social" and the "sexual" in men's networks ... identifying a distinctive category of intimacy in formally heterosexual settings which presents as non-sexual but which nevertheless involves potentially erotic desires' (213). What needs to be stressed is that these 'circuits of homosocial desire' do not (indeed, *cannot*) allow for the conscious articulation of that 'desire'. A public acknowledgement of the existence of these circuits of desire would be contrary to the dominant discourse of corporate masculinity – one defined, as we saw in the previous chapter, by publicly unambiguous heterosexuality. However, as Roper points out, these unacknowledged underlying sub-currents of same-sex 'energy' also inform the operation of corporate masculinity.

It is this sense of an ambiguous and difficult to delineate same-sex dynamic that the discussion in the remainder of this chapter attempts to tease out. As we shall see, the dynamics of homosocial interaction in anglophone organizations discussed by writers like Roper (1994, 1996) and Hearn (1992, 2002) may well also be relevant in the context of Japanese organizational culture. Accordingly, the following section discusses some of the characteristics of same-sex interaction within the context of Japanese organizations. This will then provide a framework to situate the discussion in the second half of the chapter, where I explore some of the ways in which my informants articulated their feelings about friendships and same-sex interaction within the context of the organizations they were working in, against the wider socio-historical backdrop of late 1990s, post-Bubble Japan.

Friendship and salaryman masculinity

As noted above, the 'success' of salaryman masculinity had rested on the twin pillars of heterosexual cross-sex marriage, and homosocial same-sex interaction. This same-sex interaction, expressed through various channels in a variety of settings, was traditionally regarded as crucial to success at work, particularly during the high-growth decades. As Anne Allison observes, in the context of 1980s corporate culture:

> A worker's attachment to work is meant to be cemented, (over) determined, and symbolized – making it not only lifelong but contiguous with other parts of a man's life. A *sarariiman* may find that his neighbors, golf mates, Saturday baseball team players, drinking buddies, matchmaker for marriage, wedding guests, coconspirators in sexual escapades, and counsellors for marital problems are basically drawn from the same group of coworkers.
>
> (Allison 1994: 201)

As indicated by Allison's description above, the context for the articulations of same-sex interaction and intimacy may be both 'officially' company-sponsored settings such as *bônenkai* end-of-year gatherings or company-sponsored trips and outings (*ian ryokô*), as well as settings not 'officially' sponsored, but nevertheless possessing some connection to the workplace (for instance, an after-work drinks session at an *izakaya*) (see Gagné 2010: 156–164; also Linhart 1998). The significance of this aspect of corporate culture has been discussed and commented upon quite extensively in various scholarly and non-scholarly works. These include works by authors such as Abegglen (1958), Plath (1964, 1980), Cole (1971), Vogel (1971), Dore (1973b), and Rohlen (1974), which are regarded as early 'classics' in relation to the study of Japanese organizations and organizational culture. Rohlen, for instance, dwells in some detail on various aspects of same-sex interaction among white-collar bank employees at 'Uedagin', the bank where he conducted his ethnographic research. These range from interaction at office parties, through discussion of the *senpai-kôhai* (senior–junior) relationship, to a description of the living arrangements and patterns of interaction among employees living in the single male employees' dormitory (Rohlen 1974). Robert Cole's study of an auto-parts company also discusses similar issues such as 'friendship' associations, characteristics of after-hours leisure behaviour, and workplace *oyabun-kobun* (mentor-protégé, or literally 'parent-role/child-role') relationships among blue-collar workers. Subsequent studies dealing with aspects of organizations and organizational culture continued to address issues related to same-sex interaction, whether for males or females (e.g. Rohlen 1975; Atsumi 1979, 1980; Kondo 1990; Allison 1994; Hazama 1996; Linhart 1998; Roberson 1998; Sakai 2000; Gagné 2010).

'Circuits of homosocial desire' and the oyabun/kobun, senpai/kôhai dyads

Many of the above-mentioned works drew attention to characteristics such as the *senpai–kôhai* and/or *oyabun–kobun* relationships within organizations, which were particularly important in underpinning same-sex interaction. Rohlen in particular, both in his ethnographic study of the bank (1974), and a subsequent discussion of work-group dynamics in companies (1975), addressed this aspect of same-sex interaction in white-collar organizations at some length. In talking about the intersections between the (often impersonal) hierarchical superior–subordinate pairing and the *senpai–kôhai* dyad he notes that while the latter is also hierarchical, this very hierarchy allows for intimacy:

> A *senpai* is understood to be a person who proceeds or leads with the implication that those who follow are his companions in the same pursuit, career, or institution. *Kôhai*, literally 'companion that is behind', expresses the other half of the relationship. The complete image created by the characters is one of 'friends,' one ahead and the other behind, passing along the same path of endeavor.
>   ...the term is used most often to refer to one or a few specific older individuals of the same sex who are particularly close and protective.... Among the reasons for the division along sex lines is the implied comradeship between senior and junior, a form of comradeship that does not easily cross the boundaries of sex.
>
> (Rohlen 1975: 196, 197)

The emotion underpinning this relationship is one of friendship, intimacy, and emotional closeness, reinforced by the power asymmetry between the partners – the *senpai* 'looks after' the *kôhai*, in return for gratitude and loyalty. Moreover, although *senpai–kôhai* dynamics do influence relationships between older male employees, it is, according to Rohlen, at its most intense among young, unmarried employees. As he observes, 'the great majority of *senpai–kôhai* ties among young men derive from working together, living in dorms together, or playing on a sports team together' (Rohlen 1975: 196, n.9). In talking about the features of the *senpai–kôhai* relationship, Rohlen draws an analogy with the parent/child and/or older brother/younger brother familial dynamic of interdependency and obligation. What is absent from his discussion (indeed from most discussions of Japanese organizations and organizational culture) is any reference to undercurrents of intimacy/pleasure/desire in the sense of the circuits of homosocial desire discussed above, which may inform the *senpai–kôhai* dyad.

Rather, discussions of underlying currents of sexuality in same-sex interactions in organizations tend to be found in works not specifically concerned with organizational culture such as Doi Takeo's study of the social psychology of the Japanese (1973), or anthropologist Nakane Chie's analysis of Japanese social structure (1973). While both have been extensively critiqued for their reductionism, sweeping generalizations, lack of methodological rigour, and implications of Japanese socio-cultural 'uniqueness' (see, e.g. Sugimoto and Mouer 1989; Allison 1994: 84, 85), they are among the few texts to draw attention to aspects of same-sex interaction which take into account underlying currents of homosocial desire. Nakane, for instance, draws parallels between the *oyabun–kobun* patron–client relationship within organizations, and emotionally intense homosocial (and, on occasion, homo-sexual) relationships between *samurai* retainers and their patron/lord in the centuries leading up to and during the Edo Period.[4] To reinforce her point she makes reference to the well-known legend of the Forty-Seven Rônin willing to sacrifice their lives through their devotion to their leader, Ôishi Kuranosuke. As she explains,

> The Forty-Seven Rônin reveal in extreme form the ideal personal relation-ship.... The story bears some resemblance to a love affair. In Japan there is no love story comparable in popularity to the Forty-Seven Rônin. Men so involved in such a relationship have little room left for a wife or sweetheart. In traditional morals the ideal man should not be involved in an affair with a woman. I think that if he were involved to such an extent in this kind of man-to-man relation there would seem to be no necessity for a love affair with a woman. His emotions would be completely expended in his devotion to his master. I suspect this was the real nature of *samurai* mentality, and to a certain extent the same may be true of the modern Japanese man.
>
> (Nakane 1973: 74; see also Buruma 1984: 153–157)

While the sweeping nature of Nakane's assertions and her overly simplistic con-flation of feudal relationships and those in contemporary organizations need to be regarded with some caution, she does have a point in terms of acknowledging a complexity, unacknowledged by many other writers, inherent in same-sex interaction in organizations.

The psychologist Doi Takeo, through his deployment of the concept of *amae* – the desire to be indulged, cared for, looked after by another – as underpinning interpersonal relationships also flags ideas not dissimilar to notions of homo-social desire. Doi links *amae* to what he refers to as ' "homosexual feelings" ', which are 'not homosexuality in the narrow sense ... but in the broader sense ... where the emotional links between members of the same sex take preference over those with the opposite sex. They correspond roughly ... with what is nor-mally termed "friendship" ' (Doi 1973: 113). However, Doi continues, 'where friendship usually lays emphasis on the good will existing between friends, in this case [i.e. homosexual feelings arising from *amae*] the emphasis is on the fact that the emotional links that form the basis of friendship take precedence over love between the sexes' (113). What Doi takes pains to stress – and here there are resonances with the notions of homo*social* desire discussed in the previous section, Doi's emphasis on the *Japanese*-ness of *amae* notwithstanding – is the non-*sexual* nature of these *sexual* feelings, at whose heart lies the dynamic of *amae* (113–121).

'Circuits of homosocial desire' and tsukiai

The homosocial interaction at the centre of Doi and Nakane's discussions, as well as the *senpai–kôhai*-type relationships discussed by Rohlen or Cole, are essentially vertically based, hierarchical interactions. Despite the fact that such hierarchically based interactions tend to be more visible in discussions about same-sex interaction in Japanese organizations, they intersect with other forms of interaction also in circulation. Equally pertinent as far as same-sex interactions are concerned are those that do not necessarily conform to rigid, unchanging hierarchies. These may be horizontal relationships between 'equals' (in the sense that there are no significant differences in age, status, or power). Alternatively, they may even be relationships where a disparity in status and power in one context *may* be less relevant in another context – for instance, in the context of a drinking session where alcohol may (and often does) allow for rigid hierarchies and delineations to become fluid and blurred (see, e.g. Gagné 2010: 1–9, ch. 4; also Rohlen 1974: 97–100; Allison 1994; Turner 1995: 74–91; Ben-Ari 2002). Moreover, as signalled in Roberson's (1995a, 1998) ethnographic study of blue-collar workers, or studies by Fowler (1996) and Gill (2001, also 2003) of day-labourers, patterns of friendship and same-sex interaction among men in these occupational areas may be quite different from white-collar salarymen.

Even with men who could be categorized within the rubric of the salaryman, the patterns of male–male interaction may be quite varied. Atsumi Reiko, drawing upon research conducted with white-collar male employees, found that her informants made a distinction between interaction that was connected to *tsukiai* (social interaction connected to work or community-related networks, based on obligation or a sense of social responsibility (Atsumi 1980: 64–70)), and 'relationships entered into spontaneously for their own sake (friendship)' (65). According to her, many writers have conflated the two, but in actual fact they are quite separate:

> Some Japanese company employees associate with their colleagues and other work-related people quite often after work, but the relationship is not very intimate because it is *tsukiai*. They eat and drink and/or play mahjong together after work. The frequency of association with *tsukiai* associates may be high, but it is not related to the degree of intimacy or confidence.
>
> (Atsumi 1989: 135)

The reality, though, particularly during the decades of high economic growth, but also relevant over the post-Bubble years, is that same-sex interaction based around *tsukiai* cannot be avoided. Moreover, as Anne Allison highlights in her study of the intermeshings between Bubble-era corporate masculinity and the *mizu shôbai* entertainment sector,[5] *tsukiai* relationships mediated through a female bar hostess are crucial to the collective construction of salaryman masculinity (Allison 1994; also Gagné 2010). Specifically, as she points out, it is through the bar hostess that business executives are able to 'commune with each other in a way that confirms, enhances, or sometimes creates work relations' (Allison 1994: 165). What remain unarticulated – but seem to be implied – are the underlying flows of homosocial *desire* circulating between the men, mediated through the body of the female hostess, not unlike the triangular relations of desire which Sedgwick talks about (Sedgwick 1985).

However, while such *tsukiai*-centred homosocial dynamics may be an important element within salaryman masculinity, the intensity of same-sex relationships may be greater outside of the context of the workplace. Atsumi notes that rather than forming close friendships with colleagues at work, many of her informants already had 'such close relationships with a limited number of persons' (1980: 70) predating their entry into *shakaijin* status. These friends were

> often one's former schoolmates who shared some personal experiences, such as studying the same subject together, being roommates, or participating in the same extracurricular activities.... A person may talk freely about his personal affairs with some of his close friends, and he may sometimes prefer one or two of these close friends to his wife when he needs advice and assistance. These closest ones are one's *shin-yû* (intimate friends) with whom one feels completely open and relaxed.
>
> (Atsumi 1980: 70)

The homosociality of these ties with *shin'yû* comes across in Atsumi's discussions of some of her informants. For instance, one informant who she calls 'Mr Sonoda' belonged to a tightly knit circle of close male friends dating back to a gardening club which all had belonged to in high school. Describing Mr Sonoda's relationship with the group, Atsumi explains that:

> He associates with five of them quite often, seeing them almost every weekend at one of the members' homes.... These people have been Mr Sonoda's most important and closest friends since his high school days. He admits that they know him better than his wife does. He cannot think of anything that he cannot discuss with them or anything that he will not do for them. Mr Sonoda's wife knows them all by sight; but she has never visited any of his friends' homes with her husband or alone.... The 'boys' arrange an overnight trip once a year, and they do not bring their families.... Nothing takes precedence over Mr Sonoda's association with these friends except work itself.
>
> (Atsumi 1980: 72)

What comes across from both Atsumi's discussion of Mr Sonoda, as well as from the preceding discussion of *tsukiai*-centred interaction, is the fact that same-sex homosocial relationships are an ongoing current within men's lives, which, in the context of salaryman masculinity, intersects and interacts with the other expectations with which the individual male employee may have to contend.

Informants' engagements with homosocial circuits

These reflections on the dynamics of same-sex interaction by the likes of Atsumi or Allison would have been especially pertinent during the 'Japan Inc.' decades. However, for our purposes, of greater concern is the ways in which engagements with discourses and practices of friendship and homosocial interaction were played out in the post-Bubble years, in the context of shifting cross-currents within corporate masculinity. Hence, this would be an appropriate point to bring in the voices of some of my informants in order to get a sense of these dynamics being played out on a day-to-day basis.

Matsumoto Tadashi's imagining of the 'ideal' male–male relationship at work is a good starting point. This informant, who has appeared on several occasions in earlier chapters, worked in the Accounts section of Northern Energy, and was my liaison contact in that organization. As noted previously, in terms of appearance, lifestyle, behaviour, and attitudes, he came across as embodying the salaryman masculinity 'ideal'. Yet, as we will see below, there was far more complexity to his negotiations with salaryman masculinity than was conveyed by initial appearances. His view of the 'ideal' (male) same-sex relationship in the workplace was someone 'you could hang around with (literally, "play with", *asobetari*) outside of work too' (Matsumoto, Round 2: 21). This one sentence seems to capture the sense of *amae*, closeness, and homosocial bonding discussed in the previous section.

'Good' senpai, 'bad' senpai

This sense of '*amae*' – of being looked after, guided – inherent in the *senpai/kôhai* relationship comes out in some of the others' accounts too. Shin'ya Naohiko, the former ice hockey athlete and Northern Energy systems engineer, mentioned that his happiest memory over the time he had worked at Northern Energy was of the occasion two years previously when he had gone to the beach on a day off with five of his *senpai*, all of whom had since been transferred to other branches (Shin'ya, Round 1: 29). Satô Hiroshi also worked in Northern Energy, in the Planning section, the same section as Ogasawara Takurô. Ogasawara-san was two years older than Satô-san, and hence his *senpai*. When Satô-san had first entered the workforce, he had been more anxious about his relationship with his colleagues than about the details of the work he would have to do. Fortunately for him, Ogasawara-san had stepped in and (as expected of the 'ideal' *senpai*) had 'shown him the ropes', thereby easing Satô-san's transition into organizational culture:

> the person who was here at the time of my placement after I'd completed my training (*kenshû*) was Ogasawara-san. He really took pains to teach me a whole lot of things. For instance … not so much about the details of the work [itself], but I got lots of advice about things like, this is what the company's really about, or things about interpersonal relationships (*ningen*

kankei) and the organization of the company. ... That really came in useful. If I think about it now, it was the ideal (*risôtekina*) *senpai-kohai* relationship...

...since I've joined this company, Ogasawara-san's really been like a 'lubricating oil' (*junkatsuyu*) ... I've effortlessly taken on board so many things from him, not just about the job itself, but about all sorts of things connected to the company.

(Satô, Round 1: 21)

Satô-san mentioned that he expected himself to do the same when, in due course, he too became the *senpai* in the *senpai–kôhai* pairing. Significantly, Satô-san had been told by Ogasawara-san that he himself had been 'looked after' in a similar way by a *senpai* when he had first started working at Northern Energy, something Ogasawara-san had (independently) mentioned to me too. This would be an example of homosocial reproduction as one of the arteries sustaining organizational culture along the lines suggested by Hearn (2002) and Roper (1996), above.

However, the relationship with a *senpai* does not necessarily always conform to the nurturing/caring type model. There is a flip side to homosociality, particularly given the hierarchies of power in the *senpai–kôhai* relationship, where there is the potential for bullying, intimidation, and abuse. This emerged in a rather startling way towards the end of my first interview with Matsumoto Tadashi, the Northern Energy accountant, and who was my liaison contact in that organization. Matsumoto-san, as mentioned above, had struck me as being a perfect embodiment of salaryman masculinity, more so than most of the other informants. Yet, even with him, as the following incident suggests, the situation was not necessarily a clear-cut case of an unproblematic merging with the 'ideals' of salaryman masculinity. We had been talking about the best and the worst aspects of being a *shakaijin* when he started telling me about an uneasy relationship with a senior (*senpai*) when he first entered the organization, and the stress this had caused him:

I'd only just started work, at the time I was in the sales office, and things didn't go too smoothly with the people around me. I didn't mind about how much work I had to do, even if it took time, all you had to do was do it. But with interpersonal relationships (*ningen kankei*), well,... although I had every intention of interacting properly, things didn't go too well, and that resulted in a lot of pressure, stress.

...Because at work things weren't going well with a senior (*senpai*), I was faced with some pretty horrible situations. For example,... well it was probably as a result of drunken aggression (*yopparatta ikioi*), but the door of my room in the dormitory was punched in (*buchi yaburareta*)...

...That [incident] was outside work hours. But even at work, it would have been okay if I'd been told things to my face, but instead he'd say things behind my back.... As this was around the time I'd just entered, in that sense it did cause me some stress.

(Matsumoto, Round 1: 18)

This incident had occurred some years prior to our discussion. However, it was clear from his tone that the incident had stayed with Matsumoto-san, and had had an impact on him.

Power and intimidation and corporate homosociality

Incidents such as these point to an uglier (often less talked-about) aspect of organizational masculinity – the assertion of power, whether over women (as manifested through sexual harassment, for instance) or over other men subordinate in status or age. As discussed in the previous chapter, there is a not insubstantial body of work that has examined the assertion of power over women in the framework of sexuality.[6] However, when it comes to male–male interaction, while there has been a recognition of the desire aspect of homosociality in organizations (e.g. Roper 1996), discussion of the sublimation of this desire into violence or other forms of power assertion has generally been restricted to studies centred on all-male institutions such as fraternities (Sanday 1990), boardingschools (Roden 1980), or the military (Addelston and Stirratt 1996), rather than corporate organizations.[7] Miura Tôru, the young Northern Energy new entrant, whose confusion about the 'proper' way of negotiating workplace friendships was discussed at some length in a previous chapter, also brought out some of these tensions in the power relationships between *senpai* and *kôhai*. Talking about his own situation he mentioned doing things like vacating a seat or fetching things for his *senpai*. However, compared to the way things apparently used to be in the past, he felt that his generation had it much easier. He mentioned stories heard from older colleagues about their experiences when new to the organization:

> you know, if you listen to those in their thirties and forties, it used to be much worse in the past, much more difficult.... For instance even at times like during welcome parties [for new entrants] (*kangeikai*) and so on, you had to 'scull' (*ikki*) alcohol, you don't have that now, but apparently there was that kind of stuff...
>
> ...also you'd be made to strip naked or perform tricks, they had those kind of things in the past.
>
> (Miura, Round 1: 23)

There was a sense of relief in his voice when he mentioned these rituals as being a thing of the past. At the time of this first interview, he had been unable to drink alcohol – hence the anxiety about being forced to consume large amounts of alcohol would have been greater in his case. However, by our second interview the following year, he was able to tolerate alcohol; something which, as I discuss below, was seen as important in aiding his socialization within the workplace.

Shimizu Ayaki, a Northern Print computer support officer, offered some reflections on ways of avoiding the kind of same-sex friction that often results from the assertion of power (or conflicts of power):

[If you ask me about] relationships between men ... I suppose if you get on well you don't really need to worry about such things, but ... well, you know how men and women can get on fine ... how would you put it, if you talk things get resolved smoothly, don't they? But, for men, if you clash it becomes really hard to work [together], doesn't it?

[*in response to interjection from me wondering if this was due to a sense of competition*] Yes, yes, I guess that's what it is. It'd be good if [men working together] could make compromises and consult with one another, step back where they can, try and get on together even as males.

(Shimizu, Round 1: 15)

Of friends and colleagues

Shimizu-san was quite unhappy with his work situation, and talked about some of his grievances – the atmosphere and work practices, low pay, long working hours, etc. He even mentioned actually drafting a letter of resignation. This was not empty posturing for the sake of the interview; he did not participate in the second round of interviews because by then he had ended up resigning and leaving the company. Part of his unhappiness seemed to stem from a perceived lack of friendship and camaraderie in the workplace:

Friends ... don't know if I could call them friends ... no, I don't suppose I've got any friends at the head office here now...

...

They're colleagues (*dôryô*), I suppose. Everyone, including all my *senpai*, I don't think I could call them friends. You know how even with your peers (*dôki*), there are some you become close friends with, and others you don't become friends with? Well, there's one, who's quit the company but I'm still friends with him, and I have friends in 'S-city'.

(Shimizu, Round 1: 11)

Shimizu-san's criterion for differentiating between a 'colleague' and 'friend' was the ability to spend time together on days off, to say anything at all to each other and not have to worry about the other person's feelings and sensitivities. This came out in his description of the things he and the friend who had resigned used to do together.

That friend is also really into cars. So when he was still working here at head office, we'd go [on drives] together, go out for a meal, go out drinking. You know, sometimes we'd leave for 'S-city' straight after finishing work, return around 4 a.m. in the morning, and come straight into work!

(Shimizu, Round 1: 13)

He felt that it would be good if he still had such a friend at work. This, he believed, would help him continue working at the present job (keeping in mind his desire to leave) (Shimizu, Round 1: 11, 12). As it turned out, he did end up leaving the organization.

This kind of desire for a 'true friend' rather than *tsukiai*-based superficial camaraderie was also articulated by Shin'ya Naohiko of Northern Energy. As may be recalled from discussions in earlier chapters, Shin'ya-san's journey along the life-trajectory from single, unattached employee living in the company dormitory to husband and father (with all the accompanying responsibilities) had been compressed into the space of just one year. At the time of our first interview he was still living in the company dormitory. Despite a perception of dormitory life as being one of homosocial bonding, the reality was a situation where the residents were barely aware of each others' existence. Shin'ya-san mentioned that although this had apparently not always been the case, the situation since he had started living there was one of 'wondering who might be living next door, what section he might be working in' (Shin'ya, Round 1: 26).[8] Even in the workplace itself, Shin'ya-san, at the time of our first interview, was ambivalent about his interactions with his colleagues. The *senpai* he had been close to, mentioned earlier in this section, had since been transferred elsewhere, and there seemed to be a barrier, in terms of closeness, between him and his peers. This may partly have been a consequence of his personality, which was far more introspective than others of his age. The sense of separation may also have been due to the differences in educational qualification – as someone who had only completed high school, Shin'ya-san felt himself to be at a disadvantage compared with his peers, most of whom were university graduates (Shin'ya, Round 1: 11). Whatever the reasons, this ambivalence came out in our discussions about friendship at work. He was quite explicit in telling me that he had no close friends at work. Occasionally, he did go out drinking with peers, particularly those who came to the Head Office from one of the regional centres. This, however, was mainly out of a sense of duty or *tsukiai* (along the lines suggested by Atsumi's discussion) and, as he stressed, was 'not what friends are about to me. It's different from my definition of what a friend is' (35). He then went on to expand upon his definition of a friend:

> Well, probably, I guess, a sort of vague definition would include a family element (*kazokutekina bubun*) ... more family-like on both sides, not just a relationship between the two individuals, but also, to an extent, meeting the other's [i.e. the friend's] parents, getting [the friend] to meet your own parents, that sort of thing is what's real [friendship]. As for the emotional or psychological aspects of friendship that's a completely different matter, though.
>
> ...[*in response to my question about what he meant by the 'emotional/ psychological aspects'*] The 'emotional and psychological dimension', you know, is like, well, a partner (*aite*) who encourages (*genki tsukete kureru*, literally 'empowers you'). For instance, [with friendship] there are always times when you joke around and tease each other. But, well, I think that it is really about, when the other person's really suffering, how genuinely you

can feel [their pain] – getting on the same wavelength, in both mind and body (*shinshin*).

(Shin'ya, Round 1: 35)

In many senses, Shin'ya-san's view of 'true' friendship brings out some of the nuances of those currents of homosocial desire reflected upon in the first half of this chapter. Moreover, his comment on the duty-bound *tsukiai*-type relationships would support Atsumi's assertions, discussed above, about the separation between *tsukiai*-based interactions and 'true' friendship (Atsumi 1980).[9]

Alcohol, tsukiai, *and homosocial community*

However, this is not to say that *tsukiai*-based interactions are inconsequential. As the earlier discussion of Allison's study would indicate, work-related male–male interaction (even when mediated through women) is important in shaping the contours of corporate masculinity (Allison 1994). This importance of *tsukiai* – the sense of inclusion, of having fun together – is reflected in the following comment by Nakamura Tetsuya, a technical line worker at Northern Print who had been with the organization for eight years. As we saw in Chapter 5, he most felt himself to be a 'typical salaryman' when he was unable to refuse extra work piled on by more senior colleagues, and times when he was pouring drinks for seniors (Nakamura, Round 1: 7). Yet, when I asked him what his most pleasant memory was in the eight years he had been in Northern Print, his response was: 'Surely, without having to think about it, times when I'm having fun drinking with everyone (*minna de waiwai nondeiru toki*) would be number one!' A similar sentiment was expressed by Minami Toshio from the Accounts section of Northern Energy, who also said that the best thing since joining the company for him had been the *tsukiai* and opportunities to interact with lots of different people. As he jokingly told me, he 'hung out' for opportunities to participate in such drinking occasions, and would go along 'even if I've got no money' (Minami: 13). Significantly, as both Nakamura-san's and Minami-san's comments would suggest, the role played by alcohol in shaping and reinforcing this same-sex interaction (as well as a sense of masculinity) is not unimportant. The idiomatic expression '*nomunikeishon*' sometimes used by salarymen (and others) captures this function of alcohol consumption beautifully – the term is a compound derived from the Japanese verb 'to drink' (*nomu*), and the English term 'communication' (see Spielvogel 2003: 219, n.9). As noted earlier in this chapter, this aspect of alcohol consumption has been commented upon by various authors (e.g. Rohlen 1974; Allison 1994; Linhart 1998; Roberson 1998; Ben-Ari 2000, 2002, Gagné 2010).

The significance of alcohol as an instrument in this 'crafting' process is brought out in Miura Tôru's (almost boastful) account during our second interview, of his 'progress' from being unable to tolerate alcohol to being able to drink alcohol, and to indulge in types of behaviour (including normally taboo same-sex physical intimacy) permissible when alcohol is present (see Allison 1994: 45, 46). Talking about the shifts in his behaviour when he was drinking he mentioned that prior to drinking he was very conscious of his behaviour as a respectable *kaisha no ningen* (company employee). However, this was

> before drinking. I try and bear that [the need to behave 'respectably'] in mind. Once you start drinking [though], you lose all sense of things, don't you?... I do. [I lose] control ... I don't normally drink, so once I do, I end up drinking like a dam that's burst (*damu ga kekkai shita yô ni*)!
>
> (Miura, Round 2: 20)

When in this condition, he did not become abusive or violent; rather, he described himself as 'the type that attaches himself [to people] (*kuttsuite kuru*)', someone who 'seeks bodily contact (*karada no sesshoku*)' (Miura, Round 2: 20). Although others would (jokingly) tell him off when he got into such a state, calling him an '*ahô* (idiot)' (20), everyone took into account his low alcohol tolerance and he would end up being 'forgiven (*yurusareru*)' (21). The general feeling seemed to be of an indulgent *senpai–kôhai*-type behaviour, where he would be treated (in an almost feminized manner) as a weaker, mischievous, non-adult, being called such things as '*kono gaki*' (the equivalent of something like 'little brat') (21).

Homosocial community versus heterosexual expectations?

However, there was also another side to company-based *tsukiai*, one where it was seen as an intrusion on private time that could otherwise be spent with friends, or girlfriends, or family. In terms of an aversion to *tsukiai*-related interaction, Yoshida Shun'ichi, a twenty-year-old linesman with Northern Energy, summed up the feelings of many of the younger informants. He described his feelings when out drinking with older colleagues and forced to give the appearance of participating in conversations in which he had no interest:

> [*In response to my question*] The conversation of older people? You know, when I go out drinking after work in my private time and I'm forced to listen to talk about work, at times like that, if I have to listen to work-related talk, perhaps I'm selfish, but I really detest it.
>
> (Yoshida, Round 1: 21)

Other informants echoed this kind of sentiment. For example, Kobayashi Kazushi, also of Northern Energy, resented the intrusion on his private time taken up through having to go out drinking after work, something that in the past could happen twice a week. Although this frequency had decreased to about once a month, Kobayashi-san still had to deal with other types of *tsukiai* relationships – for instance, with friends/fellow residents dropping around when he returned to the company dormitory (Kobayashi, Round 2: 22, 23).

This trend was something that came up as a topic in my discussions with some of the managers in the Personnel section of Northern Energy. The formal discussions (discussed in more detail in Chapter 4) revolved around Northern Energy's recruiting priorities and practices. This was followed by an informal *tsukiai*-type drinks session, organized by the group leader, with those who had taken part in the discussions, as well as a few other human resources junior/ middle managers joining in. It was during this more relaxed drinks session that the conversation drifted to the shifts in the ways male salarymen constructed their views of friendship and homosocial interactions related to the workplace. One of the most interesting observations was made in relation to one of the members present, an older man who did not say much for most of the evening. According to the others (and not refuted by this individual), this person, who had never married, used to spend much of his time with a work colleague. Apparently people around them would refer to them in terms of being like brothers. Given that the person in question was present, it was difficult for me to probe more, but from the tone of the conversation (and the way in which the individual himself was included) I was struck that this closeness between the two male employees was not regarded as anything particularly strange or out of the ordinary. However, significantly, this closeness was constructed in non-sexual terms (with the analogy of brothers being deployed), lending support to Roper's assertion about homosocial desire – 'intimacy in formally heterosexual settings which presents as non-sexual but which nevertheless involves *potentially* erotic desires' (Roper 1996: 213; emphasis added).

Whether such closeness was possible with younger employees was questionable. There was a general view of the shift from male employees seeing the workplace (rather than the home) as the site for (same-sex) companionship and emotional fulfilment, to a clearer demarcation between public and private, emotional fulfilment being increasingly situated within the realm of a heterosexual couple. Whereas in the past non-work socializing often incorporated activities such as going camping or to the beach with work colleagues, it was becoming increasingly unusual for younger employees to do so. If they (younger employees) did socialize with each other, it was likely to be in the company of their girlfriends or, in the case of married employees, families (rather than, interestingly, just wives). This then resulted in quite a lengthy discussion about the influences which popular culture representations of the 1950s/1960s-style 'Happy American Family' (television shows such as *Bewitched* and *Father Knows Best*) have had on how the Japanese increasingly started to construct views and ideals regarding family (discussion with Northern Energy Human resources staff, 1/12/98, Notes: 2–4). Significantly, most of the members during this discussion would have been in their late forties or fifties. This meant that they belonged to the generation (coming of age in the 1960s and 1970s) that would have been particularly exposed to the beginnings of the shifts in discourses surrounding gender, marriage, and family, *and*, at the same time, would also have been able to relate to the earlier understandings regarding these shifts.[10]

These contrasting pulls in relation to trying to reconcile often divergent discourses surrounding friendship, intimacy, interaction with colleagues, love, marriage, family, and so forth may have been at their most acute for men then in their forties and fifties. However, they were also a consideration for my informants, and their generation. An example of one informant's attempts to reconcile or come to terms with some of these shifts in priorities in his friends' and colleagues' lives is the following account provided by Satô Hiroshi, a twenty-three-year-old single Northern Energy employee. Responding to my question about what he did on weekends, he mentioned his fondness for music, and then went on to tell me, with some regret, that the band he used to play the guitar with had broken up due to other members getting married and going their separate ways (Satô, Round 1: 11). This regret – perhaps even resentment – at losing friends due to their transition to an adult, *shakaijin* masculinity came out quite poignantly in our discussion towards the end of the same interview. By way of wrapping up, I had asked about the best and worst aspects of his life at that moment. This led the conversation to take the following course:

SATÔ (S): ...the worst thing ... well, my burden of debt increasing after damaging my car [*laughs*] ... and being 'jilted' (*furareta*) a lot ... And also ... well, you know, the fact that everyone's ended up getting married.

ROMIT (R): Your friends?

S: My friends.

R: So, after they got married you haven't really...

S: Yes, that's right. You know, it's quite difficult [for them], isn't it? With children born, and stuff. So, opportunities to have fun [together] have disappeared. Possibly you end up becoming somewhat sensitive (*ki* [*o*]*tsukau*).

R: On both sides?

S: No, I do. It's like you shouldn't impose (*jama shicha ikenai*). So now, for the time being, I just go out with other single guys.

(Satô, Round 1: 12)

What come across from this brief exchange are the collisions and intermeshings between different discourses shaping salaryman masculinity, discussed previously.

Fujita Yûji: homosocial dreams, heterosexual realities

The intermingling and colliding of these various discursive 'ideals' was best brought out in my discussions with Fujita Yûji, the married Northern Print Sales employee whose views on marriage were discussed in the previous chapter. More so than other informants, 'friendship' and its importance occupied a fair share of our discussion in both interviews. Friends, in Fujita-san's view, were 'the most valuable of assets (*ichiban no zaisan*)' (Fujita, Round 2: 19). To him, the existence of a friend was just as important as his wife or children (20). Indeed, to him, 'friendship' was what made masculinity special, the one thing, more than any other, that made him glad to have been born male:

FUJITA (F): …what definitely comes to mind would be friends (*nakama*). You know, with girls you don't often hear of things like this kind of friendship (*yûjô*). It's probably largely what you'd call superficial (*uwabe*), but, on the other hand, for me, I have friends from my home-town from my high school days and university friends, who, well, would still be called close friends (*shin'yû*), so that's why, in that sense, I really think it's good to be [born] male (*otoko de yokatta*).

R: I see. So, for women … women, with each other (*onna-dôshi*), they don't have such friendships? In your view?

F: You don't really hear about it around you. So, if they don't see someone for just a short time, they lose touch, and [the relationship] ends with that. For me, there's a fellow (*yatsu*) who's been a close friend (*shin'yû*) ever since kindergarten. So there's that aspect to being glad I'm male.

(Fujita, Round 1: 25)

A close friend, such as his friend from his kindergarten years, was, according to him, 'akin to a brother (*kyôdai ni chikai*)' (Fujita, Round 1: 26) and the relationship was strong enough to endure all kinds of changes – the fact that Fujita-san was now married (and that the friend was about to be married), or even that he had moved away from his home town to another part of the country, had not weakened the bond. He was now able to meet this friend – and others who he included in his circle of good friends – only once a year or so. However, whenever they met, they were able to slip straight back into their old closeness:

this probably sounds strange, but even if there's been no contact for a year, and if I make contact, we immediately revert back to our original [relationship]. And with this, even my wife has told me that it's odd (*fushigi*).

(Fujita, Round 2: 21)

Trying to summarize his feelings towards his relationships with his friends, he stated that 'it's a source of comfort (*anshin-kan*) knowing that even if we don't keep contact the relationship won't crumble' (Fujita, Round 2: 21).

Fujita-san seemed to have a strong desire to encompass, or reconcile, or bring together all the different discourses and expectations regarding idealized friendship, marriage, and salaryman masculinity together. Thus, he repeatedly stressed that marriage had not adversely affected the intensity and closeness of his friendships. In fact the way he expressed it, he considered his wife almost like 'one of the gang'. As he explained: 'you know, everyone, including my wife, just becomes friends' (Fujita, Round 2: 22). This sense of bringing wives (including his own) into a big, happy, pre-existing circle of friends is reflected in the following words:

So, you know, it's like this – another friend is getting married soon, and in pretty much the same way, [his wife] will become part of the group, having fun with everyone, going camping and stuff. So in that sense, even as a couple, within the whole group, both become everyone's friend.

(Fujita, Round 2: 23)

He also – in contrast to the views expressed by Yoshida Shun'ichi or Kobayashi Kazushi above – placed importance on fostering friendship and camaraderie through work-related *tsukiai*. He felt – in many respects echoing the sentiments of the Northern Energy managers discussed above – that the recent trend among many of his peers of seeking their fulfilment separate from community or work networks was linked to the growing reach of 'individualism (*kojinshugi*) through mass media' (Fujita, Round 1: 26). Rather, in his view, it was valuable to participate in work-related *tsukiai*:

I think they're important. Because normally since you're so busy when you're working, you don't [talk about] anything other than work. So, in that kind of scenario, since you don't really get the opportunity to talk at a deeper level (*fukai tokoro made*), it's difficult for people to become close. That's why, regardless of whether you drink alcohol, or don't drink alcohol, I think it's really important to get away and talk together outside of work.

(Fujita, Round 1: 26)

Fujita-san's attempts to negotiate some kind of balance between the demands of homo*social* bonding with friends and colleagues, and hetero*sexual* expectations of hegemonic masculinity, are reflected in his response to my questions about whether he would have any problems showing his emotions (*kanjō*) in front of a close male friend:

Yes, I show it [feelings]. But, to an extent I'd hold back. I suppose these days it doesn't really happen [showing emotions], because I wouldn't want to make him [the friend] feel uncomfortable (*fukaikan*).

(Fujita, Round 2: 22)

On the other hand, the person he would go to if he really needed to talk about something would be his wife. However, his way of rationalizing this to me was his statement – mentioned above – that everyone *including his wife* became his friend.

Conclusion

My decision to discuss Fujita-san's views on friendship at the end of the section on informants' voices, and at some length, is deliberate. More so than the others, his narrative, I believe, best captured the juxtaposition of the sometimes conflicting strands within salaryman masculinity, particularly pronounced at that historical moment, of, on the one hand, unambiguous prescriptive heterosexuality and, on the other, ambiguous assumed homosociality. Underlying this juxtaposition are the ongoing negotiations with expectations of *tsukiai* from colleagues (and, where relevant, clients), often harking back to an older reality of homosocial intimacy, shifts in discourses surrounding 'ideals' in masculinity, marriage, companionship, and friendship reflecting wider socio-cultural changes, as well as the individual's own imaginings of 'friendship'. While all the informants engaged with these issues on a day-to-day basis, Fujita-san, not unlike Arai-san in the previous chapter, was far more *conscious* of these dynamics than was the case with many of the others.

Moreover, what this consciousness enables us to do is to feed in a consideration that has generally been absent from analyses of Japanese corporate culture – that of the undercurrents of homosocial desire which, along with the more visible influences, was also integral to the 'crafting' of salaryman masculinity. As highlighted, the 'success' of salaryman masculinity was as dependent on homosocial bonds as was the public subscription to an ideology of hegemonic heterosexuality (see Frank 1987). In this regard, relationships like the *senpai/kôhai* and *oyabun/kobun* dyads were integral to the homosocial reproduction of salaryman masculinity. Thus, in the context of my informants being 'crafted' into salaryman masculinity, this aspect of organizational culture was one that had to be taken into account. As the various accounts revealed, as was the case with engagements with other aspects of salaryman masculinity, the engagements with the expectations of homosociality were characterized by shades of ambiguity and contradiction. The informants often had to contend simultaneously with a variety of competing expectations. These included idealized imaginings of what constituted same-sex friendship, both in general and specifically at the workplace. At the same time, as Miura Tôru's account of being reprimanded for bringing notions of pre-*shakaijin* friendship into adult *shakaijin* spaces, or Matsumoto Tadashi's recollections of bullying and intimidation at the hands of a senior colleague suggest, the reality of negotiating homosocial relationships does not always conform to idealized imaginings. Moreover, as the accounts of the younger informants brought out, shifting expectations about heterosexual relationships (with wives or girlfriends) outside the workplace meant that homosocial demands within the organization became increasingly regarded with ambivalence. Yet, at the same time, as the accounts of informants like Fujita Yûji and Satô Hiroshi reveal, acknowledged homosocial relations as well as *unacknowledged* 'circuits' of homosocial desire (Roper 1996: 212, 213) were still relevant as undercurrents informing salaryman masculinity.

My decision to situate this chapter as the final ethnographic chapter was a deliberate one. This chapter, more so than the others, touched upon areas within salaryman masculinity that could only really be brought out through interactive, one-on-one discussions with individuals. The subtle nuances of Matsumoto-san's recollections of being bullied by a senior, or Fujita-san's reflections on the importance of friendship, would have been much harder to tap into had an interactive relationship between us not existed. As highlighted when discussing the research methodology in the Introduction, the use of semi-structured, intensive interviews was integral to the multi-pronged, multi-layered research approach adopted in my discussion, allowing for an added, richer layer of material to complement the 'macro' view of the dynamics of salaryman masculinity. This, in turn, has allowed us to appreciate Ken Plummer's reflection that 'lives, situations,... societies are always and everywhere evolving, adjusting, emerging, becoming' (Plummer 1996: 224). This is regardless of whether we are talking about that historical moment in late 1990s Japan at the focus of this book, or, for that matter, reflecting back from our position today, a decade down the track.

8 Beyond the 'JTB-Man'

Looking back from the 2010s

In this final chapter, we fast-forward a decade or so to the opening years of the 2010s and reflect back on the conversations and personal voices of the preceding chapters. As highlighted when setting out the mappings and arguments of this book in Chapter 1, the underlying 'spine' bringing the chapters together is the proposition that an appreciation of the conditions of the post-Bubble years, in particular the post-1995 period, is important in order to gain a fully nuanced understanding of the socio-economic, political, and cultural conditions in the first decades of the twenty-first century. This applies to framings of masculinities too, in particular the position of salaryman *masculinity* in postwar Japan. As pointed out in that first chapter, while the salaryman and all that he has represented has been extensively researched and studied from a variety of angles, what has generally been overlooked has been an examination of the *man* in the salaryman. This is despite the figure of the salaryman and the values and lifestyle associated with him having become something of a metonym for all Japanese men over the postwar decades, particularly over the pre-1990s decades.

Thus, a primary aim of this book has been to explore the discourse of the salaryman as a particular discourse of *masculinity* embedded within particular ideologies of gender, sexuality, class, and, indeed, the nation. In this sense, 'masculinity' *and* the discourse of the salaryman cannot be disentangled from the processes of industrial-capitalist modernity and late modernity in Japan from the late nineteenth century up until the present. 'Masculinity' as deployed in my argument has not been in the sense of some kind of essentialized biological essence cutting across all individuals genetically classified as 'male', and fixed over time. Rather, my understanding of the term has been one that sees 'masculinity' – what it means to be a 'male' person, 'manhood' – 'as a constantly changing collection of meanings that we construct through our relationships with ourselves, with each other, and with our world' (Kimmel 1994: 120). Thus, it would be more realistic to talk in terms of masculini*ties* – multiple constructions and representations of 'maleness'. I have argued, moreover, that among these various masculinities, at any particular point in time in a given society one discourse of masculinity has the greatest ideological power and hold over the others. This is what Connell (1987, 1995, 2000) and other writers have labelled 'hegemonic' masculinity. This hegemonic masculinity may be conceived of as a cultural 'ideal' or 'blueprint', which exerts a powerful influence over the lives of men and women.

However, as I have also argued, while the hegemonic form of masculinity may well have the greatest ideological power, this power is not absolute. Rather, at stake is a complex process whereby the hegemonic discourse intersects and interacts with other forms of masculinity in varying ways. These processes of engagement may incorporate dynamics of appropriation, subjugation, and marginalization, as well as resistance, subversion, playful engagement, and modification. As a whole, these dynamics constitute what Demetriou (2001: 348) terms a 'hybrid bloc' (348). Within the context of these dynamics, hegemonic masculinity is constantly shaped by other masculinities, and by surrounding social, cultural, economic, and political institutions, structures, and practices. The non-hegemonic masculinities are in turn shaped through this process. In this sense hegemonic masculinity is an ongoing, constantly shaping and re-shaping gender *project* (Connell 2002: 81, 82). This is what I referred to as the 'crafting' and 're-crafting' of masculinity, which occurs both at the wider societal level, and within individual males over their life-paths. The term 'crafting', as Dorinne Kondo noted, implies that 'identity is not a static *object*, but a creative *process*' (Kondo 1990: 48). Thus, I have argued that identity built around being gendered as 'masculine' is a constantly shifting, re-shaping, re-enacting process occurring at the intersections of individual agency and discourses and ideologies circulating within and through society. Accordingly, the discussion of this crafting process in this book has focused on two levels of analysis – the 'macro' societal level, and the 'micro' level of the individual male on the ground.

As I have highlighted, over the postwar decades accompanying Japan's transition to a global industrial power, the discourse of masculinity surrounding the salaryman emerged as the hegemonic form of masculinity. This was despite the fact that even at the high point of Japan's economic success story in the 1960s and 1970s, only a limited number of men would have fallen under the strictest definitional rubric of the term salaryman. Rather, as I stressed, it was the *ideology* (of gender, of sexuality, of class, of nation) embodied in the salaryman that was far more extensive in its reach. At the core of this ideology was the equation of masculinity with the public work sphere, and femininity with the private, household sphere. Within this ideological framework, the two sides of the binary were linked together through the institution of publicly acknowledged and sanctioned heterosexual marriage. Thus, it was the notion of the adult man, the socially responsible *shakaijin*, as producer *and* reproducer (in other words, the *daikokubashira* mainstay of the household) that lay at the heart of the ideology embedded in the discourse of salaryman masculinity. Moreover, despite the various socio-economic and cultural shifts which became pronounced over the 1980s and have intensified since the 1990s, this equation of hegemonic masculinity with production and reproduction continues to remain entrenched. However, at the same time, as mentioned above, hegemonic masculinity is in a constant state of being crafted and recrafted in response to the wider socio-economic and cultural context. Such forces as the emergence of a late capitalist society with a greater range (through choice, or otherwise) of employment and lifestyle spaces, increases in women's workforce participation, the impact of almost two decades of economic slowdown forcing many organizations to rethink assumptions about corporate culture and management practices, and the influence of increasingly globalized discourses of gender and sexuality (including masculinity), have exerted a shaping influence on the articulations of hegemonic masculinity.

Thus, in this regard, the moment in history when the 'micro' level conversations with the young men informing this book occurred was a significant one. While at the time they themselves (or I, for that matter) were not necessarily aware of it, they were negotiating their way through the expectations of salaryman masculinity, as many of the old pre-Lost Decade assumptions and expectations were starting to be superseded by a new set of expectations. Hence, drawing upon the deeply personal and nuanced accounts of these young men allowed us to gain a sense of the complexity of the 'on-the-ground' dynamics of crafting salaryman masculinity at that moment in history; a complexity that may not have been conveyed to the same extent had the focus of discussion been limited to the macro level. However, at the same time, the macro-level of analysis allowed us to situate and contextualize these individual complexities and contradictions and negotiations within the wider socio-cultural and economic framework.

These conversations were taking place against a backdrop of a collective socio-cultural psyche still haunted by the twin traumas of 1995, mentioned in Chapter 1 – the Hanshin Earthquake in January and the Aum Shinrikyô terrorist attack on the Tokyo subway system in March of that year. A decade or so down the track, at the time of writing (late 2011), Japan is dealing with the fallouts from another set of traumas: the earthquake and tsunami of 11 March 2011 and the subsequent (and still ongoing) nuclear crisis. In this sense, the 'micro'-level voices of my informants as they negotiated their ways through the cross-currents and shifts in hegemonic expectations of salaryman masculinity were situated within a wider time-frame episode bounded at either end by the two sets of natural and human-generated national traumas (1995 and 2011). While it is still premature to conjecture with any certainty, we may well be entering the next chapter in the ongoing narrative of Japan's modernity and late modernity (see Chandler *et al.* 2011; Uno and Hamano 2012). In this respect, this may be a suitable historical moment to reflect back upon post-Bubble years, and the ways in which discourses around masculinities (including salaryman masculinity) may have shifted.

At the 'macro' socio-economic level, the intervening years since the conversations with my informants occurred have not been encouraging ones for Japan. The 'Lost Decade' of the 1990s has now become two 'Lost Decades', as many of the socio-economic and cultural unravellings set in motion in the early post-Bubble years have continued through the 2000s. Even before the devastating impact of the March 2011 earthquake/tsunami and subsequent nuclear crisis, socio-economic indicators and media and academic assessments offered a less than healthy evaluation. Despite occasional signs of recovery, such as in the mid-2000s prior to the negative impact of the global financial crisis, the economy continued its jerky, lacklustre performance through the 2000s (see Kingston 2010: 273, n.5). While indicators such as the unemployment rate, hovering between 5 and 6 per cent, may not, on the surface, look too bad compared with European and North American rates, underlying these figures have been serious (and widening) inequalities. First, 'official' unemployment in the fifteen to twenty-four age category has been above the average, increasing as much as 10 per cent in 2003, a reflection of the gloomy prospects facing many young people in twenty-first-century Japan (Kingston 2010: 93; also Yuzawa and Miyamoto 2008: 156, 157). Second, within the employed labour force, the proportion comprising easily dispensable part-time, contract, and dispatch workers has grown quite noticeably (see Japan Institute for Labour Policy and Training (JILPT) 2011: 2–7). As Jeff Kingston (2010: 35) points out, over the ten years from 1992 to 2002, full-time workers fell by 3.5 million, while non-regular workers increased by 5.67 million. By 2008 non-regular workers constituted 34.1 per cent of the workforce (Kingston 2010: 35), and they were the first group to be laid off during the 2008/2009 global financial crisis (JILPT 2011: 15). A new term, *precariat* ('precarious proletariat'), popularized by the *freeter* activist and writer Amamiya Karin, has entered into public discourse to describe these (around twenty million) workers employed on an unstable, non-permanent basis (Obinger 2009; Kingston 2010: 84; see also Standing 2011: 7–13). The economic precariousness of members of this sector of society, as well as their socio-cultural alienation, was best exemplified in the 2008 Akihabara incident, when Katô Tomohiro, a twenty-five-year-old socially alienated non-regular worker, drove a mini-van into a crowded pedestrian mall and then went on a stabbing rampage in the Akihabara district of Tokyo (popularly known as an electronics and *anime*/gaming hub), killing seven people, and injuring several others. It subsequently emerged that Katô had left a trail of desperately lonely and self-loathing online posts that, while not necessarily explaining his actions, put them in the wider psycho-social (and indeed, economic) context of day-to-day reality for *precariat* Japan. As I noted in Chapter 1, the post-Bubble years have been punctuated by numerous instances of seemingly spontaneous, often bizarre incidents of violent crime attracting frenzied media attention. So, in this regard, the intense media scrutiny of the Akihabara incident was not unusual. However, as Slater and Galbraith (2011) point out, in this instance, both mainstream and new media analysis shifted from an initial focus on individual pathology to contextualizing Katô's actions with reference to the wider socio-economic structural conditions of post-Bubble, late capitalist, neo-liberal Japan – specifically the *precarious*, disconnected, and seemingly future-less on-the-ground reality for large swathes of young (*and* middle-aged and elderly) Japanese women and men. Thus the (never accurate) imagining of Japan as an overwhelmingly 'middle-class' society has quite definitely been debunked, and replaced by a recognition of Japan as a society characterized by class-based distinctions (*kakusa shakai*). As I will discuss further on, however, the *appeal* of the discourse of the middle class, and what it symbolizes, continues to exert socio-cultural influence.

Foregrounding these economic and labour market shifts has been the amplification of demographic trends of an ageing population and low birth rates that started surfacing in the 1990s. In 2009, for instance, 23 per cent of the population was over 65, and is projected to reach 40 per cent by the mid-twenty-first century (Kingston 2010: 41). At the same time, the working-age population share will continue to decline, dropping to fewer than fifty million (from a peak of eighty-seven million in the mid-1990s) by 2050 (*The Economist*, 20–26 November 2010: 16). This will have, indeed is already having, myriad ramifications for the economy, one example being the implications for public expenditure – in 2010 around 70 per cent of social security payments went to the over-sixty-five age cohort (ibid.). Consequently, public debt levels have continued to balloon, reaching 200 per cent of GDP in 2010 (Kingston 2010: 42), radically altering the global imagining of Japan as a frugal, fiscally 'responsible' socio-economy to one dangerously close to going into fiscal tailspin along the lines of some Latin American economies in the 1990s and 2000s, or, more recently, Eurozone economies like Greece. Thus, over the span of less than two decades, Japan in the global imaginary appears to have gone from a blueprint for economic success to being touted by some as the 'Argentina of Asia' – a previously affluent economy with a seemingly rosy future that failed to live up to its potential (Lehmann 2002).

Beyond the 'JTB-Man': salaryman masculinity in the 2010s

In light of the above, where, and how, do we situate the salaryman a decade down the track? Specifically, how relevant is the type of salaryman presented in the JTB guide with which this book opened to the socio-cultural and economic conditions of 2010s Japan? At one level, given all the upheavals, particularly within the labour market and corporate sector, of the past two decades, it would make sense to dismiss the salaryman, and the discourse of masculinity he embodied, as an anachronistic vestige of a past era. Contemporary public imaginings of Japanese masculinity are increasingly dominated by tropes such as the *otaku*/technogeek, the *freeter*, the male escorts (*hosuto*) of 'host clubs', or the seemingly asexual/feminized *sôshokukei danshi* ('herbivorous men'). All of these discourses (indeed, practices) of masculinity come across as complete antitheses of the salaryman, and may well *appear* to be displacing him in a struggle for a new hegemonic masculinity. Indeed, these shifts may be indicative of what Sabine Frühstück and Anne Walthall, in their introduction to a recent edited volume, refer to as 'numerous microcosms of "(hegemonic) masculinities"' (emphasis added) (Frühstück and Walthall 2011a: 10). Frühstück and Walthall draw upon cultural theorist Azuma Hiroki to suggest that a virtual reality, or '"game-ish realism (*gêmuteki riarizumu*)"' (Azuma cited in Frühstück and Walthall 2011a: 11), as embodied and enacted through modes of masculinity like the *otaku*, have replaced the salaryman in the national psyche; in their words: 'the "techno geeks" or "database animals" have won' (12). This may be seen as resonating with Connell's reflection that:

> [n]ew groups may challenge old solutions and construct a new hegemony. The dominance of *any* group of men may be challenged.... Hegemony ... is a historically mobile relation [and] [i]ts ebb and flow is a key element of the picture of masculinity.
>
> (Connell 1995: 77, 78)

However, we need to be careful about reading too much into practices/styles (rather than discourses/ideologies) of subcultural masculinities like the *otaku* or *sôshokukei danshi*, whose socio-cultural impact often gets disproportionately magnified as a result of media commodification. This is particularly pertinent in the case of *otaku* masculinity, whose mainstream appeal has, in no small part, been the consequence of cultural industry packaging, and even official cultural policy. For instance, the enhanced (domestic and global) profile of the *otaku* from the mid-2000s was propelled by the commercial success of the 2004/2005 book, film, and TV series, *Densha Otoko* ('Train Man'), as well as the incorporation of technogeek attributes within the framework of official and semi-official 'Cool Japan' initiatives (see Allison 2009; Freedman 2009; Napier 2011).[1] Rather, what we do need to consider when reflecting on articulations of masculinities in the supposed 'game-ish realism' context of post-Bubble Japan is the extent to which core assumptions about socio-culturally hegemonic expectations of masculinity are being dislodged. In particular, we need to contemplate whether the ostensibly consumption-mediated, seemingly 'anti-salaryman' masculinities, like the *otaku* or *sôshokukei danshi*, are *really* dismantling the work/production/masculinity nexus. Indeed, Ian Condry, in his essay on *otaku* masculinity in the Frühstück and Walthall collection mentioned above, draws attention to the ways in which some interpretations of *otaku* masculinity 'share a common assumption with salaryman masculinity, namely that value (a man's worth) tends to be grounded in productivity' (Condry 2011: 265). This 'productivity' can vary from 'producing' violence, as in the case of *otaku* he labels as 'bad otaku', to producing animated films or video games in the case of 'good otaku' (265). The common denominator thus remains the link between masculinity and production/work.

In fact, as pointed out in Chapter 1, despite all the socio-economic *and* corporate culture upheavals and shifts over the post-Bubble era, the discourse of the salaryman has continued to be remarkably tenacious. This comes through in the persisting presence of the salaryman in the popular cultural landscape of twenty-first-century Japan – for instance, the ongoing popularity of icons like *Sarariiman Kintarô* and *Shima Kôsaku*, or the success of the band Ketsumeishi's *Tatakae! Sarariiman* ('Fight! Salaryman') single in 2010, or even the continuing profile of the business novel as a popular literary genre, as evidenced by business novelist Ikeido Jun's winning of the prestigious Naoki Prize for fiction in 2011. Moreover, as suggested in earlier chapters, the ongoing economic slowdown and harsh labour market conditions of the past two decades have actually worked to *enhance* the socio-cultural appeal of salaryman masculinity. At first glance, this may come across as counter-intuitive. However, as I pointed out in Chapters 5 and 6, the post-Bubble years have seen a widening divide, in terms of financial security and socio-cultural status, between those male graduates able (or lucky enough) to enter into the parameters of salaryman masculinity, and those (increasing numbers) who find themselves relegated to low-paying, insecure jobs in the non-permanent sector. This divide is not merely at an abstract, theoretical level. Rather, it translates through to real, on-the-ground financial and quality-of-life indicators. Taga Futoshi, for instance, drawing upon Health and Welfare Ministry statistics, points out that there is a considerable disparity in lifetime income between a man employed as a regular, permanent employee and someone in a non-permanent position – even if the latter works for forty hours a week from age twenty to fifty-nine, his total lifetime income will still be less than his permanent counterpart's by as much as 130 million yen (Taga 2011b: 191). This, as I suggested in Chapter 6, has ramifications for such considerations as the ability to attract potential marriage partners, start a family, get a bank loan to purchase a house, pay childcare costs, etc. – essentially access to all the discursive and ideological markers of 'middle-class' respectability. Despite the not insignificant shifts in attitudes towards gender, sexuality, and family over the past two decades, the notion of the husband being the primary household provider (essentially, the *daikokubashira*) remains stubbornly entrenched, as reflected in the much higher rates of singlehood among men in non-permanent work (Taga 2011b: 192, 193). As Taga also observes, while young women today are much less likely than their mothers' generation to be *sengyō shufu* ('full-time housewives'), there is still a continuing desire to marry a man with job and income stability (Taga 2011b: 193).

Thus, the discourse of the 'salaryman', may well, in some respects, be returning to the socio-culturally idealized elite status it occupied when works such as Ronald Dore's *City Life in Japan* and Ezra Vogel's *Japan's New Middle-Class* were published. At the time, in the late 1950s and 1960s, access into 'salaryman-ness' (through university education, for instance) translated into economic and financial security (and consequently socio-cultural status) not available to men who may have only had a junior high or high school education. In the post-Bubble era, this finds echoes in the divide between the growing population of men restricted to unstable, irregular contract or *freeter* work (the *precariat*), and those able or lucky enough to enter into the domain of full-time, permanent work, with all the social, financial, and economic dividends that go with the status (see Taga 2011b: 190–193). However, at the same time, there is absolutely no denying that the on-the-ground reality of being a salaryman in neo-liberal, economically downbeat 2010s Japan is quite different from what being a salaryman entailed in the economically buoyant 1960s, 1970s, 1980s, and even into the 1990s. To echo Akiko Takeyama's words, in the context of the harsher, globalized, neo-liberal realities of (both private *and* public sector) organizational culture, idealized (and expected) attributes and behaviour no longer focus around values like 'hard work (*kinben*), perseverance (*nintai*), and group harmony

(*kyôchôsei*)', but rather around 'entrepreneurial spirit (*kigyôka seishin*), competitive society (*kyôsô shakai*), and self-responsibility (*jikosekinin*)' (Takeyama
2010: 234).

Thus, the new post-Bubble shapings of corporate culture have foregrounded
the emergence and discursive privileging of a newer form of idealized corporate
masculinity, influenced by a Euro-American multinational global hypermasculinity. This is a 'style' of masculinity that, in contrast to the company-centred
articulations of 'traditional' salaryman masculinity, is marked by 'increasing
egocentrism, very conditional loyalties (even to the corporation), and a declining
sense of responsibility for others' (Connell 2000: 52). Significantly, this is a
style of corporate masculinity/corporate ideology that is seen, in some quarters,
as providing the key to resuscitating Japan's sluggish economy, and reinvigorating its creative potential (see, for instance, many of the essays in Chandler *et al.*
2011).[2] In some respects, this newer form of salaryman/corporate masculinity
may well come across as more 'liberating', in the sense of opening up spaces for
expression of individuality and flexibility. Thus, linking this back to my informants, within the framework of this kind of economic rationalist, numbers-driven,
egocentric emergent hegemonic masculinity that, at the time of our conversations was starting to gain visibility, a slightly idiosyncratic, nonconformist high-
performer like Kimura Kenji of Northern Print would more likely be an exemplar
than someone like Matsumoto Tadashi of Northern Energy. The latter's strong
sense of responsibility and conformity, as well as his sober, conservative,
'respectable' demeanour and outlook, it may be recalled from our earlier chapters, if anything, made him an exemplar of 'traditional' salaryman masculinity
along the lines of the JTB guide referred to in the Introduction.

Significantly, in relation to gender in the context of corporate culture, while
on the surface the newer shapings of corporate masculinity may come across as
less patriarchal and gender exclusivist than the 'Japan Inc.'-era discourses, the
reality is more complex. As authors such as Connell (2000: 39–66) and Kimmel
(2001) have cautioned, despite their (superficially) 'increasingly libertarian sexuality' (Connell 2000: 52), these newer discourses of corporate masculinity may
be no less patriarchal and heteronormative than older forms of hegemonic masculinity, albeit in different ways. Indeed, in the harsher, more efficiency-driven
post-Bubble organizational culture, if anything, the qualities and attributes defining 'success' in the workplace, rather than being 'gender neutral', have become
even more 'masculine' (see Taga 2011b: 193). Compared with this harder, more
aggressive, 'take-no-prisoners' style of corporate masculinity that is seen as
defining 'success', the older model of salaryman masculinity, along the lines
depicted in the JTB guide, appears almost 'feminine'. Thus, while the *form* of
salaryman masculinity may have altered in response to some of the pressures
and contestations discussed, the core ideological assumptions at the heart of the
discourse, such as the work/masculinity nexus and the expectations of the man
as heterosexual reproducer, have not altered significantly.

The juxtaposition of the two 'styles' of salaryman masculinity are skilfully
captured in one particular scene in Kurosawa Kiyoshi's 2008 award-winning

feature film, *Tokyo Sonata*. The film, which I have discussed at length elsewhere (see Dasgupta 2011), revolves around the impact of corporate restructuring upon a seemingly average, everyday, middle-class family (a '*goku futsû kazoku*'), with a salaryman father, a *sengyô shufu* mother, and two sons, living in the anywhere/everywhere landscape of suburban Japan. The father, Sasaki Ryûhei, initially comes across as something of a 'poster boy' for 'Japan Inc.-era salaryman masculinity – a forty-six-year-old middle-management *kachô* (section manager) in the administrative division of a large organization. Ryûhei's seemingly predictable middle-class salaryman life is abruptly shattered when, as a result of organizational outsourcing to China, he is suddenly laid off, a victim of the coldly efficient economic rationalist realities of post-Bubble Japan. Unable to reveal his 'unemployed' status at home, Ryûhei spends his days alternating between killing time at a city-centre park populated by homeless 'down-and-outs' and unemployed salarymen like himself, and visiting *Hello Work*, the (ironically named) official employment exchange, in search of a job commensurate with his white-collar managerial expertise.

At first these efforts seem to be in vain, but he finally gets short-listed for a white-collar management position. The scene where Ryûhei is being interviewed for the job brings into sharp relief the contrast between the discourse of salaryman masculinity privileged when Ryûhei was being 'crafted' into it (as during the Bubble years), and the dominant articulations of its twenty-first-century counterpart. In contrast to Ryûhei's almost frumpily old-fashioned presentation, his interviewer comes across as a fashionably groomed, slick young thirties-something embodiment of the new post-Bubble generation of salarymen. In language normally reserved for subordinates, the interviewer asks (the age-wise, senior) Ryûhei what specific skills or talents he can bring to the organization. Ryûhei fumbles at trying to come up with anything convincing, other than the ability to sing *karaoke* and his long experience of maintaining smooth interpersonal relations in the workplace – well-recognized attributes of the earlier generation of generalist managers, but clearly out of synch with the requirements of the new specific-skills-based workplace ideology. Ryûhei's humiliation is sealed when his sneering younger interviewer orders him to demonstrate his *karaoke* skills there-and-then, using a pen as a proxy microphone.

This scene in the film signals the juncture when the reality that he has slipped out of the markers of hegemonic masculinity finally sinks in, and the remainder of the film deals with the spin-offs from this on himself and each member of his family. I have zoomed in on this particular scene here because it *visually* articulates the dynamics and undercurrents within hegemonic masculinity that have informed the discussion in this book; that, to return to Connell's words, hegemony 'is a historically mobile relation [and] [i]ts ebb and flow is a key element of the picture of masculinity' (Connell 1995: 77, 78). Within this quote I believe the 'ebb-and-flow' aspect is particularly significant. What we see in the above scene in *Tokyo Sonata* is not so much a sudden disconnected jump from one style of privileged masculinity to another. Rather, underlying the shift from when Ryûhei would have been an embodiment of the hegemonic ideal, to his trendy young interviewer becoming the 'ideal', are the processes of 'internal hegemony' that, drawing on Demetriou (2001), I have discussed previously – the 'ebb and flow', referred to above, is constituted through undercurrents and cross-currents of appropriation, incorporation, resistance, subversion, and playful engagement, between the hegemonic and other discourses of masculinity. Thus, the hegemonic ideals as we see them today incorporate within them aspects both from the older 'Japan Inc.'-era discourse of salaryman masculinity *as well as* aspects from other discourses of masculinity – for instance, the *otaku*, or *sôshokukei danshi*, or for that matter, the pro-feminist sentiments of some of the 1990s men's groups.

Moreover, foregrounding these shifting articulations are both the broader, longer-term socio-historical framework of Japanese modernity and late modernity *and* the specific historical moment. Thus, in 2011, in the wake of the earthquake/tsunami on 11 March and subsequent nuclear crisis in Fukushima, a new discourse of 'disaster masculinity' appears to be taking shape. The expression of this comes through, for instance, in the coolly composed grit and perseverance of the then Chief Cabinet Secretary Edano Yukio during media appearances (in contrast to the bumbling ineptitude shown by many other officials and politicians) in the immediate post-crisis weeks and months, or in the spirit of selflessness, harking back to the *messhi hôkô* ('selfless devotion') of feudal *samurai* and 'Economic Miracle'-era *kigyô senshi* discussed in Chapter 2, of the so-called 'Fukushima 50' who (apparently) chose to stay on at the crippled Fukushima nuclear reactor, battling exhaustion and potentially jeopordizing their health and even lives, in an effort to prevent the reactor from going into meltdown (see, for instance, *BBC News Asia-Pacific*, 17 March 2011).

How this plays out in years to come, in terms of shaping the contours of socio-culturally hegemonic masculinity, will be worth tracking.[3] At the end of the day, underlying the articulations of the one discourse of masculinity, that within the interplay of multiple discourses presents as the socio-culturally privileged hegemonic one, are, to borrow from Nana Okura Gagné's insightful and richly nuanced doctoral thesis on everyday practices of salarymen, 'socio-cultural processes by which an individual, as far as possible, receives, interprets, negotiates with, and further acts upon issues within the limits of the existing ideologies, practices and institutions that have been inherited from the past' (Gagné 2010: 15). In this sense, the 'micro' negotiations in which the young men of Northern Energy and Northern Print were engaging in the threshold years of the twenty-first century continue to have ripples for the 'craftings' of salaryman masculinity today.

Coda: back to the 'micro'

Finally, in light of the above comments, we cannot but help speculate about where those young Northern Energy and Northern Print salarymen are today, a decade on from our conversations. How might they have coped with some of the pressures, discussed in the preceding section, of being a 'successful' salaryman in the 2000s and 2010s? Or, for that matter, do they still define themselves against the markers of salaryman masculinity? Did Kimura Kenji, as he so confidently predicted he would in the late 1990s, really end up quitting his salaryman job at Northern Print (assuming that Northern Print itself, like so many other small to medium organizations, did not end up folding)? Or did the responsibility of fatherhood and having to be a *daikokubashira* whittle away his bravado and risk-taking? What about his personality-wise polar opposite counterpart at Northern Energy, Matsumoto Tadashi? Has he, as he approaches the age of forty, moved into management as he expected he would, and as would have been almost automatic under the 'Japan Inc.'-era lifetime employment/seniority system? Did he indeed, as he had predicted he would when talking about his future life-path, end up as a *tanshin funin*, living away from his family for an extended period due to work transfers? What about some of the others a decade or so down the track? Is Arai Jun still with the same male partner, and have they managed to arrange to live together in the same city? Did he end up 'coming out' at work? If not, how has he continued using the *gomakasu* strategies discussed in Chapter 6 to negotiate with heteronormative expectations in the workplace, particularly if he has moved up the organizational hierarchy?[4]

However, of all those young men with whom I interacted for almost two years, I wonder most about Shin'ya Naohiko of Northern Energy, perhaps my 'favourite' informant, the one I came closest to in blurring the line between 'research informant' and friend, something good, 'objective' researchers are supposed not to do, but which invariably happens (see, for instance, Newton 1993).[5] Shin'ya-san, as we may recall, despite only having a high school education, was far more introspective and analytical in his responses than most of his university-educated peers. As may be recalled, he had hoped to become a professional ice hockey player, but this career dream was aborted through injury. When we first met he was a carefree single young man with lots of dreams, such as going back to study, or travelling to places like Egypt. We quickly clicked at the Northern Energy focus group discussion. We subsequently went out together for drinks, and he introduced me to his new girlfriend. His girlfriend had just returned to study, so they had no intention in the short/medium term to get into a permanent arrangement like marriage. Shin'ya-san also once invited me to the Northern Energy dormitory for single employees, thus giving me an opportunity to observe dormitory life on the ground. As we know, despite having no intention of 'settling down', by the time of our second round of interviews he was married and father to a newborn baby girl. Becoming a father, as he told me in our final meeting, had, on the one hand, resulted in him gaining added trust and respect from his colleagues. However, at the same time, it had made it 'that much harder to quit the company' (Shin'ya, Round 2: 6). That was really our last meaningful interaction. I have often wondered how his life has shaped up since. His daughter, newly born at the time, would now be in the upper grades of primary school. How has he dealt with the *daikokubashira* realities, as his daughter progressed from infancy to childhood and now towards adolescence? Or, for that matter, are he and his wife (formerly girlfriend) still together, or are they among the growing statistics of divorce in post-Bubble Japan? What about at work – has he moved up towards management, or, in a system where seniority no longer guarantees automatic promotion, has his lack of a university qualification been an obstacle? Or, for that matter, is he still at Northern Energy?

Given the above musings about Shin'ya-san and the others, it is tempting to go back and do a longitudinal follow-up study, similar to Kaori Okano's recently published research on a group of women whom she first started interviewing in the late 1980s as part of a school-to-work transition study, and subsequently followed through into adulthood and towards middle age (Okano 2009). In the future, I may well consider doing something similar – returning to those Northern Energy and Northern Print informants who I am able to trace, to map out their life trajectories and narratives since our conversations in the late 1990s. However, for the purpose of *this* book, I have deliberately chosen to focus on that particular historical moment when they were manoeuvring their way through the shifting discursive currents of what it meant to be a man and a salary*man* in post-Bubble Japan. As I emphasized in the opening chapter, their voices (and my reflections on them) were, and always will be, a deliberate pause in the ongoing narrative of masculinit*ies* – hegemonic or otherwise – situated within the overall historical trajectory of Japanese industrial capitalism, and associated conditions of modernity and late modernity.

Glossary of Japanese terms

Bônenkai	End-of-year party, often organization/workplace based
Buchô	Head of department in an organization; (department) director
Buka	Workplace subordinate/junior
Daikokubashira	Literally, central support pillar of a house; more generally, the (typically male) mainstay or provider of a household
Dansei	Male, man, masculine
Ian-ryokô	Company-sponsored recreational trip
Ichininmae	Literally one full serving (of food) for one person; more generally (acquiring) the status of fully mature social adult through marriage and/or regular employment
Izakaya	Relatively informal, relaxed eating/drinking establishment which acts as both a bar/pub serving alcoholic (and non-alcoholic) drinks, as well as serving a variety of Japanese and non-Japanese finger-foods and snacks. These establishments are popular for after-work drinks and social gatherings
Jômu	Managing director
Josei	Female, woman, feminine
Jôshi	Workplace superior
Jôshiki	Common sense; general (social) knowledge; socially sanctioned etiquette
Kachô	Section chief/section manager within an organization
Kaichô	Chairperson of an organization
Kaisha	private firm, company
Kakarichô	Subsection chief within an organization
Kenshyû	Training; study (generally of a professional/technical nature)
Kobun	Literally, child-role (in a parent-role/child-role pairing). More generally refers to the junior/younger partner in mentor/protégé-type relationships
Kôhai	One's junior in an organization, school, university, sports team, etc.

Manga	Comic
OL	Stands for 'Office Lady'. Term used to denote female clerical employees in organizations, performing general secretarial/support work
Onna	Woman, female, girl (especially when used with suffix ~*no ko*)
Otoko	Man, male, boy (especially when used with suffix ~*no ko*)
Otokorashii	Manly, masculine
Otokorashisa	Manliness, masculinity
Oyabun	The 'parent-role' in the *oyabun/kobun* mentor/protégé-pairing
Sarariiman	From 'salaryman'. In theory, any employee receiving a monthly salary; however, generally understood to designate male, full-time, white-collar permanent employees of private sector (sometimes public sector) organizations
Seken	The 'world'; society; public opinion; social consensus
Sengyô Shufu	'Full-time' housewife; a woman who is primarily a homemaker
Senpai	One's senior in an organization, school, university, sports club
Shachô	President of a private corporate organization
Shakaijin	Literally, 'society/social person'. Generally refers to a fully mature adult with responsibilities. Typically the status is acquired upon entry into full-time work
Shataku	Company housing
Shinnyû Shain	New entrant into a company
Tanshin Funin	Workers forced to live away from their families for an extended period of time for reasons related to work (such as job transfers)
Tenkei	Model; stereotype; archetype
Torishimariyaku	Member of a Board of Directors
Tsukiai	Socializing between individuals, generally work based

Appendix: profile of informants

Northern Energy (NE)

Pseudonym	Age (+)	No. of years with firm (+)	Area of work	Education	Marital status	Other comments
Murayama Satoshi	30	5	General Admin.	U	Married	• Father of newborn
Shin'ya Naohiko	22	4	Systems Support	HS	Married	• Single at first interview • Became father over course of interaction
Minami Toshio	19	1	Sales	U		
Matsumoto Tadashi	28	3.5	Accounts	U	Single	• Liaison person for NE • Engaged
Taoka Kiyoshi	25	1	Technical Planning	U	Single (but engaged)	• Transferred after first interview
Nohara Nori	19	2	Repair	HS	Single	
Imai Shinji	26	4	Customer Relations	U	Single	
Miura Tôru	20	5 months	Accounts	TC	Single	
Ogasawara Takurô	25	2.5	Design/ Planning	U	Single	
Matsuzaka Kôhei	20	3	Accounts	HS	Single	
Kobayashi Kazushi	24	3	Accounts	U	Single	
Ishida Naoki	21	3	Accounts	HS	Single	
Murai Yukihiro	25		Customer Relations	U	Single	• Only participated in focus interview • Initial NE liaison but transferred
Makimura Keisuke	23	1.5	Design/ Planning	U	Single	
Satô Hiroshi	23	3	Planning	U	Single	
Yoshida Shun'ichi	20	6 months	Repairs	TC	Single	
Yamazaki Tsuyoshi	28		Engineering	U	Married	• Only focus group
Kishida Takuya	27		Engineering	U	Single	• Only focus group

Notes
(+): At the time of first individual interview.
U: University, HS: High School, TC: Technical College.

Northern Print (NP)

Pseudonym	*Age (+)*	*No. of years with firm (+)*	*Area of work*	*Education*	*Marital status*	*Other comments*
Kimura Kenji	25	3	Sales	U	Married	• NP Liaison person • Became father over course of interaction
Saiki Yasuo	23	5	Technical/ Shop-floor	HS	Single	
Tanaka Tetsu	27			TC	Single	• Only participated in focus group
Fujita Yûji	27	2	Sales	HS	Married	• Changed jobs to Northern Print from elsewhere
Shimizu Ayaki	26	1.5	Computer Systems	U	Single	• Quit before 2nd interview
Kajima Daisuke	28	7	Technical/ Shopfloor Manager	TC	Married	
Takahashi Yoshio	23	3	Technical/ Shopfloor	TC	Single	
Hamada Shigeru	25	Less than 1	Shop-floor (but intern)	U	Single	• President's son • Previously in different firm • Was being groomed for eventual takeover
Katayama Katsuhiko	26	4	Sales	U	Single	• Transferred after 1st interview
Inoue Toshifumi	26	1.5	Technical/ shop-floor	U	Single	
Kurihara Hidetoshi	28	5	Shop-floor but Accounts related	U	Married	
Nakamura Tetsuya	26	7	Shopfloor	HS	Single	

Notes

(+): At the time of first individual interview.

U: University, HS: High School, TC: Technical College.

Other

Pseudonym	*Age*	*No of years with firm*	*Area of work*	*Education*	*Marital status*	*Other comments*
Arai Jun	25	1	Public Corporation: Customer Service	University	In a relationship with boyfriend in another city	• Not part of regular pool of informants • Self-identified as gay

Notes

1 Introduction: salarymen in the 'Lost Decade'

1 Emphasis dropped henceforth, unless specifically marking out the term.

2 Another 'exemplar' of this new style of corporate masculinity is the *zainichi* (Korean-Japanese) founder and CEO of telecommunications corporation Softbank.

3 I am grateful to Chikako Nihei for drawing my attention to this band. Another example in contemporary youth/popular culture is some of the 'tongue-in-cheek' representations of the salaryman in the music group World Order's music video clips.

4 This applies even to works such as Ogasawara (1998) and Sakai (2000) that may appear to focus on the salaryman as a *gendered* construct, but only skirt around the issue. However there are exceptions. Anne Allison's early ethnographic study of a hostess bar explores the ways in which the salarymen frequenting the establishment engaged with dominant discourses and ideologies surrounding gender, sexuality, and corporate masculinity (Allison 1994). Some of the Japanese works emerging from the interrogations of masculinity (discussed below) in the 1990s also addressed issues related to the model of masculinity embodied in the salaryman (Inoue *et al.* 1995: 215–233; Nakamura 1996; Toyoda 1997: 91–156).

5 The essence of *daikokubashira* masculinity is best conveyed by Tom Gill's observation that 'in the image of the *daikokubashira*, man merges with pillar. It is an image of reliability, strength, of statis' (Gill 2003: 144).

6 For a detailed discussion of the teasing out and unpacking of the actual term 'masculinity', see Dasgupta 2005a: 22–30.

7 The term *dansei*, comprised of *dan*, the Chinese reading of the *kanji* character for the Japanese word, *otoko* (man/male) and *sei*, the suffix used to denote 'sex', could connote either male *gender* or male *sex* (in the biological sense). Thus, *danseigaku* was/is used as a descriptor for research on masculinities, and men's/masculinity studies as an academic discipline, along with the somewhat less common *dansei kenkyû* (research into men). In terms of everyday parlance the term *otoko*, or *otoko no hito* (adult man/male person)/*otoko no ko* (male child), is more widespread than the more formal, academic-sounding *dansei*. The term 'masculinity' is translated either as *danseisei* (literally, 'the quality of maleness'), or, more commonly, *otokorashisa*. Strictly speaking, *otokorashisa* would refer to 'manliness' rather than 'masculinity'. However, scholars, including Itô Kimio, the academic associated with bringing *danseigaku* into the mainstream in the 1990s, often apply the term to refer to 'masculinity' (see Dasgupta (2009: 85, 86, n.9) for a discussion of the complexities of discussing terminology related to gender and masculinity across languages, specifically Japanese and English).

8 For an excellent discussion of the genealogy of research into men and masculinities in Japan, see Taga 2003a; also Taga 2005.

9 I use both *ideology* and *discourse* as theoretical underpinnings framing my discussion. While the two concepts may be (and often are) treated independently, they are,

nevertheless intertwined, particularly in my application of them. While ideology has myriad meanings and applications (see Eagleton 1991; Cavallaro 2001), my deployment of the term references it as 'a set of ideas through which people fashion themselves and others within specific socio-historical contexts, and through which the prosperity of certain groups is concerned' (Cavallaro 2001: 76). In this regard, ideology may be thought of as one of the 'tools' through which hegemony operates, a 'particular set of effects *within* discourses' (Eagleton 1991: 194; emphasis in original). I use *discourse* in the sense of a body of knowledge built around specific culturally and historically produced meanings – thus the discourse of the salaryman would refer to all the meanings, articulations, actions, associations, and practices built up around the term. Moreover, discourses are processes that have *ideologies* – of class, of gender, of nation, for instance – embedded within them. In this sense, discourse is not only a process in and of itself, but also an *ideological* process (Steinberg 1991: 187).

2 Framing the 'macro': historicizing salaryman masculinity

1 Like 'salaryman', the term 'white-collar' too can be fraught with definitional inconsistencies. White-collar, in terms of a broad categorization, refers to workers engaged in 'managerial or intellectual work' (Levison cited in Southern 2000: 193; also Mills 1956). Conversely, the label blue-collar is applied to workers performing physical/manual labour. However, as Southern points out, such watertight distinctions are far from rigorous. This is particularly the case in the context of Japanese companies (see Taga 2011c: 8). For example, some of my own informants who were performing technical/manual work still considered themselves salarymen, since they were regular employees of an organization, and received a monthly salary. Indeed, Okamoto and Sasano, in their discussion of media representations of the salaryman during the postwar era, mention the brief media appearance of the term 'female salaryman (*joshi sarariiman*)' in the 1950s (Okamoto and Sasano 2001: 24), and I have heard women employed in non-clerical roles, refer to themselves as a 'salaryman'.

2 As William Kelly, writing in the mid-1980s, noted, it was the 'wide-appeal, not universal attainment of this [middle-class] ideal' (Kelly 1986: 605) that traditionally accounted for high rates of middle-class self-identification until very recently. This was a perception that was particularly entrenched during the economic prosperity years of the 1970s and 1980s. Although it has shifted considerably in the wake of the social and economic upheavals of the 1990s, with greater public discourse on social inequality (Ishida and Slater 2010b: 6–8), the 'ideal' (perhaps 'myth') of the middle class, in relation to lifestyle and values, continues to exert a powerful influence into the present. For discussion of the debates relating to class in postwar Japan over the years see Kishimoto 1978; Steven 1983; Ishida 1993; Satô 2000; Kelly 2002; Ishida and Slater 2010a, 2010b.

3 Andrew Gordon, for instance, points out that the term was around in the 1910s alongside other more generic terms for middle-class salary earners such as *hôkyû seikatsu-sha* (people receiving a salary), *chishiki kaikyû* (intellectual class), *zunô rôdôsha* (brain workers), *shinchûkan kaikyû* (new middle class), as well as the older pre-Meiji *koshi-ben* (Gordon 2002: 113; also Kinmonth 1981: 289). There is a substantial body of both academic and non-academic literature – primarily in Japanese – dealing with the history of the salaryman; for instance, the detailed study by Matsunari *et al.* (1957) of the salaryman in prewar and immediate postwar Japan (with some comparison with the salaryman's counterpart in the Soviet Union and the United States), Suyama's discussion of the history of *manga* representations of the salaryman (Suyama 1965), Takeuchi's analysis of the history of the salaryman (Takeuchi 1996, 1997), Chapter 1 of Umezawa's detailed study of the salaryman (Umezawa 1997), Tanaka and Nakamura's discussion of the 1920s/1930s periodical *Sarariiman* (Tanaka

and Nakamura 1999), and Iwase's comprehensive study of urban middle-class life during the 1920s/1930s (Iwase 2006). For an excellent discussion of the emergence of the salaryman in English, see Kinmonth 1981, esp. ch. 8.

4 Similarly, Harry Oshima, discussing labour force distribution by occupational category, gives a percentage of 5.4 falling into the category of 'professional, technical, managerial' in 1920, which by 1930 had increased to 6.1 per cent (Oshima 1982: 34; also Iwase 2006: 25, 26). Takeuchi (1996: 131) notes that in Taishô 9 (1920) the 'salaryman' accounted for 5.5 per cent of the employed population, with one in five employed persons in Tokyo being salaried employees (*gekkyû-tori*) (see also Kelly 2002: 127 n.2).

5 For a fascinating discussion of the cartoon and *manga* depictions of the salaryman (and his antecedents) from the Meiji period right up until the mid-twentieth century see Suyama 1965.

6 Tanaka and Nakamura (1999) discuss *Sarariiman* at some length in their study of this periodical, which had until their 'rediscovery' of it largely been forgotten.

7 Arguably, had Japan not gone down the path of fascism and military aggression from the mid-1930s, and had the emerging civil society and economy of the 1920s and early 1930s continued to expand, salaryman masculinity may well have become dominant earlier. Indeed, as Iwase notes, the immediate postwar slogan of *Shôwa hachinen ni kaerô* ('Let's Return to Shôwa 8 [1933]') supports such speculation. This was the year when the Japanese economy appeared to have shaken off the worst effects of the global Great Depression triggered by the 1929 Wall Street Crash, and seemed on track to renewed economic growth and prosperity (Iwase 2006: 255–257). However, this sense of optimism was short-lived with a succession of domestic and international political and military crises forming the backdrop to the growing grip of military-backed authoritarianism through the mid- and late 1930s.

8 For a discussion of the influence of the war and wartime experience (including experience in the military) on the corporate executives and salarymen who shaped the recovery and the 'Economic Miracle' see Hazama 1996; Amano 2006; and Kimura 2006.

9 The 'Income Doubling Plan' was initiated by the administration of Prime Minister Ikeda Hayato in 1960. Through a combination of macro-economic policies (in particular, boosting domestic consumption), the Plan aimed to double national income (measured by real GNP) within a period of ten years. In reality, this target was reached within seven years (see Uchino 1983: chs 4, 5; Hein 1993: 112–115).

10 As Brinton in her study of the gender dynamics of the 'Economic Miracle' points out, the structure of the taxation regime also detracted from married women working full-time. If a spouse earned above a set ceiling amount, the husband (as primary income earner) would lose the tax exemption that applied to any spousal income earned below that ceiling (Brinton 1993: 89, n.10). In addition, we need to remember that we are talking about *culturally privileged* ideals here. The reality, even at the high point of this salaryman/*sengyô shufu* hegemony's pervasiveness in the 1960s, was that the *sengyô shufu* was actually more than likely to be a *kengyô shufu*, a 'part-time housewife', i.e. a housewife with a part-time job (Ueno 1988: 173–174; Uno 1993: 304).

11 Personal household savings, which became an important pool to tap into for financing investment without the need for overseas borrowing, was a significant component of economic growth over these decades. Over these decades, the household savings rate increased from 12.2 per cent in 1955 to 20.5 per cent in 1973 (Tipton 2008: 194; see also Horioka 1993: 280–289).

12 Evidence for this appeal of the middle-class ideal is perhaps provided by the progressive standardization and convergence of lifestyle patterns (including leisure activities and consumption) of both white-collar and blue-collar workers over these years; as Tipton points out: 'A 1970 NHK survey of blue-collar and white-collar workers revealed almost identical uses of time in a "typical" day for sleeping, meals and personal hygiene' (Tipton 2008: 193; see Hazama (1976: 45, table 14) for breakdown of the survey).

13 *Kigyô shôsetsu* were – and continue to be – a visible genre within popular literature alongside *sarariiman manga*. Such works, as noted earlier in the chapter, date at least as far back as the 1920s with the publication of Maeda Hajime's *Sarariiman Monogatari* ('Tales of the Salaryman') and its sequel. For a discussion of this genre, particularly in the context of the postwar high economic growth era, see Sataka 1991; Tao 1996; also Umezawa 1997: 45–47. For discussion of *manga*, see Schodt 1986: 111–114; Kinsella 2000: 79–84; Matanle *et al.* 2008.

14 The second and third parts of Tessa Morris-Suzuki's very engaging oral history account of the Shôwa era convey a keen sense of the upheavals and excitement surrounding the student protests in the 1960s, as seen through the eyes of her informants who lived through the events (Morris-Suzuki 1984: parts 3 and 4; also McCormack 1971; Krauss 1974).

15 The Oil Crisis of 1973 when OPEC quadrupled the price of oil, and the preceding 'Nixon Shock' of 1972 when the Nixon Administration in the USA ended the fixed dollar/yen exchange rate and imposed surcharges on Japanese imports, are generally regarded as the watershed between the end of the high-growth era, and the subsequent years of slower economic growth (Tipton 2008: 202, 203). The repercussions of these two successive 'shocks' had the immediate effect of putting the brakes on economic growth – whereas GNP growth in 1972 had been 8.5 per cent, by 1974 it had fallen to *minus* 1.4 per cent, and the inflation rate was over 30 per cent (Itô 1992: 70, 71). However, in the long term the economy was able to recover within a couple of years. Moreover, the Oil Crisis prompted a shift away from energy-intensive manufacturing industries to an emphasis on more value-added, technology-intensive sectors like electronics and information technology (Tipton 2008: 206, 207). In this respect, the post-Oil Crisis years not only signified the transition to a post-industrial, mature economy, but also contained the seeds for the 'Bubble Economy' boom of the 1980s and its collapse in the 1990s.

16 The immediate trigger for the recession of the 1990s was the 'bursting' of the artificially inflated land and stock 'bubble' that had built up over the late 1980s, in January 1991. Over the following years the total value of stock and land prices dropped sharply by around $16 trillion, or, according to Jeff Kingston, 'equivalent to three times the size of Japan's GDP' (Kingston 2011: 24). The real economic growth rate fell from 3.1 per cent in 1991 to 0.4 per cent in 1992, and by 1994 unemployment had climbed to 3 per cent, and continued to edge upwards through the rest of the decade (Tipton 2008: 225). For more discussion of the background factors see Yoshikawa 2002; Kingston 2011.

17 The total number of 'dispatched workers', for instance, increased from just over 200,000 in 1990 to close to half a million in 2000, and close to two million by 2008 (Japan Institute for Labour Policy and Training 2011: 14).

18 A combination of the English 'freelance' and the German-derived Japanese term for casual/temporary work, *arubaito*.

19 The birth rate had been decreasing steadily since the early 1970s, and by the late 1990s had fallen to 1.34, well below the population replacement figure (Roberson and Suzuki 2003a: 10; Taga 2005: 156).

20 See, for instance, Ujigawa (1981), *Gekkan Rôdô Kumiai* (1990), Ôtani (1993), Uchihashi *et al.* (1994), *Shûkan Daiyamondo* (1995), Shimada *et al.* (1996), Ôta (1997), Umezawa (1997), *Asahi Shinbun* Shakai-bu (1998), *Dame-Ren* (1999: 19–82), Okamoto and Sasano (2001) for some of the discussion during the 1990s problematizing the salaryman, but not necessarily through a lens of gender.

21 In fact, there had been the odd newspaper or magazine article focusing on masculinity, even in the prewar decades. See, for instance, Ôta Yôko's reflection on 'maleness' (*Otoko to iu mono*) in the November 1935 issue of the journal *Nihon Hyôron*, and the panel discussion between three contemporary (and well-known) female literary figures – Uno Chiyo, Enchi Fumiko, and Hirabayashi Taiko – which appeared in a

March 1959 issue of the women's magazine *Fujin Kôron*. See Taga (2005; also Naka-mura and Nakamura 1997) for examples of some of the early academic works focus-ing on masculinity. Taga (155) locates the emergence of masculinity as a focus of *academic* scrutiny to the publication in 1986 of Watanabe Tsuneo's *Datsu-dansei no jidai* ('The Post-Male Age').

22 Despite the use of a name (Men's Liberation) suggestive of a more conservative, anti-feminist agenda along the lines of some of the men's groups in countries like the United States (such as the Promise Keepers), right from the onset, these groups have had considerable intersections – both at an intellectual and a personal level – with academic and community-based women's groups and feminist organizations. There were also intersections with other social activist and interest groups gaining in promi-nence and visibility through the 1990s, such as advocacy groups for sexual minorities (e.g. OCCUR), and other specific interest groups, such as fatherhood and childcare groups like *Ikujiren* (see Roberson and Suzuki 2003a: 11).

3 Men's stories of becoming *otoko*

1 All names of the informants are pseudonyms. When discussing specific individuals, I refer to them either by their full 'name' in Japanese order (family name, followed by personal name) or, when referring to an individual previously mentioned, through the use of the suffix '-*san*' attached to the family name. The use of *san* (usually after the family name, but, in some situations, also after the personal name) is the most common (though by no means, the only) form of address in Japan.

2 It was only after entering the workforce, where he encountered quite a few women doing technical work, that Shin'ya-san started to question his earlier assumptions about the non-suitability of women for 'men's work'. Ironically, as mentioned, his own mother had engaged in conventionally 'unfeminine' types of work.

3 There may have been a few considerations at play here. First, unlike many of the school ethnographies I referred to, my informants were *adults* recalling their experi-ences, rather than as adolescents still coming to terms with their sexualities. In addi-tion, the specifics of the researcher/informant relationship may also have precluded reference to such 'sensitive' issues.

4 Arai Jun was not actually part of my 'pool' of informants. However, due to the sensi-tivities surrounding breaching the mutually maintained façade of heteronormativity between the informants in Northern Energy and Northern Print, I arranged, through networks, to conduct a discussion with Arai-san as he was willing to talk to me about his 'non-heterosexual' identity.

5 The Ni-chome precinct in Tokyo's Shinjuku locality contains over 200 gay bars and clubs concentrated within a few urban blocks, making the area a 'gay ghetto' that, particularly in the 1990s, attracted media attention, often of a sensationalist nature.

4 Becoming *shakaijin:* 'craftings' into salaryman masculinity

1 Ogasawara, for instance, points out that in large organizations with more than 1,000 employees (and Northern Energy would fall into this category) women accounted for only 1 per cent of managers of the *buchô* class (general or department managers), 2 per cent of *kachô* (section managers), and 6 per cent of even the lowest managerial rank of *kakarichô* (chief, or subsection managers) (Ogasawara 1998: 20).

2 At this point in time (in the late 1990s), the issue of (apparently) delinquent youth 'hanging out' (or rather squatting on the ground) in public places like entrances to con-venience stores had become something of a 'moral panic' social phenomenon, seen by many conservative observers and commentators as symptomatic of a general moral decline among youth.

3 The relationship between dyed hair and workplace appearance is significant, particularly at that historical moment. Dyeing hair as a fashion statement started to become increasingly noticeable from the 1990s; prior to then it had largely been restricted to particular subcultures or industries like fashion or music. However, despite the widespread public visibility from the 1990s of dyed or bleached hair, employees in 'respectable' organizations are looked upon unfavourably if they have visibly tinted hair. This is especially so in the case of male employees (Lee 2003: 40; see also *Asahi Shinbun* (1998) for a series on attitudes during these years to male employees wearing ear-studs/earrings).

4 When describing these practices for which the recruits underwent training, he also mentioned 'serving tea' (*ocha-kumi*). This took me by surprise, as this practice in particular marks the gendered boundary between salaryman masculinity and OL femininity in the workplace (see Ogasawara 1998: 40–43). Northern Energy would have been a *very* progressive organization indeed if it instructed *both* female and male recruits in the correct way of serving tea! However, this was not the case, as Imai-san quickly corrected himself and clarified that the male entrants were not instructed in the etiquette of serving tea.

5 Dorinne Kondo's description of the 'Ethics School' where she and her co-workers underwent a gruelling physical and mental schedule of 'self-improvement' provides an excellent account of the incorporation of these practices into the workplace arena as a means of 'crafting' bodies and minds (Kondo 1990: 76–104). See also Frühstück and Ben-Ari (2002: 19) on 'courses' offered by the Self Defence Force to private organizations.

5 Working with salaryman masculinity

1 For some of these works, particularly over the initial decades of the emergence of masculinity studies, see, for instance, Willis 1979; Game and Pringle 1983; Collinson and Collinson 1989; Collinson 1992; Hood 1993; Roper 1994; Cheng 1996a, 1996b; Collinson and Hearn 1996a, 1996b, 1996c; Beynon 2002; Hearn 2002; McDowell 2003; Wilson 2003.

2 Similarly, many of the early Japanese-language works on masculinity, such as Nakamura (1996) or the *danseigaku* special edition in the Japanese Feminism series edited by Inoue *et al.* (1995), spotlighted the nexus between work and salaryman masculinity.

3 Not a single informant made reference to the military (in the Japanese context, the *jieitai*, the Self Defence Force) when talking about occupations associated with *otoko-rashisa*. As noted in Chapter 2, the military effectively ceased to be a masculine 'ideal' following Japan's defeat in World War Two.

4 The informant who mentioned this noted that his association of a lack of masculinity was restricted to the sales staff (*uriko*), and not to actual bakers (*yaku-hito*) (Imai, Round 1: 8).

5 From the term used – 'stewardess' – it seemed that flight attendants were exclusively female in the mind of the informant who mentioned this occupation (Matsumoto, Round 1: 9).

6 See my discussion of the *tanshin-funin* phenomenon in Chapter 2.

6 Working with heterosexuality: sexuality, marriage, fatherhood, and salaryman masculinity

1 A sample of this literature would includes Burrell and Hearn 1989; Acker 1990; Hearn *et al.* 1989; Collinson 1992; Hearn 1992, 2002; Roper 1994; McDowell 1995; Cheng 1996a; Collinson and Hearn 1996b; Pringle 1993; Mills 1998; Aaltio and Mills 2002; Wilson 2003; Alvesson and Due Billing 2009.

2 The media spotlight on the never-married Tim Cook, who took over as the new CEO of Apple Inc. in August 2011, is an example of this – the fact that his sexual orientation was ambiguous in a corporate landscape dominated by (apparently) *unambiguously* heterosexual CEOs was reason enough for widespread speculation about his sexuality.

3 For discussion of the film, see Buckley (2000) and McLelland (2000: 98–101). The title plays upon a modified version of the slang term for a male homosexual, *okama*. An *okama* can also refer to the pot in which rice was traditionally cooked. The burnt rice that sticks to the bottom and sides of the pot is known as *okoge*. Hence, if the other meaning of *okama* (i.e. homosexual male) is deployed, *okoge* refers to (heterosexual) women who 'stick' to gay men – i.e. prefer the company of, or are infatuated with, gay men. In English the equivalent street term would be 'fag hag', which is the English title that has been used for Nakajima's film (see McLelland 2000: 8, 9; also Pflugfelder 1999: 323, 324).

4 See Dales (2005) for a discussion of the problematics of such an overly simplistic and skewed representation of these women.

5 This combination of attributes traditionally associated with blue-collar/working-class masculinity (hard drinking, fighting) with salaryman masculinity made Kajima-san not unlike the hero of the *manga* series *Sarariiman Kintarô* mentioned in earlier chapters. One could even argue that (like the character Kintarô), by integrating such a history of 'wild' and 'dangerous' masculinity into his present respectable life, he was in fact strengthening and reinforcing hegemonic masculinity, in a way that other informants with a less 'wild' past could not.

6 Both of us then joked that it may be possible to conceive of situations where an unmarried male employee might wear a wedding band-style ring to work, just to gain 'trust'; what this seems to underscore is the element of *projecting*, even *performing* the heterosexual ideal, regardless of what the underlying reality may be.

7 Significantly, this shift in official policy was driven not so much by a genuine commitment to challenging dominant paradigms on gender, but rather by the economic and demographic implications of declining birth rates. Regardless of the motive, one fall-out of this official reassessment of gender roles within the family was a focus on the role of the father within the family. There had, in fact, been an ongoing debate surrounding fatherhood and the place of the father within the household over much of the postwar period, and there is a substantial body of literature in Japanese that reflects some of this richness. See Nakamura and Nakamura (1997) for a list of works dealing with fatherhood published in Japanese; also Hoshi 1995; Ikujiren 1995; Murase 1995; Kodama 2001; Kaizuma 2004; in English, see Ishii-Kuntz 1993, 2003; Jolivet 1997: 61–76; Roberts 2002; Hidaka 2010: 147–154; Taga 2011a. However, they gained heightened prominence in the 1990s, and formed the backdrop to the series of equal opportunity and 'family-friendly' laws and policy initiatives, such as the 'Angel Plan' (1994), the Childcare/Familycare Leave Law 1992 (1999), Basic Law for a Gender-Equal Society (1999), and a strengthened Equal Employment Opportunity Law (1999), aimed at allowing women to remain in the workforce *and* get married and have children, partly through trying to encourage men to take a more active role in childcare and domestic activities. An example of this official 'sanctioning' of active fatherhood through public campaigns was the Ministry of Health and Welfare's 1999 poster promotion featuring Sam, the partner of the (at the time) popular female musician, Namuro Amie, holding the couple's baby son, with the accompanying caption stating that 'Men who do not participate in child-rearing are not called fathers' (*ikuji o shinai otoko o chichi-oya to wa yobanai*) (see Roberts 2002; Taga 2011a: 100, 101). One spin-off of this kind of official sanctioning has been greater visibility in popular culture of men's involvement in child-rearing. This, in turn, led to the growing strength of a public discourse (as evidenced in the pronouncements of some of my informants) that saw fatherhood as somehow 'cool' and glamorous.

8 In general, it is much easier in Japanese (compared with English) to be vague about gender pronouns, something that fitted in perfectly with strategies of *gomakasu* in which Arai-san was engaging.

7 Working with homosociality

1 The term 'homosocial', as I expand on below, has been deployed in varied ways, ranging from purely social superficial interaction within same-sex groups and/or between individuals, to relations infused with erotic tension (for some of these various readings of the term and its associations, see, e.g. Sedgwick 1985; Crowley 1987; Bird 1996; Roper 1996; Buchbinder 1998; McBee 1999).

2 See, e.g. Herdt 1981; Crowley 1987; Sherrod 1987; Papataxiarchis 1991; Nardi 1992a, 1992b; Spangler 1992; Bird 1996; Gutmann 1996; Vale de Almeida 1996: 85–112; McBee 1999.

3 See her *Between Men*, ch. 1, 'Gender Asymmetry and Erotic Triangles', for a discussion of the theoretical constructs bound to her conceptualization of homosocial desire in the context of the literary texts examined (Sedgwick 1985: 21–27).

4 For an engaging and comprehensive discussion of same-sex interaction in feudal Japan see Pflugfelder 1999.

5 Literally, the 'water trade', but more loosely, the bars, restaurants, nightclubs, massage parlours, hostess clubs, and other forms of 'entertainment', which constitute the night-time hospitality sector (see Allison 1994: 33, 34).

6 See, for instance, the various chapters in Hearn *et al.* (1989), Witz *et al.* (1996), and Paetzold (2004).

7 Collinson's descriptions of some of the (often sexually) humiliating initiation rituals targeting new apprentices on the shop-floor is an exception (Collinson 1992: 110–122). Other studies which address similar dynamics of same-sex violence/intimidation/harassment in the context of organizational culture include Vaught and Smith (1980) and Lee (2000: 147–152). Ackroyd and Thompson (1999: passim) and Wilson (2003: 193–195, 201–203) discuss some of the literature in the area. Importantly, it was from around these years that a public discourse about *ijime* (bullying) in the workplace started to become visible in Japan. For instance, in the late 1990s the popular weekly magazine *SPA!* (11 November 1998: 37–42) carried an exposé-style feature (complete with case studies) on violence in corporate organizations (*shanai bôryoku*), and letters to 'problem pages' in salaryman magazines such as *Big Tomorrow*, as well as postings on salaryman websites often featured (and continue to do so) complaints from salarymen who have been the target of bullying by *senpai*, colleagues, or managers.

8 This lack of a cohesive sense of community in Shin'ya-san's dormitory was brought home to me one night when he invited me to stay over in his room, after I had missed the last train during a night out drinking with him (and some of the other head office informants). Over the couple of hours I spent with him in the dormitory I did not encounter a single other resident that night or in the morning. This (lack of interaction), however, as Shin'ya-san mentioned, had not always been the situation. Moreover, talking to informants who were residents in some of Northern Energy's dormitories in other cities, I got the impression that there was greater interaction between residents at these other locations. See Rohlen (1974: 212–225) and Lo (1990: 51–71) for detailed discussions of company dormitory life; also Unami (1994) for a discussion of the surveillance element of company dormitory design.

9 Of interest is the fact that, as discussed at some length in the previous chapter, by the time of our second interview, fatherhood had bestowed a new prestige upon Shin'ya-san. This, as noted, had worked towards *reducing* the distance he perceived between himself and the married men in his workplace.

10 Ronald Dore, writing in the early 1970s, captures some of these shifts:

> Another … recent coinage is *mai-hômu-shugi* or 'my-home-ism'. This refers to the 'privatized concerns of the man of small ambition – chiefly concerned to get a pretty little house and a pretty little wife and two model children, to have a colour TV and a cooler and to join the ranks of *maikaa-zoku*, the 'my car tribe'. The

word has ambiguous connotations. The popular weekly magazines do in part encourage the my-home-ist. They feed his fantasies, extol the pleasures of the consumer society, treat it as natural to be in love with one's wife, and refer to my-home-ism as the trend of the times.... But at the same time they feed the older sensual fantasies of the bar-girl/geisha mistresses and lascivious weekends at hot-spring resorts – enjoyed in the company of one's *workmates* rather than of the wife one married from a sense of family duty, and thus a use of leisure which binds one more closely to one's work and workmates rather than drawing one away from them.

(Dore 1973b: 212, 213) (see also my discussion in Chapter 2)

8 Beyond the 'JTB-Man': looking back from the 2010s

1 In a sense, the disproportionate importance given to technogeek masculinities as evidence of the demise of a hegemonic discourse of masculinity (salaryman, or otherwise) in 2000s Japan resonates with similar claims made in the 1980s about *shinjinrui* masculinities, or for that matter the *mobo* as a trope of masculinity in 1920s Japan (see my discussion in Chapter 2).
2 'Going global', along the lines of 'successful' (and exemplary) corporations like e-business giant Rakuten, which in 2011 introduced English (rather than Japanese) as the language for all internal meetings, seems to be a key theme in much of the literature on 'reinvigorating Japan'.
3 Significantly, both Edano and the 'Fukushima 50' ended up entering into the lexicon of contemporary popular Japan. The top keywords of 2011 included both the 'Fukushima 50' and a newly coined verb '*edaru*' to imply working without taking a break! See Gakuranman.com, 'Top 60 Japanese Buzzwords of 2011'. I am grateful to Alisa Freedman for alerting me to the release of the list.
4 In fact, my conversation with Arai Jun triggered my interest in looking at the intersections between corporate masculinity and non-normative sexualities. I am currently, at the time of writing (December 2011), in the process of completing a research project on gay salarymen's engagements with workplace heteronormativity.
5 Also see Dasgupta (2005a: 54–60) for a detailed discussion of the 'shades-of-grey' in informant/researcher relations, and the overall research process.

References

Aaltio, Iiris and Mills, Albert J. (eds) (2002) *Gender, Identity and the Culture of Organizations*, London: Routledge.

Abegglen, James C. (1958) *The Japanese Factory: Aspects of Its Social Organization*, Glencoe, IL: The Free Press.

Abe, Tsunehisa, Obinata, Sumio, and Amano, Masako (eds) (2006) *Danseishi 3: 'Otokorashia' no Gendaishi* (History of Masculinity Series No. 3: The Contemporary History of 'Manliness/Maleness'), Tokyo: Nihon Keizai Hyôron-sha.

Acker, Joan (1990) 'Hierarchies, Jobs, Bodies: A Theory of Gendered Organizations', *Gender and Society*, 4 (2): 139–158.

Ackroyd, Stephen and Thompson, Paul (1999) *Organizational Misbehaviour*, London: Sage.

Addelston, Judi and Stirratt, Michael (1996) 'The Last Bastion of Masculinity: Gender Politics at the Citadel', in Cliff Cheng (ed.) *Masculinities in Organizations*, Thousand Oaks, CA: Sage, pp. 54–76.

Adkins, Lisa and Merchant, Vicki (eds) (1996) *Sexualizing the Social: Power and the Organization of Sexuality*, New York: St Martin's Press.

Allison, Anne (1994) *Nightwork: Sexuality, Pleasure, and Corporate Masculinity in a Tokyo Hostess Club*, Chicago, IL: University of Chicago Press.

Allison, Anne (2006) *Millennial Monsters: Japanese Toys and the Global Imagination*, Berkeley: University of California Press.

Allison, Anne (2009) 'The Cool Brand, Affective Activism and Japanese Youth', *Theory, Culture and Society*, 26(2–3): 89–111.

Alvesson, Mats and Due Billing, Yvonne (2009, 2nd edn) *Understanding Gender and Organizations*, London: Sage.

Amano, Masako (2006) 'Sôron: "Otoko de Aru Koto" no Sengoshi: Sarariiman, Kigyô Shakai, Kazoku' (Introduction: The Postwar History of 'Being Male/Being a Man': The Salaryman, Corporate Society, Family), in Tsunehisa Abe, Sumio Obinata, and Masako Amano (eds) *Danseishi 3: 'Otokorashia' no Gendaishi* (History of Masculinity Series No. 3: The Contemporary History of 'Manliness/Maleness'), Tokyo: Nihon Keizai Hyôron-sha, pp. 1–32.

Amano, Masako and Kimura, Ryoko (eds) (2003) *Jendaa de Manabu Kyôikugaku* (Studying Education Through Gender), Kyoto: Sekai Shisôsha.

Arai, Shinya (trans. Chieko Mulhern) (1991) *Shôshaman: A Tale of Corporate Japan*, Berkeley: University of California Press.

Asahi Shinbun (1998) 'Dansei Shain no Piasu' (Earrings of Male Employees), 8, 9, 10 April.

Asahi Shinbun Shakai-bu (ed.) (1998) *'Kaisha Ningen'-tachi no Matsuro: Tsugi wa Saraiiman ni Naritakunai* (The End of the 'Company Persons': No one Will want to be Salarymen Next), Tokyo: Daiyamondo-sha.

Asai, Haruo, Itô, Satoru, and Murase, Yukihiro (eds) (2001) *Nihon no Otoko wa Doko kara Kite, Doko e Iku no ka: Dansei Sekushuariti Keisei (Kyôdô Kenkyûkai)* (Where have Japanese Men Come From, Where Are They Going? Construction of Male Sexuality [Collaborative Research]), Tokyo: Jûgatsusha.

Atsumi, Reiko (1979) 'Tsukiai – Obligatory Personal Relationships of Japanese White-collar Company Employees', *Human Organization*, 38(1): 63–70.

Atsumi, Reiko (1980) 'Patterns of Personal Relationships: A Key to Understanding Japanese Thought and Behaviour', *Social Analysis*, 5 (6): 63–78.

Atsumi, Reiko (1989) 'Friendship in Cross-cultural Perspective', in Yoshio Sugimoto and Ross Mouer (eds) *Constructs for Understanding Japan*, London: Kegan Paul International, pp. 130–153.

Ballon, Robert J. (ed.) (1969) *The Japanese Employee*, Tokyo: Sophia University.

Beck, John C. and Beck, Martha N. (1994) *The Change of a Lifetime: Employment Practices Among Japan's Managerial Elite*, Honolulu: University of Hawaii Press.

Ben-Ari, Eyal (2000) '"Not-Precisely-Work": Golf, Entertainment and Imbibement Among Japanese Business Executives in Singapore', in Eyal Ben-Ari and John Clammer (eds) *Japan in Singapore: Cultural Occurrences and Cultural Flows*, Richmond, Surrey: Curzon, pp. 150–174.

Ben-Ari, Eyal (2002) 'At the Interstices: Drinking, Management, and Temporary Groups in a Local Japanese Organization', in Joy Hendry and Massimo Raveri (eds) *Japan at Play: The Ludic and Logic of Power*, London: Routledge, pp. 129–151.

Beynon, John (2002) *Masculinities and Culture*, Buckingham, UK: Open University Press.

Bird, Sharon R. (1996) 'Welcome to the Men's Club: Homosociality and the Maintenance of Hegemonic Masculinity', *Gender and Society*, 10(2): 120–132.

Brinton, Mary C. (1993) *Women and the Economic Miracle: Gender and Work in Postwar Japan*, Berkeley: University of California Press.

British Broadcasting Corporation (BBC) News Asia-Pacific (2011) 'Japan Hails the Heroic "Fukushima 50"', 17 March. Available at www.bbc.co.uk/news/world-asia-pacific-12779510 (last accessed 7 December 2011).

Broadbent, Kaye (2003) *Women's Employment in Japan: The Experience of Part-time Workers*, London: RoutledgeCurzon.

Brod, Harry (ed.) (1987) *The Making of Masculinities: The New Men's Studies*, Boston, MA: Unwin Hyman.

Brod, Harry and Kaufman, Michael (eds) (1994) *Theorizing Masculinities*, Thousand Oaks, CA: Sage.

Buchbinder, David (1998) *Performance Anxieties: Re-producing Masculinity*, St Leonards, NSW: Allen & Unwin.

Buckley, Sandra (2000) 'Sexing the Kitchen: *Okoge* and Other Tales of Contemporary Japan', in Cindy Patton and Benigno Sánchez-Eppler (eds) *Queer Diasporas*, Durham, NC: Duke University Press, pp. 215–244.

Burrell, Gibson, and Hearn, Jeff (1989) 'The Sexuality of Organization', in Jeff Hearn *et al.* (eds) *The Sexuality of Organization*, London: Sage, pp. 1–28.

Buruma, Ian (1984) *A Japanese Mirror: Heroes and Villains of Japanese Culture*, London: Jonathan Cape.

Castro-Vázquez, Genaro (2007) *In the Shadows: Sexuality, Pedagogy and Gender Among Japanese Teenagers*, Lanham, MD: Lexington Books.

Castro-Vázquez, Genaro and Kishi, Izumi (2003) 'Masculinities and Sexuality: The Case of a Japanese Top Ranking Senior High School', *Journal of Gender Studies*, 12(1): 21–33.

Cavallaro, Dani (2001) *Critical and Cultural Theory: Thematic Variations*, London: The Athlone Press.

Chandler, Clay, Chhor, Heang, and Salsberg, Brian (executive eds) (2011) *Reimagining Japan: The Quest for a Future That Works*, San Francisco, CA: Viz Media, LLC.

Cheng, Cliff (ed.) (1996a) *Masculinities in Organizations*, Thousand Oaks, CA: Sage.

Cheng, Cliff (1996b) 'Men and Masculinities Are Not Necessarily Synonymous: Thoughts on Organizational Behavior and Occupational Sociology', in Cliff Cheng (ed.), *Masculinities in Organizations*, Thousand Oaks, CA: Sage, pp. xi–xx.

Cheng, Mariah Mantsun and Kallenberg, Arne L. (1997) 'How Permanent was Permanent Employment? Patterns of Mobility in Japan, 1916–1975', *Work and Occupations*, 24(1): 12–32.

Clark, Rodney (1979) *The Japanese Company*, New Haven, CT: Yale University Press.

Cole, Robert E. (1971) *Japanese Blue Collar: The Changing Tradition*, Berkeley: University of California Press.

Cole, Robert E. and Tominaga, Ken'ichi (1976) 'Japan's Changing Occupational Structure and Its Significance', in Hugh Patrick (ed.) *Japanese Industrialization and its Social Consequences*, Berkeley: University of California Press, pp. 53–95.

Collinson, David L. (1988) ' "Engineering Humour": Masculinity, Joking and Conflict in Shop-floor Relations', *Organization Studies*, 9(2): 181–199.

Collinson, David L. (1992) *Managing the Shopfloor: Subjectivity, Masculinity and Workplace Culture*, Berlin: Walter de Gruyter.

Collinson, David L. and Collinson, Margaret (1989) 'Sexuality in the Workplace: The Domination of Men's Sexuality', in Jeff Hearn *et al.* (eds) *The Sexuality of Organization*. London: Sage, pp. 91–109.

Collinson, David L. and Hearn, Jeff (1996a) 'Breaking the Silence: On Men, Masculinities and Managements', in David L. Collinson and Jeff Hearn (eds) *Men as Managers, Managers as Men: Critical Perspectives on Men, Masculinities and Managements*, London: Sage, pp. 1–24.

Collinson, David L. and Hearn, Jeff (eds) (1996b) *Men as Managers, Managers as Men: Critical Perspectives on Men, Masculinities and Managements*, London: Sage.

Collinson, David and Hearn, Jeff (1996c) ' "Men" at "Work": Multiple Masculinities/ Multiple Workplaces', in Máirtín Mac an Ghaill (ed.) *Understanding Masculinities: Social Relations and Cultural Arenas*, Buckingham, UK: Open University Press, pp. 61–76.

Condry, Ian (2011) 'Love Revolution: Anime, Masculinity, and the Future', in Sabine Frühstück and Anne Walthall (eds) *Recreating Japanese Men*, Berkeley: University of California Press, pp. 262–283.

Connell, R.W. (1987) *Gender and Power: Society, the Person and Sexual Politics*, Cambridge: Polity Press.

Connell, R.W. (1989) 'Cool Guys, Swots and Wimps: The Interplay of Masculinity and Education', *Oxford Review of Education*, 15(3): 291–303.

Connell, R.W. (1995) *Masculinities*, St Leonards, NSW: Allen & Unwin.

Connell, R.W. (2000) *The Men and the Boys*, St Leonards, NSW: Allen & Unwin.

Connell, R.W. (2002) *Gender*, Cambridge, UK: Polity Press.

Connell, R.W. and Messerschmidt, James W. (2005) 'Hegemonic Masculinity: Rethinking the Concept', *Gender and Society*, 19 (6): 829–859.

Crichton, Michael (1992) *Rising Sun*, London: Arrowsmith.

Crowley, John W. (1987) 'Howells, Stoddard, and Male Homosocial Attachment in Victorian America', in Harry Brod (ed.) *The Making of Masculinities: The New Men's Studies*, Boston, MA: Unwin Hyman, pp. 301–324.

Dales, Laura (2005) 'Lifestyles of the Rich and Single: Reading Agency in the "Parasite Single" Issue', in Lyn Parker (ed.) *The Agency of Women in Asia*, Singapore: Marshall Cavendish Academic, pp. 133–157.

Dales, Laura (2009) *Feminist Movements in Contemporary Japan*, London: Routledge.

Dame-Ren ('Useless' Association) (ed.) (1999) *Dame-Ren Sengen: Dame-Ren Manifest*, Tokyo: Sakuhinsha.

Dasgupta, Romit (2000) 'Performing Masculinities? The "Salaryman" at Work and Play', *Japanese Studies*, 20(2): 189–200.

Dasgupta, Romit (2002) 'Karôshi', in Sandra Buckley (ed.) *Encyclopedia of Contemporary Japanese Culture*, London: Routledge, pp. 247, 248.

Dasgupta, Romit (2003a) 'Creating Corporate Warriors: The "Salaryman" and Masculinity in Japan', in Kam Louie and Morris Low (eds) *Asian Masculinities: The Meaning and Practice of Manhood in China and Japan*, London: RoutledgeCurzon, pp. 118–134.

Dasgupta, Romit (2003b) 'Cybermasculinities: Masculine Identities and the Internet in Japan', in Nanette Gottlieb and Mark McLelland (eds) *Japanese Cybercultures*, London: Routledge, pp. 109–125.

Dasgupta, Romit (2005a) 'Crafting Masculinities: Negotiating Masculine Identity in the Japanese Workplace', Unpublished Ph.D. thesis, Perth, Australia: Curtin University.

Dasgupta, Romit (2005b) 'Salarymen Doing Straight: Heterosexual Men and the Dynamics of Gender Conformity', in Mark McLelland and Romit Dasgupta (eds) *Genders, Transgenders, and Sexualities in Japan*, London: Routledge, pp. 168–182.

Dasgupta, Romit (2009) 'The "Lost Decade" of the 1990s and Shifting Masculinities in Japan', *Culture, Society and Masculinity*, 1(1): 79–95.

Dasgupta, Romit (2010) 'Globalization and the Bodily Performance of "Cool" and "Uncool" Masculinities in Corporate Japan', *Intersections: Gender and Sexuality in Asia and the Pacific*, Issue 23 (January). Available at http://intersections.anu.edu.au/issue23/dasgupta.htm (last accessed 23 September 2011).

Dasgupta, Romit (2011) 'Emotional Spaces and Places of Salaryman Anxiety in Kurosawa Kiyoshi's *Tokyo Sonata*', *Japanese Studies*, 31(3): 373–386.

Dawson, Chester (2002) 'Ghosn's Way: Why Japan Inc. is Following a *Gaijin*', *Business Week*, 20 May: 27.

Demetriou, Demetrakis Z. (2001) 'Connell's Concept of Hegemonic Masculinity: A Critique', *Theory and Society*, 30(3): 337–361.

D'Emilio, John (1997) 'Capitalism and Gay Identity', in Roger N. Lancaster and Micaela di Leonardo (eds) *The Gender/Sexuality Reader: Culture, History, Political Economy*, New York: Routledge, pp. 169–178.

Doi, Takeo (trans. John Bester) (1973) *The Anatomy of Dependence*, Tokyo: Kôdansha International.

Dore, Ronald (1973a) *British Factory-Japanese Factory: The Origins of National Diversity in Industrial Relations*, Berkeley: University of California Press.

Dore, Ronald P. (1973b) (reprint edn) *City Life in Japan: A Study of a Tokyo Ward*, Berkeley: University of California Press.

Dower, John W. (1993) 'Peace and Democracy in Two Systems: External Policy and Internal Conflict', in Andrew Gordon (ed.) *Postwar Japan as History*, Berkeley: University of California Press, pp. 3–33.

Duberman, Martin (1991) '"Writhing Bedfellows" in Antebellum South Carolina: Historical Interpretation and the Politics of Evidence', in Martin Duberman *et al.* (eds) *Hidden From History: Reclaiming the Gay and Lesbian Past*, London: Penguin Books, pp. 153–168.

Duus, Peter (1998 (2nd edn) *Modern Japan*, Boston, MA: Houghton Mifflin.

Eagleton, Terry (1991) *Ideology: An Introduction*, London: Verso.

Economist, The (2008) 'Sayonara, Salaryman', 386 (8561), 5–11 January: 56–58.

Economist, The (2010) 'Special Report Japan: Into the Unknown', 397 (8709), 20–26 November.

Edwards, Tim (1990) 'Beyond Sex and Gender: Masculinity, Homosexuality and Social Theory', in Jeff Hearn and David Morgan (eds) *Men, Masculinities and Social Theory*, London: Unwin Hyman, pp. 110–123.

Edwards, Walter (1989) *Modern Japan Through its Weddings: Gender, Person, and Society in Ritual Portrayal*, Stanford, CA: Stanford University Press.

Epstein, Debbie (2001) 'Boyz' Own Stories: Masculinities and Sexualities in Schools', in Wayne Martino and Bob Meyenn (eds) *What About the Boys? Issues of Masculinities in Schools*, Buckingham, UK: Open University Press, pp. 96–109.

Faderman, Lillian (1981) *Surpassing the Love of Men: Romantic Friendship and Love between Women from the Renaissance to the Present*, New York: Morrow.

Fine, Michelle *et al.* (1997) '(In)Secure Times: Constructing White Working-class Masculinities in the Late 20th Century', *Gender and Society*, 11(1): 52–68.

Fôramu Josei no Seikatsu to Tenbô (Women's Lifestyle and Prospects Forum) (ed.) (1994) *Zuhyô de Miru Onna no Genzai: Danjo Kyôsei e no Shihyô* (Women Today Seen Through Charts: Indices Towards Males and Females Living in Harmony), Kyôto: Minerva Shobô.

Foucault, Michel (1979) *Discipline and Punish: The Birth of the Clinic*, London: Penguin Books.

Fowler, Edward (1996) *San'ya Blues: Laboring Life in Contemporary Tokyo*, Ithaca, NY: Cornell University Press.

Frank, Blye (1987) 'Hegemonic Heterosexual Masculinity', *Studies in Political Economy*, 24: 159–170.

Freedman, Alisa (2009) '*Train Man* and the Gender Politics of Japanese "*Otaku*" Culture: The Rise of New Media, Nerd Heroes and Consumer Communities', *Intersections: Gender and Sexuality in Asia and the Pacific*, Issue 20 (April). Available at http://intersections.anu.edu.au/issue20/freedman.htm (last accessed 2 December 2011).

Freedman, Alisa (2011) *Tokyo in Transit: Japanese Culture on the Rails and Road*, Stanford, CA: Stanford University Press.

Frühstück, Sabine and Ben-Ari, Eyal (2002) ' "Now We Show It All!" Normalization and the Management of Violence in Japan's Armed Forces', *Journal of Japanese Studies*, 28(1): 1–39.

Frühstück, Sabine and Walthall, Anne (2011a) 'Introduction: Interrogating Men and Masculinities', in Sabine Frühstück and Anne Walthall (eds) *Recreating Japanese Men*, Berkeley: University of California Press, pp. 1–21.

Frühstück, Sabine and Walthall, Anne (eds) (2011b) *Recreating Japanese Men*, Berkeley: University of California Press.

Fruin, W. Mark (1978) 'The Japanese Company Controversy', *Journal of Japanese Studies*, 4(2): 267–300.

Fujii, Harue (1995) *Nihon-gata Kigyô Shakai to Josei Rôdô: Shokugyô to Katei no Ryôritsu o Mezashite* (The Japanese Model of Industrial Society and Female Labour: Aiming to Balance Work and Home), Tokyo: Minerva Shobô.

Fujimura, Masayuki (2006) 'Wakamono Sedai no "Otokorashisa" to Sono Mirai' (The 'Masculinity' of the Younger Generation and its Prospects), in Tsunehisa Abe, Sumio Obinata, and Masako Amano (eds) *'Otokorashia' no Gendaishi* (The Contemporary History of 'Manliness/Maleness'), Tokyo: Nihon Keizai Hyôron-sha, pp. 191–216.

Gagné, Nana Okura (2010) ' "Salarymen" in Crisis: The Collapse of Dominant Ideologies and Shifting Identities of Salarymen in Metropolitan Japan', Ph.D. thesis, Yale University, Connecticut, NH.

Gakuranman.com (2011) 'Top 60 Japanese Buzzwords of 2011', 18 November. Available at http://gakuranman.com/top-60-japanese-buzzwords-of-2011/ (last accessed 7 December 2011).

Game, Anne and Pringle, Rosemary (1983) *Gender at Work*, Sydney: George Allen & Unwin.

Gekkan Rôdô Kumiai (1990) 'Tokushû "Kaisha Ningen" no Kaimei: Kigyô Shakai to Kaisha Ningen' (Special Issue Explaining the 'Company Person': Industrial Society and the Company Person), June: 16–23.

Genda, Yûji (trans. Jean Connell Hoff) (2005) *A Nagging Sense of Job Insecurity: The New Reality Facing Japanese Youth*, Tokyo: Internation House of Japan.

Genji, Keita (trans. Hugh Cortazzi) (1972) *The Ogre and Other Stories of the Japanese Salaryman*, Tokyo: The Japan Times.

Gill, Tom (2001) *Men of Uncertainty: The Social Organization of Day Laborers in Contemporary Japan*, Albany, NY: State University of New York Press.

Gill, Tom (2003) 'When Pillars Evaporate: Structuring Masculinity on the Japanese Margins', in James E. Roberson and Nobue Suzuki (eds) *Men and Masculinities in Contemporary Japan: Dislocating the Salaryman Doxa*, London: RoutledgeCurzon, pp. 144–161.

Gordon, Andrew (1985) *The Evolution of Labor Relations in Japan: Heavy Industry, 1853–1955*, Cambridge, MA: Council of East Asian Studies, Harvard University.

Gordon, Andrew (ed.) (1993) *Postwar Japan as History*, Berkeley: University of California Press.

Gordon, Andrew (2002) 'The Short Happy Life of the Japanese Middle Class', in Olivier Zunz, Leonard Schappa, and Nobuhiro Hiwatori (eds) *Social Contracts Under Stress: The Middle Classes of America, Europe, and Japan at the Turn of the Century*, New York: Russell Sage Foundation, pp. 108–129.

Gutmann, Matthew C. (1996) *The Meanings of Macho: Being a Man in Mexico City*, Berkeley: University of California Press.

Hall, Marny (1989) 'Private Experiences in the Public Domain: Lesbians in Organizations', in Jeff Hearn *et al.* (eds) *The Sexuality of Organization*, London: Sage, pp. 125–138.

Hamabata, Matthews Masayuki (1990) *Crested Kimono: Power and Love in the Japanese Business Family*, Ithaca, NY: Cornell University Press.

Hanke, Robert (1992) 'Redesigning Men: Hegemonic Masculinity in Transition', in Steve Craig (ed.) *Men, Masculinity and the Media*, Newbury Park, CA: Sage, pp. 185–198.

Harootunian, Harry (2000) *Overcome by Modernity: History, Culture, and Community in Interwar Japan*, Princeton, NJ: Princeton University Press.

Hayashi, Tomoyuki (1995) ' "Wanted": Shinnyû Shain no Inishiêshon' ('Wanted': New Recruit Initiation), *Shûkan Asahi*, 12 May: 13–18.

Hazama, Hiroshi (1976) 'Historical Changes in the Life Style of Industrial Workers', in Hugh Patrick (ed.) *Japanese Industrialization and Its Social Consequences*, Berkeley: University of California Press, pp. 21–51.

Hazama, Hiroshi (1996) *Keizai Taikoku o Tsukuriageta Shisô: Kôdo Keizai Seichô-ki no Rôdô-êtosu* (The Philosophy that Built Up the Economic Superpower: The Labour Ethos of the High-Speed Economic Growth Period), Tokyo: Kôshindô.

Hazama, Hiroshi (trans. Mari Sako and Eri Sako) (1997) *The History of Labour Management in Japan*, Basingstoke, UK: MacMillan.

Hearn, Jeff (1992) *Men in the Public Eye: The Construction and Deconstruction of Public Men and Public Patriarchies*, London: Routledge.

Hearn, Jeff (1994) 'Research in Men and Masculinities: Some Sociological Issues and Possibilities', *The Australian and New Zealand Journal of Sociology*, 30(1): 47–70.

Hearn, Jeff (2002) 'Alternative Conceptualizations and Theoretical Perspectives on Identities and Organizational Cultures: A Personal Review of Research on Men in Organizations', in Iiris Aaltio and Albert J. Mills (eds) *Gender, Identity and the Culture of Organizations*, London: Routledge, pp. 39–56.

Hearn, Jeff and Morgan, David (eds) (1990) *Men, Masculinities and Social Theory*, London: Unwin Hyman.

Hearn, Jeff *et al.* (eds) (1989) *The Sexuality of Organization*, London: Sage.

Hein, Laura (1993) 'Growth Versus Success: Japanese Economic Policy in Historical Perspective', in Andrew Gordon (ed.) *Postwar Japan as History*, Berkeley: University of California Press, pp. 99–122.

Herdt, Gilbert H. (1981) *Guardians of the Flute: Idioms of Masculinity*, New York: McGraw Hill.

Hidaka, Tomoko (2006) 'Corporate Warriors or Company Animals? An Investigation of Japanese Salaryman Masculinities Across Three Generations', Ph.D. thesis, University of Adelaide, Australia.

Hidaka, Tomoko (2010) *Salaryman Masculinity: Continuity and Change in Hegemonic Masculinity in Japan*, Leiden: Brill.

Higashino, Mitsunari (2011) 'Kawaru Hatarakasarekata, Hatarakikata: Rôdô Hôsei no Henka to Jiko-Sekinin no Ronri' (The Changing Ways of Being Made to Work and Working: Labour Law Transitions and Debates on Self-responsibilty), in Futoshi Taga (ed.) *Yuragu Sarariiman Seikatsu: Shigoto to Katei no Hazama de* (Unstable Salaryman Life: Caught Between Work and Family), Tokyo: Minerva Shobô, pp. 35–63.

Hirota, Masaki (trans. Suzanne O'Brien) (1999) 'Notes on the "Process of Creating Women" in the Meiji Period', in Haruko Wakita, Anne Bouchy, and Chizuko Ueno (eds) *Gender and Japanese History – Volume 2: The Self and Expression/Work and Life*, Osaka: Osaka University Press, pp. 197–219.

Hood, Jane C. (ed.) (1993) *Men, Work, and Family*, Newbury Park, CA: Sage.

Horioka, Charles Yuji (1993) 'Consuming and Saving', in Andrew Gordon (ed.) *Postwar Japan as History*, Berkeley: University of California Press, pp. 259–292.

Hoshi, Tateo (1995) 'Ko-sodate kara Haruka Hanarete: "Otoko" no Ko-sodate kara' (Distanced from Childrearing: From the Child-rearing of a 'Male'), in Teruko Inoue, Chizuko Ueno, and Yumiko Ehara (eds) *Danseigaku: Nihon no Feminizumu Bessatsu* (Men's Studies: Special Edition of Japanese Feminism Series), Tokyo: Iwanami Shoten, pp. 191–209.

Iida, Yumiko (2000) 'Between the Technique of Living on Endless Routine and the Madness of Absolute Ground Zero: Japanese Identity and the Crisis of Modernity in the 1990s', *Positions: East Asian Cultural Critique*, 8(2): 423–464.

Iida, Yumiko (2002) *Rethinking Identity in Modern Japan: Nationalism as Aesthetics*, London: Routledge.

Ikujiren (Otoko mo Onna mo Ikuji o! Renrakukai) (Childcare Hours for Men and Women

Network) (1995) *Ikuji de Kaisha o Yasumu yôna Otokotachi* (The Kind of Men Who Take Leave for Childcare), Tokyo: Yukkusha.

Imamura, Anne E. (1984) 'Review of *Classes in Contemporary Japan*, by Rob Steven', *Political Science Quarterly*, 99(3): 580–581.

Inagami, Takeshi and Whittaker, D. Hugh (2005) *The New Community Firm: Employment, Governance and Management Reform in Japan*, Cambridge, UK: Cambridge University Press.

Inoue, Teruko, Ueno, Chizuko, and Ehara, Yumiko (eds) (1995) *Danseigaku: Nihon no Feminizumu Bessatsu* (Men's Studies: Special Edition of Japanese Feminism Series), Tokyo: Iwanami Shôten.

Ishida, Hiroshi (1993) *Social Mobility in Contemporary Japan: Educational Credentials, Class and the Labour Market in Cross National Perspectives*, Stanford, CA: Stanford University Press.

Ishida, Hiroshi and Slater, David H. (eds) (2010a) *Social Class in Contemporary Japan: Structures, Sortings and Strategies*, London: Routledge.

Ishida, Hiroshi and Slater, David H. (2010b) 'Social Class in Japan', in Hiroshi Ishida and David H. Slater (eds) *Social Class in Contemporary Japan: Structures, Sortings and Strategies*, London: Routledge, pp. 1–29.

Ishii, Kazumi and Jarkey, Nerida (2002) 'The Housewife is Born: The Establishment of the Notion and Identity of the *Shufu* in Modern Japan', *Japanese Studies*, 22(1): 35–47.

Ishii-Kuntz, Masako (1993) 'Japanese Fathers: Work Demands and Family Roles', in Jane C. Hood (ed.) *Men, Work, and Family*, Newbury Park, CA: Sage, pp. 45–67.

Ishii-Kuntz, Masako (2003) 'Balancing Fatherhood and Work: Emergence of Diverse Masculinities in Contemporary Japan', in James E. Roberson and Nobue Suzuki (eds) *Men and Masculinities in Contemporary Japan: Dislocating the Salaryman Doxa*, London: RoutledgeCurzon, pp. 198–216.

Itô, Kimio (1993) *'Otokorashisa' no Yukue: Dansei Bunka no Bunka Shakaigaku* (The Direction of 'Manliness/Masculinity': The Cultural Sociology of Male Culture), Tokyo: Shinyôsha.

Itô, Kimio (1996) *Danseigaku Nyûmon* (Introduction to Men's Studies), Tokyo: Sakuhinsha.

Itô, Kimio (1998) 'Umareru: Tsukurareru "Otoko" to "Onna"' (Being Born: The Making of 'Male' and 'Female'), in Kimio Itô and Kazue Muta (eds) *Jendâ de Manabu Shakaigaku* (Studying Sociology through Gender), Kyoto: Sekai Shisôsha, pp. 16–29.

Itô, Takatoshi (1992) *The Japanese Economy*, Cambridge, MA: MIT Press.

Ivy, Marilyn (1993) 'Formations of Mass Culture', in Andrew Gordon (ed.) *Postwar Japan as History*, Berkeley: University of California Press, pp. 239–258.

Iwabuchi, Koichi (2008) 'Lost in TransNation: Tokyo and the Urban Imaginary in the Era of Globalization', *Inter-Asia Cultural Studies*, 8(2): 543–556.

Iwase, Akira (2006) *'Gekkyû Hyaku-en' Sarariiman: Senzen Nihon no 'Heiwa'na Seikatsu* (The 'Hundred Yen Per Month' Salaryman: The 'Peaceful' Lifestyle of Prewar Japan), Tokyo: Kôdansha.

Jagose, Annamarie (1996) *Queer Theory*, Carlton South: Melbourne University Press.

Japan Institute of Labour (ed.) (2003) *Japanese Working Life Profile 2003*, Tokyo: Japan Institute of Labour.

Japan Institute for Labour Policy and Training (JILPT) (2011) *Labor Situation and Analysis: Detailed Exposition 2011/2012*, Tokyo: The Japanese Institute for Labour Policy and Training.

Japan Tourist Bureau (JTB) (2006) *Illustrated 'Salaryman' in Japan*, Japan in Your

Pocket! JTB Illustrated Book Series, no. 8, Tokyo: JTB Nihon Kôtsû Kôsha Shuppan-jigyô Kyoku.

Johnson, Chalmers (1982) *MITI and the Japanese Miracle: The Growth of Industrial Policy, 1925–1975*, Stanford, CA: Stanford University Press.

Johnson, Thomas Wayne (1975) *Shônendan: Adolescent Peer Group Socialization in Rural Japan*, Taipei: The Orient Cultural Service.

Jolivet, Muriel (1997) *Japan: A Childless Society?*, London: Routledge.

Kaizuma, Keiko (2004) *Kindai Nihon no Fusei-ron to Jendaa Poritikusu* (Gender Politics and Debates on Fatherhood in Modern Japan), Tokyo: Sakuhinsha.

Kamata, Satoshi (trans. Tatsuru Akimoto) (1982) *Japan in the Passing Lane: An Insider's Account of Life in a Japanese Auto Factory*, London: Unwin Paperbacks.

Kanter, Rosabeth Moss (1977) *Men and Women of the Corporation*, New York: Basic Books.

Karlin, Jason G. (2002) 'The Gender of Nationalism: Competing Masculinities in Meiji Japan', *Journal of Japanese Studies*, 28(1): 41–77.

Katz, Jonathan (1976) *Gay American History: Lesbians and Gay Men in the USA – A Documentary*, New York: Thomas J. Crowley.

Katz, Richard (1998) *Japan: The System That Soured*, Armonk, NY: M.E. Sharpe.

Kaufman, Michael (ed.) (1987) *Beyond Patriarchy: Essays by Men on Pleasure, Power, and Change*, Toronto: Oxford University Press.

Kaufman, Michael (1994) 'Men, Feminism, and Men's Contradictory Experiences of Power', in Harry Brod and Michael Kaufman (eds) *Theorizing Masculinities*, Thousand Oaks, CA: Sage, pp. 142–163.

Kelly, William W. (1986) 'Rationalization and Nostalgia: Cultural Dynamics of New Middle-class Japan', *American Ethnologist*, 13(4): 603–618.

Kelly, William W. (1993) 'Finding a Place in Metropolitan Japan: Ideologies, Institutions, and Everyday Life', in Andrew Gordon (ed.) *Postwar Japan as History*, Berkeley: University of California Press, pp. 189–216.

Kelly, William W. (2002) 'At the Limits of New Middle-class Japan: Beyond "Mainstream Consciousness"', in Olivier Zunz, Leonard Schappa, and Nobuhiro Hiwatori (eds) *Social Contract Under Stress: The Middle Classes of America, Europe, and Japan at the Turn of the Century*, New York: Russell Sage Foundation, pp. 232–254.

Kelly, William W. and White, Merry I. (2006) 'Students, Slackers, Singles, Seniors, and Strangers: Transforming a Family-Nation', in Peter J. Katzenstein and Takashi Shiraishi (eds) *Beyond Japan: The Dynamism of East Asian Regionalism*, Ithaca, NY: Cornell University Press, pp. 63–82.

Kimmel, Michael S. (1994) 'Masculinity as Homophobia: Fear, Shame, and Silence in the Construction of Gender Inequality', in Harry Brod and Michael Kaufman (eds) *Theorizing Masculinities*, Thousand Oaks, CA, pp. 119–141.

Kimmel, Michael S. (2001) 'Global Masculinities: Restoration and Resistance', in Bob Pease and Keith Pringle (eds) *A Man's World? Changing Men's Practices in a Globalized World*, London: Zed Books, pp. 21–37.

Kimura, Ryôko (2006) 'Sengo Tsukurareru "Otoko" no Imêji: Senso-eiga ni Miru Danseisei no Kaifuku no Dôtei' (Constructing the Postwar 'Male' Image: The Path to the Restoration of Masculinity as Seen in War Films), in Tsunehisa Abe, Sumio Obinata, and Masako Amano (eds) *Danseishi 3: 'Otokorashia' no Gendaishi* (History of Masculinity Series No. 3: The Contemporary History of 'Manliness/Maleness'), Tokyo: Nihon Keizai Hyôron-sha, pp. 60–91.

Kingston, Jeff (2004) *Japan's Quiet Transformation: Social Change and Civil Society in the Twenty-first Century*, London: RoutledgeCurzon.

Kingston, Jeff (2011) *Contemporary Japan: History, Politics, and Social Change Since the 1980s*, Chicester, West Sussex: Wiley-Blackwell.

Kinmonth, Earl H. (1981) *The Self-made Man in Meiji Japanese Thought: From Samurai to Salaryman*, Berkeley: University of California Press.

Kinsella, Sharon (2000) *Adult Manga: Culture and Power in Contemporary Japan*, Richmond, UK: Curzon.

Kishimoto, Shigenobu (1978) *Chûryû no Gensô* (The Illusion of Middle Class), Tokyo: Kôdansha.

Kitazawa Rakuten Kenshô Kai (Kitazawa Rakuten Memorial Association) (ed.) (1973) *Rakuten Manga-shû Taisei: Taishô-hen* (Compilation of Collected Rakuten *Manga*: Taishô Collection), Tokyo: Gurafikku-sha.

Kodama, Ryôko (2001) 'Chichioya-ron no Genzai: Nana-jû Nendai Ikô o Chûshin Toshite' (Contemporary Fatherhood Debates: Focusing on the Seventies Onwards), in Haruo Asai, Satoru Itô, and Yukihiro Murakami (eds) *Nihon no Otoko wa Doko kara Kite, Doko e Iku no ka: Dansei Sekushuariti Keisei (Kyôdô Kenkyûkai)* (Where Have Japanese Men Come From, Where Are They Going?: Construction of Male Sexuality [Collaborative Research]), Tokyo: Jûgatsusha, pp. 122–149.

Kohso, Sabu (2006) 'Angelus Novus in Millenial Japan', in Tomiko Yoda and Harry Harootunian (eds) *Japan after Japan: Social and Cultural Life from the Recessionary 1990s to the Present*, Durham, NC: Duke University Press, pp. 415–438.

Kondo, Dorinne K. (1990) *Crafting Selves: Power, Gender, and Discourses of Identity in a Japanese Workplace*, Chicago, IL: University of Chicago Press.

Kondo, Dorinne K. (1994) '*Uchi no Kaisha:* Company As Family?', in Jane M. Bachnik and Charles J. Quinn, Jr. (eds) *Situated Meaning: Inside and Outside in Japanese Self, Society, and Language*, Princeton, NJ: Princeton University Press, pp. 170–191.

Kosugi, Reiko (trans. Ross Mouer) (2008) *Escape from Work: Freelancing Youth and the Challenge to Corporate Japan*, Melbourne: TransPacific Press.

Krauss, Ellis S. (1974) *Japanese Radicals Revisited: Student Protest in Postwar Japan*, Berkeley: University of California Press.

Kumazawa, Makoto (ed. Andrew Gordon/trans. Andrew Gordon and Mikiso Hane) (1996) *Portraits of the Japanese Workplace: Labor Movements, Workers, and Managers*, Boulder, CO: Westview Press.

LeBlanc, Robin M. (2010) *The Art of Gut: Manhood, Power, and Ethics in Japanese Politics*, Berkeley: University of California Press.

Lee, Deborah (2000) 'Hegemonic Masculinity and Male Feminisation: The Sexual Harassment of Men at Work', *Journal of Gender Studies*, 9(2): 141–155.

Lee, Kang On (2003) 'Any Color as Long as It's Brown', *Look Japan*, April: 40.

Leheny, David (2006) *Think Global, Fear Local*, Ithaca, NY: Cornell University Press.

Lehmann, Jean-Paul (2002) 'Argentina's Decline Holds Lessons for Japan: Japan in the Global Era', *Japan Times Online*, 11 February. Available at www.japantimes.co.jp/text/eo20020211jl.html (last accessed 30 November 2011).

Levine, Solomon B. (1983) 'Careers and Mobility in Japan's Labor Markets', in David W. Plath (ed.) *Work and Lifecourse in Japan*, Albany, NY: State University of New York Press, pp. 18–33.

Light, Richard (2000) 'From the Profane to the Sacred: Pre-game Ritual in Japanese High School Rugby', *International Review for the Sociology of Sport*, 35(4): 451–463.

Lincoln, James R. (1984) 'Review of *Classes in Contemporary Japan*, by Rob Steven', *Contemporary Sociology*, 13(6): 748–750.

Linhart, Sepp (1998) '*Sakariba*: Zone of "Evaporation" Between Work and Home?', in

Joy Hendry (ed.) *Interpreting Japanese Society: Anthropological Approaches*, London: Routledge, pp. 231–242.

Lo, Jeannie (1990) *Office Ladies, Factory Women: Life and Work at a Japanese Company*, New York: M.E. Sharpe.

Louie, Kam and Low, Morris (eds) (2003) *Asian Masculinities: The Meaning and Practice of Manhood in China and Japan*, London: RoutledgeCurzon.

Lunsing, Wim (2001) *Beyond Common Sense: Sexuality and Gender in Contemporary Japan*, London: Kegan Paul.

Mac an Ghaill, Máirtín (1994) *The Making of Men: Masculinities, Sexualities and Schooling*, Buckingham, UK: Open University Press.

Mackie, Vera (2000a) 'The Dimensions of Citizenship in Modern Japan: Gender, Class, Ethnicity and Sexuality', in Andrew Vandenberg (ed.) *Citizenship and Democracy in a Global Era*, Basingstoke, UK: Macmillan, pp. 245–257.

Mackie, Vera (2000b) 'Modern Selves and Modern Spaces', in Elise K. Tipton and John Clark (eds) *Being Modern in Japan: Culture and Society from the 1910s to the 1930s*, Sydney: Australian Humanities Research Foundation, pp. 185–199.

Mackie, Vera (2002) 'Embodiment, Citizenship and Social Policy in Contemporary Japan', in Roger Goodman (ed.) *Family and Social Policy in Japan: Anthropological Approaches*, Cambridge, UK: Cambridge University Press, pp. 200–229.

Mackie, Vera (2003) *Feminism in Modern Japan: Citizenship, Embodiment and Sexuality*, Cambridge, UK: Cambridge University Press.

Maeda, Hajime (1928) *Sarariiman Monogatari* (Tales of the Salaryman), Tokyo: Tôyô Keizai Shinpôsha.

Martino, Wayne (1999) ' "Cool Boys", "Party Animals", "Squids" and "Poofters": Interrogating the Dynamics and Politics of Adolescent Masculinities in Schools', *British Journal of Sociology of Education*, 20(2): 239–263.

Matanle, Peter (2006) 'Beyond Lifetime Employment? Re-fabricating Japan's Employment Culture', in Peter Matanale and Wim Lunsing (eds) *Perspectives on Work, Employment and Society in Japan*, Basingstoke and New York: Palgrave Macmillan, pp. 58–78.

Matanle, Peter and Lunsing, Wim (eds) (2006) *Perspectives on Work, Employment and Society in Japan*, Basingstoke and New York: Palgrave Macmillan.

Matanle, Peter, McCann, Leo, and Ashmore, Darren (2008) 'Men Under Pressure: Representations of the "Salaryman" and his Organization in Japanese Manga', *Organization*, 15(5): 639–664.

Matsunari, Yoshie, Izutani, Hajime, Tanuma Hajime, and Noda, Masaho (1957) *Nihon no Sarariiman* (The Japanese Salaryman), Tokyo: Aoki Shoten.

Matsuno, Hiroshi (ed.) (2001) *Sarariiman Shakai Shô-Jiten* (A Concise Dictionary of Salaryman Society), Tokyo: Kôdansha Gendai Shinsho.

McBee, Randy D. (1999) ' "He Likes Women More Than He Likes Drink and That Is Quite Unusual": Working-class Social Clubs, Male Culture, and Heterosocial Relations in the United States, 1920s–1930s', *Gender and History*, 11(1): 84–112.

McCann, Leo, Hassard, John, and Morris, Jonathan (2006) 'Hard Times for the Salaryman: Corporate Restructuring and Middle Managers' Working Lives', in Peter Matanale and Wim Lunsing (eds) *Perspectives on Work, Employment and Society in Japan*, Basingstoke and New York: Palgrave Macmillan, pp. 98–116.

McLelland, Mark (2001) 'Live Life More Selfishly: An On-line Gay Advice Column in Japan', *Journal of Media and Cultural Studies*, 15(1): 103–116.

McCormack, Gavan (1971) 'The Student Left in Japan', *New Left Review*, 65: 37–53.

McCormack, Gavan (1998) 'From Number One to Number Nothing: Japan's *Fin de Siècle* Blues', *Japanese Studies*, 18(1): 31–44.

McCormack, Gavan (2000) 'The Japanese Movement to "Correct" History', in Laura Hein and Mark Selden (eds) *Censoring History: Citizenship and Memory in Japan, Germany, and the United States*, Armonk, NY: M.E. Sharpe, pp. 53–73.

McCreery, John L. (2000) *Japanese Consumer Behavior: From Worker Bees to Wary Shoppers*, Richmond, UK: Curzon.

McDowell, Linda (1995) 'Body Work: Heterosexual Gender Performances in City Workplaces', in David Bell and Gill Valentine (eds) *Mapping Desire: Geographies of Sexualities*, London: Routledge, pp. 75–95.

McDowell, Linda (2001a) '"It's that Linda again": Ethical, Practical and Political Issues Involved in Longitudinal Research with Young Men', *Ethics, Place and Environment*, 4(2): 87–100.

McDowell, Linda (2001b) *Young Men Leaving School: White, Working-class Masculinity*, Leicester: Youth Work Press.

McDowell, Linda (2002) 'Transitions to Work: Masculine Identities, Youth Inequality and Labour Market Change', *Gender, Place and Culture*, 9(1): 39–51.

McDowell, Linda (2003) *Redundant Masculinities? Employment Change and White Working class Youth*, Oxford: Blackwell.

McLelland, Mark J. (2000) *Male Homosexuality in Modern Japan: Cultural Myths and Social Realities*, Richmond, UK: Curzon.

McLelland, Mark (2005) 'Salarymen Doing Queer: Gay Men and the Heterosexual Public Sphere', in Mark McLelland and Romit Dasgupta (eds) *Genders, Transgenders, and Sexualities in Japan*, London: Routledge, pp. 96–110.

McLelland, Mark and Dasgupta, Romit (eds) (2005) *Genders, Transgenders, and Sexualities in Japan*, London: Routledge.

Mills, Albert J. (1998) 'Cockpits, Hangars, Boys and Galleys: Corporate Masculinities and the Development of British Airways', *Gender, Work and Organization*, 5(3): 172–188.

Mills, C. Wright (1956) *White Collar: The American Middle Class*, London: Oxford University Press.

Mills, Martin (2001) 'Pushing it to the Max: Interrogating the Risky Business of Being a Boy', in Wayne Martino and Bob Meyenn (eds) *What About the Boys? Issues of Masculinities in Schools*, Buckingham, UK: Open University Press, pp. 53–65.

Minichiello, Sharon A. (ed.) (1998) *Japan's Competing Modernities: Issues in Culture and Democracy, 1900–1930*, Honolulu: University of Hawaii Press.

Ministry of Health, Labour and Welfare (MHLW) (2005) *White Paper on the Labour Economy 2005*, ch. 2, 'Current Situation and Issues in the Labour Supply'. Available at www.mhlw.go.jp/english/wp/l-economy/2005/dl/02–02–01.pdf (last accessed 17 September 2011).

Miyadai, Shinji, Tsuji, Izumi, and Okai, Takayuki (eds) (2009) *'Otokorashia' no Kairaku: Popyurâ Bunka kara Mita sono Jittai* (The Pleasures of 'Manliness': The Reality as Seen through Popular Culture), Tokyo: Keisô Shobô.

Miyamoto, Michiko (2008) 'Koyô Ryûdôka no moto de no Kazoku Keisei: Hôkai-suru Jyakunen-sô no "Kindai Kazoku" Keisei Kiban' (Family Formation Under Employment Flexibilization: The Crumbling Base of the Younger Generation's 'Modern Family' Formation), in Keiko Funabashi and Michiko Miyamoto (eds) *Koyô Ryûdôka no naka no Kazoku: Kigyô-shakai, Kazoku, Seikatsu-hoshô Shisutemu* (The Family in Employment Flexibilization: Corporate-society, Family, and Social Security Systems), Tokyo: Minerubua Shôbo, pp. 79–98.

Miyazaki, Hirokazu (2006) 'Economy of Dreams: Hope in Global Capitalism and Its Critiques', *Cultural Anthropology*, 21(2): 147–172.

Moon, Seungsook (2005) *Militarized Modernity and Gendered Citizenship in South Korea*, Durham, NC: Duke University Press.

Morgan, David (1981) 'Men, Masculinity and the Process of Sociological Enquiry', in Helen Roberts (ed.) *Doing Feminist Research*, London: Routledge & Kegan Paul, pp. 83–113.

Morgan, David (1992) *Discovering Men*, London: Curzon.

Morris-Suzuki, Tessa (1984) *Shôwa: An Inside History of Hirohito's Japan*, North Ryde, NSW: Methuen Australia.

Mugikura, Testsu (2006) 'Otokorashisa to Hômuresu' (Masculinity and the Homeless), in Tsunehisa Abe, Sumio Obinata, and Masako Amano (eds) *Danseishi 3: 'Otokorashia' no Gendaishi* (History of Masculinity Series No. 3: The Contemporary History of 'Manliness/Maleness'), Tokyo: Nihon Keizai Hyôron-sha, pp. 92–123.

Murakami, Yasusuke (1978) 'The Reality of the New Middle Class', *Japan Interpreter*, 12(1): 1–15.

Murase, Haruki (1995) 'Hausu-hazubando Sengen' (House-husband Manifesto), in Teruko Inoue, Chizuko Ueno, and Yumiko Ehara (eds) *Danseigaku: Nihon no Feminizumu Bessatsu* (Men's Studies: Special Edition of Japanese Feminism Series), Tokyo: Iwanami Shoten, pp. 185–190.

Murata, Yôhei (2000) 'Chûnen Shinguru Dansei o Sogai-suru Basho' (The Places Where Middle-Aged Single Men Feel Alienated), *Jinbun Chirigaku* (Human Geography), 52(6): 533–551.

Nakamura, Akira (1996) *Zenryoku Shissô shita Otoko-tachi: Kigyô Senshi no Danseigaku* (Men who Ran with All Their Strength: Men's Studies for the Corporate Warrior), Tokyo: Kindai Bungeisha.

Nakamura, Akira and Nakamura, Tadashi (eds) (1997) *Otoko ga Mietekuru Jibun-sagashi no 100 satsu* (100 Books For Men To Find Themselves), Kyôto: Kamogawa Shuppan.

Nakamura, Tadashi (2003) 'Regendering Batterers: Domestic Violence and Men's Movements', in James E. Roberson and Nobue Suzuki (eds) *Men and Masculinities in Contemporary Japan: Dislocating the Salaryman Doxa*, London: Routledge, pp. 162–179.

Nakamura, Takafusa (trans. Jacqueline Kaminski) (1981) *The Postwar Japanese Economy: Its Development and Structure*, Tokyo: University of Tokyo Press.

Nakane, Chie (1973) *Japanese Society*, Harmondsworth, Middlesex: Penguin Books.

Nakanishi, Shintarô (2008) *1995-nen: Miryô no Mondaiken* (The Year 1995: Spheres of Unresolved Problems), Tokyo: Ôtsuki Shoten.

Napier, Susan (2011) 'Where Have All the Salarymen Gone? Masculinity, Masochism, and Technomobility in *Densha Otoko*', in Sabine Frühstück and Anne Walthall (eds) *Recreating Japanese Men*, Berkeley: University of California Press, pp. 154–176.

Nardi, Peter M. (ed.) (1992a) *Men's Friendships*, Newbury Park, CA: Sage.

Nardi, Peter M. (1992b) '"Seamless Souls": An Introduction to Men's Friendships", in Peter M. Nardi (ed.) *Men's Friendships*, Newbury Park, CA: Sage, pp. 1–14.

Nathan, John (2004) *Japan Unbound: A Volatile Nation's Quest for Pride and Purpose*, New York: Houghton Mifflin.

Newton, Esther (1993) 'My Best Informant's Dress: The Erotic Equation in Fieldwork', *Cultural Anthropology*, 8(1): 3–23.

Noble, Gregory W. (1989) 'The Japanese Industrial Policy Debate', in Stephen Haggard and Chung-in Moon (eds) *Pacific Dynamism: The International Politics of Industrial Change*, Boulder, CO: Westview Press, pp. 53–95.

Noguchi, Yukio (1994) 'The "Bubble" and Economic Policies in the 1980s', *Journal of Japanese Studies*, 20(2): 291–329.

Nolte, Sharon and Hastings, Sally Ann (1991) 'The Meiji State's Policy toward Women, 1890–1910', in Gail Lee Bernstein (ed.) *Recreating Japanese Women, 1600–1945*, Berkeley: University of California Press, pp. 151–174.

'Northern Energy' Corporation Ltd (1999) *Heisei Jû-ichi Nendo Daigaku(in) Sotsu Shin-nyû-shain Kyôiku Puroguramu* (Heisei 11 [1999] New Entrant Training Programme for University and Postgraduates), unpublished in-house manual).

Obinger, Julia (2009) 'Working on the Margins: Japan's *Precariat* and Working Poor', *Electronic Journal of Contemporary Japanese Studies* (Discussion Paper 1). Available at www.japanesestudies.org.uk/discussionpapers/2009/Obinger.html (last accessed 2 December 2011).

Odani, Sean (2001) 'Freeters: Japan's Carefree Young Wage Workers', *Via*, 22(4): 24, 25.

Ogasawara, Yuko (1998) *Office Ladies and Salaried Men: Power, Gender, and Work in Japanese Companies*, Berkeley: University of California Press.

Okamoto, Tomochika and Sasano, Etsuko (2001) 'Sengo Nihon no "Sarariiman" Hyôzô no Henka: "Asahi Shinbun" o Jirei ni' (Changes in Representation of 'Salaried men' in Postwar Japanese Newspapers: A Re-examination of *Asahi Shimbun*, 1945–1999), *Shakaigaku Hyôron*, 52(1):16–32.

Okano, Kaori (2009) *Young Women in Japan: Transition to Adulthood*, London: Routledge.

Ôsawa, Mari (1993) *Kigyô Chûshin Shakai o Koete: Gendai Nihon o 'Jendâ' de Yomu* (Moving Beyond a Company-Centred Society: Reading Modern Japan through 'Gender'), Tokyo: Jiji Tsûshinsha.

Oshima, Harry T. (1982) 'Reinterpreting Japan's Postwar Growth', *Economic Development and Cultural Change*, 31(1): 1–43.

Ôta, Hajime (1997) *Shigoto-jin no Jidai* (The Age of the Work-Centred Person), Tokyo: Shinchosha.

Ôta, Mutsumi (1999) 'Dad Takes Childcare Leave', *Japan Quarterly*, 146: 83–89.

Ôta, Yôko (1935) 'Otoko to iu Mono wa' (What is a Man?), *Nihon Hyôron*, November: 476–488.

Ôtani, Akihiro (1993) *Sarariiman no Wasuremono* (Things Forgotten by Salarymen), Tokyo: Magajin Hausu.

Ouchi, William G. (1981) *Theory Z: How American Business Can Meet the Japanese Challenge*, Reading, MA: Addison-Wesley.

Ôya, Sôichi (1981) *Ôya Sôichi Zenshû* (Collected Works of Ôya Sôichi) (vol. 2), Tokyo: Sôyôsha.

Paetzold, Ramona L. (2004) 'Sexual Harassment as Dysfunctional Behavior in Organiations', in Ricky W. Griffin and Anne M. O'Leary-Kelly (eds) *The Dark Side of Organizational Behavior*, San Francisco, CA: Jossey-Bass, pp. 159–186.

Papataxiarchis, Evthymios (1991) 'Friends of the Heart: Male Commensal Solidarity, Gender, and Kinship in Aegean Greece', in Peter Loizos and Evthymios Papataxiarchis (eds) *Contested Identities: Gender and Kinship in Modern Greece*, Princeton, NJ: Princeton University Press, pp. 156–179.

Pempel, T.J. (1982) *Policy and Politics in Japan: Creative Conservatism*, Philadelphia, PA: Temple University Press.

Pflugfelder, Gregory M. (1999) *Cartographies of Desire: Male–Male Sexuality in Japanese Discourse, 1600–1950*, Berkeley: University of California Press.

Plath, David W. (1964) *The After Hours: Modern Japan and the Search for Enjoyment*, Westport, CT: Greenwood Press.

Plath, David. W. (1980) *Long Engagements: Maturity in Modern Japan*, Stanford, CA: Stanford University Press.

Plath, David W. (ed.) (1983a) *Work and Lifecourse in Japan*, Albany, NY: State University of New York Press.

Plath, David W. (1983b) 'Introduction: Life is Just a Job Résumé?', in David W. Plath (ed.) *Work and Lifecourse in Japan*, Albany, NY: State University of New York Press, pp. 1–13.

Plath, David W. (1986) 'Review of *Classes in Contemporary Japan*, by Rob Steven', *Journal of Japanese Studies*, 12(1): 155–158.

Plummer, David (1999) *One of the Boys: Masculinity, Homophobia, and Modern Manhood*, New York: Harrington Park Press.

Plummer, Ken (1996) 'Symbolic Interactionism in the Twentieth Century: The Rise of Empirical Social Theory', in Bryan S. Turner (ed.) *The Blackwell Companion to Social Theory*, Oxford: Blackwell, pp. 223–251.

Pringle, Rosemary (1989) 'Bureaucracy, Rationality and Sexuality: The Case of Secretaries', in Jeff Hearn *et al.* (eds) *The Sexuality of Organization*, London: Sage, pp. 150–177.

Pringle, Rosemary (1993) 'Male Secretaries', in Christine L. Williams (ed.) *Doing 'Women's Work': Men in Nontraditional Occupations*, Newbury Park, CA: Sage, pp. 128–151.

Queer Japan (2000) 'Hentai-suru Sarariiman: Tokushû' (Queering the Salaryman: Special Feature), 2, April: 5–107.

Rebick, Marcus E. (1998) 'The Japanese Labour Market for University Graduates: Trends in the 1990s', *Japan Forum*, 10(1): 17–29.

Rich, Adrienne (1980) 'Compulsory Heterosexuality and Lesbian Experience', *Signs*, 5(4): 631–660.

Roberson, James E. (1995a) 'After Hours and Private Time: Class, Leisure and Identity in Japan', *American Asian Review*, 13(2): 213–255.

Roberson, James E. (1995b) 'Becoming *Shakaijin*: Working-class Reproduction in Japan', *Ethnology*, 34(4): 293–313.

Roberson, James (1998) *Japanese Working Class Lives: An Ethnographic Study of Factory Workers*, London: Routledge.

Roberson, James (2005) 'Fight! *Ippatsu*!! "*Genki*" Energy Drinks and the Making of Masculine Ideology in Japan', *Men and Masculinities*, 7(4): 365–384.

Roberson, James E. and Suzuki, Nobue (2003a) 'Introduction', in James E. Roberson and Nobue Suzuki (eds) *Men and Masculinities in Contemporary Japan: Dislocating the Salaryman Doxa*, London: RoutledgeCurzon, pp. 1–19.

Roberson, James E. and Suzuki, Nobue (eds) (2003b) *Men and Masculinities in Contemporary Japan: Dislocating the Salaryman Doxa*, London: RoutledgeCurzon.

Roberts, Glenda S. (1994) *Staying on the Line: Blue-collar Women in Contemporary Japan*, Honolulu: University of Hawaii Press.

Roberts, Glenda S. (2002) 'Pinning Hopes on Angels: Reflections from an Aging Japan's Urban Landscape', in Roger Goodman (ed.) *Family and Social Policy in Japan: Anthropological Approaches*, Cambridge, UK: Cambridge University Press, pp. 54–91.

Roden, Donald (1980) *Schooldays in Imperial Japan: A Study in the Culture of a Student Elite*, Berkeley: University of California Press.

Rohlen, Thomas P. (1974) *For Harmony and Strength: Japanese White-collar Organization in Anthropological Perspective*, Berkeley: University of California Press.

Rohlen, Thomas P. (1975) 'The Company Work Group', in Ezra F. Vogel (ed.) *Modern Japanese Organization and Decision Making*, Berkeley: University of California Press. 185–209.

Ronald, Richard and Alexy, Allison (2011) 'Continuity and Change in Japanese Homes and Families', in Richard Ronald and Allison Alexy (eds) *Home and Family in Japan: Continuity and Transformation*, London: Routledge, pp. 1–24.

Roper, Michael (1994) *Masculinity and the British Organization Man Since 1945*, Oxford: Oxford University Press.

Roper, Michael (1996) '"Seduction and Succession": Circuits of Homosocial Desire in Management', in David L. Collinson and Jeff Hearn (eds) *Men as Managers, Managers as Men: Critical Perspectives on Men, Masculinities and Managements*, London: Sage, pp. 210–226.

Rose, Caroline (2006) 'The Battle for Minds and Hearts: Patriotic Education in Japan in the 1990s and Beyond', in Naoko Shimazu (ed.) *Nationalisms in Japan*, London: Routledge.

Rotundo, E. Anthony (1989) 'Romantic Friendship: Male Intimacy and Middle-class Youth in the Northern United States, 1800–1900', *Journal of Social History*, 23(1): 1–25.

Saitô, Takao (2002) 'Business Fiction in a New Era', *Japanese Book News*, 38: 1–3.

Sakai Junko (2000) *Japanese Bankers in the City of London: Language, Culture and Identity in the Japanese Diaspora*, London: Routledge.

Sand, Jordan (1998) 'At Home in the Meiji Period: Inventing Japanese Domesticity', in Stephen Vlastos (ed.) *Mirror of Modernity: Invented Traditions of Modern Japan*, Berkeley: University of California Press, pp. 191–207.

Sanday, P.R. (1990) *Fraternity Gang Rape: Sex, Brotherhood, and Privilege on Campus*, New York: New York University Press.

Sataka, Makoto (1991) *Keizai Shôsetsu no Yomikata: Keizai Shôsetsu ga Kaita Nihon no Kigyô* (How to Read Business Novels: Japanese Firms as Depicted in Business Novels), Tokyo: Tokuma Bunko.

Satô, Toshiki (2000) *Fubyôdô Shakai Nihon* (Japan the Unequal Society), Tokyo: Chuo Kôron Shinsha.

Schilling, Mark (2000) 'Into the Heartland with Tora-san', in Timothy J. Craig (ed.) *Japan Pop! Inside the World of Japanese Popular Culture*, Armonk, NY: M.E. Sharpe, pp. 245–255.

Schodt, Frederick (1986) *Manga!Manga! The World of Japanese Comics*, Tokyo: Kôdansha International.

Schodt, Frederik L. (1996) *Dreamland Japan: Writings on Modern Manga*, Berkeley, CA: Stone Bridge Press.

Sedgwick, Eve Kosovsky (1985) *Between Men: English Literature and Male Homosocial Desire*, New York: Columbia University Press.

Sedgwick, Mitchell W. (2007) *Globalisation and Japanese Organizational Culture: An Ethnography of a Japanese Firm in France*, London: Routledge.

Sherrod, Drury (1987) 'The Bonds of Men: Problems and Possibilities in Close Male Friendships', in Harry Brod (ed.) *The Making of Masculinities: The New Men's Studies*, Boston, MA: Unwin Hyman, pp. 213–239.

Shibuya, Tomomi (2001) '"Feminisuto Dansei Kenkyû" no Shiten to Kôsô: Nihon no Danseigaku oyobi Dansei Kenkyû Hihan o Chûshin ni' (A View and Vision of 'Feminist Studies on Men and Masculinities': Focusing on a Critique of Men's Studies and Research on Men in Japan), *Shakaigaku Hyôron* (Japan Sociological Review), 51(4): 447–463.

Shimada, Haruo *et al.* (1996) *Sarariiman Hakai: Nihonteki Koyô ga Dai-Hôkai suru!* (The Ruin of the Salaryman: The Great Collapse of Japanese-style Management!), Tokyo: Chûkei Shuppan.

Shimoda, Tomoko (2008) 'Representations of Parenting and Gender Roles in the *Shôshika* Era: Comparisons of Japanese and English-language Parenting Magazines', *Electronic Journal of Contemporary Japanese Studies*, 14 January. Available at www.japanesestudies.org.uk/articles/2008/Shimoda.html (last accessed 17 September 2011).

Shimokawa, Kôichi (2006) *'Ushinawareta Jû-nen' wa Norikoerareta ka* (Has the 'Lost Decade' Been Overcome?), Tokyo: Chûkô Shinsho.

Shûkan Daiyamondo: The Diamond Weekly (1995) 'Sarariiman no Nazo' (Riddle of the Salaryman), 15 April, Special Issue.

Sievers, Sharon L. (1983) *Flowers in the Salt: The Beginnings of Feminist Consciousness in Modern Japan*, Stanford, CA: Stanford University Press.

Silverberg, Miriam (1992) 'Constructing the Japanese Ethnography of Modernity', *Journal of Asian Studies*, 51(1): 30–54.

Slater, David H. and Galbraith, Patrick W. (2011) 'Re-narrating Social Class and Masculinity in Neoliberal Japan', *Electronic Journal of Contemporary Japanese Studies*. Available at www.japanesestudies.org.uk/articles/2011/SlaterGalbraith.html (last accessed 5 November 2011).

Southern, Jacquelyn (2000) 'Blue Collar, White Collar: Deconstructing Classification', in J.K. Gibson-Graham, Stephen A. Resnick, and Richard D. Wolff (eds) *Class and its Others*, Minneapolis: University of Minnesota Press, pp. 191–224.

SPA! (1998) 'Gen'in-betsu "Shanai Bôryoku" Yotsu no Patân' (Four Patterns of 'Company Violence' By Cause), 11 November: 37–42.

Spangler, Lynn C. (1992) 'Buddies and Pals: A History of Male Friendships on Prime-time Television', in Steve Craig (ed.) *Men, Masculinity, and the Media*, Newbury Park, CA: Sage, pp. 93–110.

Spielvogel, Laura (2003) *Working Out in Japan: Shaping the Female Body in Tokyo Fitness Clubs*, Durham, NC: Duke University Press.

Standing, Guy (2011) *The Precariat: The New Dangerous Class*, London: Bloomsbury Academic.

Standish, Isolde (2000) *Myth and Masculinity in Japanese Cinema: Towards a Political Reading of the 'Tragic Hero'*, Richmond, UK: Curzon.

Steinberg, Marc W. (1991) 'The Re-making of the English Working Class?', *Theory and Society*, 20(2): 173–197.

Steven, Rob (1983) *Classes in Contemporary Japan*, Cambridge, UK: Cambridge University Press.

Sugimoto, Yoshio and Mouer, Ross (1989) 'Introduction: Cross-currents in the Study of Japanese Society', in Yoshio Sugimoto and Ross Mouer (eds) *Constructs for Understanding Japan*, London: Kegan Paul International, pp. 1–35.

Suyama, Teiichi (1965) 'Manga ni Yoru Sarariiman no Hyakunen-shi' (A Hundred-year History of the Salaryman through *Manga*), *Bessatsu Chuo Koron*, 4(2): 135–142.

Taga, Futoshi (2001) *Dansei no Jendâ Keisei: 'Otokorashisa' no Yuragi no Naka de* (The Gender Formation of Men: Inside the Instabilities of 'Masculinity/Manliness'), Tokyo: Tôyôkan Shuppan-sha.

Taga, Futoshi (2003a) 'Recent Trends in Men's Studies in Japan'. Unpublished Paper Presented at the 13th Biennial Japanese Studies Association of Australia Conference, Brisbane, Australia.

Taga, Futoshi (2003b) 'Rethinking Male Socialization: Life Histories of Japanese Male

Youth', in Kam Louie and Morris Low (eds) *Asian Masculinities: The Meaning and Practice of Manhood in China and Japan*, London: RoutledgeCurzon, pp. 137–154.

Taga, Futoshi (2005) 'Rethinking Japanese Masculinities: Trends of Research on Men and Masculinities in Japan', in Mark McLelland and Romit Dasgupta (eds) *Genders, Transgenders, and Sexualities in Japan*, London: Routledge, pp. 153–167.

Taga, Futoshi (2006a) *Otokorashisa no Shakaigaku: Yuragu Otoko no Raifukôso* (The Sociology of Masculinity/Manliness: The Unstable Lifecourse of Men), Kyoto: Sekai Shisô-sha.

Taga, Futoshi (2006b) 'Tsukareta Otoko no Raifusaikuru' (The Constructed Life Cycle of Men), in Tsunehisa Abe, Sumio Obinata, and Masako Amano (eds) *Danseishi 3: 'Otokorashia' no Gendaishi* (History of Masculinity Series No. 3: The Contemporary History of 'Manliness/Maleness'), Tokyo: Nihon Keizai Hyôron-sha, pp. 158–190.

Taga, Futoshi (2011a) 'Ikuji-suru Sarariiman: Ikuji ga Dekinai Tsurasa, Shigoto ga Dekinai Tsurasa' (Childrearing Salarymen: The Pain of Not Being Able to Engage in Childrearing, The Pain of Not Being Able to Work), in Futoshi Taga (ed.) *Yuragu Sarariiman Seikatsu: Shigoto to Katei no Hazama de* (Unstable Salaryman Life: Between Work and Family), Tokyo: Minerva Shobô, pp. 99–126.

Taga, Futoshi (2011b) 'Kojin-ka Shakai ni okeru "Otokorashisa" no Yukue: Sarariiman no Ima-tokore kara' (The Future Direction of 'Masculinity/Manliness' in an Individualized Society: From the Salaryman's Present Position'), in Futoshi Taga (ed.) *Yuragu Sarariiman Seikatsu: Shigoto to Katei no Hazama de* (Unstable Salaryman Life: Between Work and Family), Tokyo: Minerva Shobô, pp. 187–217.

Taga, Futoshi (2011c) 'Yuragu Rôdô-kihan to Kazoku-kihan: Sarariiman no Kako to Genzai' (The Unstable Labour Model and Family Model: The Salaryman's Past and Present'), in Futoshi Taga (ed.) *Yuragu Sarariiman Seikatsu: Shigoto to Katei no Hazama de* (Unstable Salaryman Life: Between Work and Family), Tokyo: Minerva Shobô, pp. 1–33.

Taga, Futoshi (ed.) (2011d) *Yuragu Sarariiman Seikatsu: Shigoto to Katei no Hazama de* (Unstable Salaryman Life: Caught Between Work and Family), Tokyo: Minerva Shobô.

Takeda, Hiroko (2005) *The Political Economy of Reproduction in Japan: Between Nation-state and Everyday Life*, London: RoutledgeCurzon.

Takeuchi, Hiroshi (1996) 'Sarariiman to iu Shakai-teki Hyôchô' (The Salaryman as Social Symbol), in Shun Inoue *et al.* (eds) *Nihon Bunka no Shakaigaku* (The Sociology of Japanese Culture), Iwanami Kôza: Gendai Shakaigaku (Iwanami Seminar Series: Contemporary Sociology), Tokyo: Iwanami Shoten, pp. 125–142..

Takeuchi, Hiroshi (1997) 'Sarariiman-gata Ningen-zô no Tanjô to Shûen' (The Birth and Demise of the Salaryman-model Archetype), in Hirochika Nakamaki and Kôichirô Hioki (eds) *Keiei Jinruigaku Kotohajime: Kaisha to Sarariiman* (Towards an Anthropology of Administration: The Company and the Salaryman), Tokyo: Tôhô Shuppan, pp. 223–235.

Takeyama, Akiko (2010) 'Intimacy for Sale: Entrepreneurship and Commodity Self in Japan's Neoliberal Situation', *Japanese Studies*, 30(2): 231–246.

Tanaka, Hidetomi and Muneyoshi Nakamura (1999) 'Wasurerareta Keizai-shi "Sarariiman" to Hasegawa Kunio' (Hasegawa Kunio and the Forgotten Business Journal 'Sarariiman' ['The Salaryman']), *Festschrift for the 30th Anniversary of Jôbu University*, Joint Publication of the Department of Commercial Science 10(2), and Department of Management and Information Science 20, Jôbu University: 1–22.

Tanaka, Miyoko (1974) 'Gendai Dansei-ron' (Contemporary Theories on the Male), *Chûo Kôron*, January: 88–98.

Tanaka, Toshiyuki (2009) *Danseigaku no Shin-tenkai* (New Developments in Men's/ Masculinity Studies), Tokyo: Seikyûsha.

Tao, Masao (1996) *Kigyô Shôsetsu ni Manabu Soshiki-ron Nyûmon* (An Introduction to Studying Organizational Theory in Business Novels), Tokyo: Yûhikaku Sensho.

Thorne, Barrie (1993) *Gender Play: Girls and Boys in School*, New Brunswick, NJ: Rutgers University Press.

Tipton, Elise K. (2008) *Modern Japan: A Social and Political History*, London: Routledge.

Tipton, Elise K. and Clark, John (eds) (2000a) *Being Modern in Japan: Culture and Society from the 1910s to the 1930s*, Sydney: Australian Humanities Research Foundation.

Tipton, Elise K. and Clark, John (2000b) 'Introduction', in Elise K. Tipton and John Clark.(eds) *Being Modern in Japan: Culture and Society from the 1910s to the 1930s*, Sydney: Australian Humanities Research Foundation, pp. 7–13.

Tobin, Joseph J. (1992) 'Introduction: Domesticating the West', in Joseph J. Tobin (ed.) *Re-made in Japan: Everyday Life and Consumer Taste in a Changing Society*, New Haven, CT: Yale University Press, pp. 1–41.

Toyoda, Masayoshi (1997) *Otoko ga 'Otokorashisa' o Suteru Toki* (When Men Discard 'Manliness'), Tokyo: Asuka Shinsha.

Turner, Christena L. (1995) *Japanese Workers in Protest: An Ethnography of Consciousness and Experience*, Berkeley: University of California Press.

Uchihashi, Katsuto, Okumura, Hiroshi, and Sataka, Makoto (eds) (1994) *Kaisha Ningen no Shûen* (The Death of the Company Person), Tokyo: Iwanami Shoten.

Uchino, Tatsurô (trans. Mark A. Harbison) (1983) *Japan's Postwar Economy: An Insider's View of Its History and Its Future*, Tokyo: Kôdansha International.

Ueno, Chizuko (1988) 'The Japanese Women's Movement: The Counter Values to Industrialism', in Gavan McCormack and Yoshio Sugimoto (eds) *The Japanese Trajectory: Modernization and Beyond*, Cambridge, UK: Cambridge University Press, pp. 167–185.

Ueno, Chizuko (1995) 'Kigyô Senshitachi' (Corporate Warriors), in Teruko Inoue, Chizuko Ueno, and Yumiko Ehara (eds) *Danseigaku: Nihon no Feminizumu Bessatsu* (Men's Studies: Special Edition of Japanese Feminism Series), Tokyo: Iwanami Shôten, pp. 215–216.

Ueno, Chizuko (2004) (trans. Beverley Yamamoto) *Nationalism and Gender*, Melbourne: TransPacific Press.

Ujigawa, Makoto (1981) *Jikkanteki Sarariiman-ron: Kaisha Ningen kara Dappi* (A Realistic Study of the Salaryman: Casting off the Skin of the Company Person), Tokyo: Nihon Seisansei Honbu.

Umezawa, Tadashi (1997) *Sarariiman no Jikakuzô* (Salarymen's Self-images), Tokyo: Minerva Shobô.

Unami, Akira (1994) 'Kaisha koso Sekai da: Shain-ryô Kenchiku no Kansatsu Shisutemu' (The Company Itself is the World: The Surveillance System of Company Dormitory Architecture), in Katsuto Uchihashi, Hiroshi Okumura, and Makoto Sataka (eds) *Kaisha Ningen no Shûen* (The End of the Company Person), Tokyo: Iwanami Shoten, pp. 103–120.

Uno, Chiyo, Enchi, Fumiko, and Hirabayashi, Taiko (1959) 'Dansei Mondai Tokushû: Dansei-ron Yokozuna Shingikai' (Special Issue on the Male Problem: The Great Discussion on Masculinity Theory), *Fujin Kôron*, 20 March: 116–120.

Uno, Kathleen S. (1993) 'The Death of "Good Wife, Wise Mother"?', in Andrew Gordon (ed.) *Postwar Japan as History*, Berkeley: University of California Press, pp. 293–322.

198 References

Uno, Tsunehiro (2008) *Zero Nendai no Shisôryoku* (The Ideological Power of the Zero Decade), Tokyo: Hayakawa Shobô.

Uno, Tsunehiro and Hamano, Satoshi (2012) *Kibôron: 2010 Nendai no Bunka to Shakai* (On Hope: Culture and Society in the 2010s), Tokyo: NHK Shuppan.

Vale de Almeida, Miguel (1996) *The Hegemonic Male: Masculinity in a Portuguese Town*, Providence, RI: Berghahn Books.

van Helvoort, Ernest (1979) *The Japanese Working Man: What Choice? What Reward?*, Tenterden, Kent, UK: Paul Norbury Publications.

Vaught, Charles and Smith, David L. (1980) 'Incorporation and Mechanical Solidarity in an Underground Coal Mine', *Sociology of Work and Occupations*, 7(2): 159–187.

Vicinus, Martha (1991) 'Distance and Desire: English Boarding School Friendships, 1870–1920', in Martin Duberman *et al.* (eds) *Hidden From History: Reclaiming the Gay and Lesbian Past*, London: Penguin Books, pp. 212–229.

Vogel, Ezra F. (1971) (2nd edn) *Japan's New Middle Class: The Salaryman and His Family in a Tokyo Suburb*, Berkeley: University of California Press.

Vogel, Ezra F. (1979) *Japan as Number One: Lessons for America*, Cambridge, MA: Harvard University Press.

Walker, J.C. (1988) *Louts and Legends: Male Youth Culture in an Inner-city School*, Sydney: Allen & Unwin.

Wedgwood, Nikki (2009) 'Connell's Theory of Masculinity: Its Origins and Influences on the Study of Gender', *Journal of Gender Studies*, 18(4): 329–339.

White, Merry (1993) *The Material Child: Coming of Age in Japan and America*, New York: The Free Press.

White, Merry (2002) *Perfectly Japanese: Making Families in an Era of Upheaval*, Berkeley: University of California Press.

Whitehead, Stephen (1998) 'Disrupted Selves: Resistance and Identity Work in the Managerial Arena', *Gender and Education*, 10(2): 199–215.

Williams, Christine L. (1993) 'Introduction', in Christine L. Williams (ed.) *Doing 'Women's Work': Men in Nontraditional Occupations*, Newbury Park, CA: Sage, pp. 1–9.

Willis, Paul E. (1977) *Learning to Labour: How Working Class Kids Get Working Class Jobs*, Aldershot, UK: Gower.

Willis, Paul (1979) 'Shop Floor Culture, Masculinity and the Wage Form', in John Clarke, Chas Critcher, and Richard Johnson (eds) *Working Class Culture: Studies in History and Theory*, London: Hutchinson, pp. 185–198.

Wilson, Fiona M. (2003 (2nd edn) *Organizational Behaviour and Gender*, Aldershot, UK: Ashgate.

Wiltshire, Richard (1995) *Relocating the Japanese Worker: Geographical Perspectives on Personnel Transfers, Career Mobility and Economic Restructuring*, Kent, UK: Japan Library.

Witz, Anne, Halford, Susan, and Savage, Mike (1996) 'Organized Bodies: Gender, Sexuality and Embodiment in Contemporary Organizations', in Lisa Adkins and Vicki Merchant (eds) *Sexualizing the Social: Power and the Organization of Sexuality*, New York: St Martin's Press, pp. 173–190.

Yamada, Masahiro (1999) *Parasaito Shinguru no Jidai* (The Age of Parasite Singles), Tokyo: Chikuma Shinsho.

Yamasaki, Hiroshi (2001) 'Kindai Dansei no Tanjô' (The Birth of the Modern Male), in Haruo Asai, Satoru Itô, and Yukihiro Murase (eds) *Nihon no Otoko wa Doko Kara Kite, Doko e Iku no ka: Dansei Sekushuariti Keisei ('Kyôdô kenkyû')* (Where Have

Japanese Men Come From, Where Will They Go? Construction of Male Sexuality [Collaborative Research]), Tokyo: Jûgatsusha, pp. 32–53.

Yano, Christine R. (1998) 'Defining the Modern Nation in Japanese Popular Song, 1914–1932', in Sharon A. Minichiello (ed.) *Japan's Competing Modernities: Issues in Culture and Democracy 1900–1930*, Honolulu: University of Hawaii Press, pp. 247–264.

Yano, Ichirô and Yano-Tsuneta Kinenkai (Tsuneta Yano Memorial Society) (eds) (1970) *Nippon: A Charted Survey of Japan*, Tokyo: Kokuseisha.

Yoda, Tomiko (2006) 'A Roadmap to Millenial Japan', in Tomiko Yoda and Harry Harootunian (eds) *Japan after Japan: Social and Cultural Life from the Recessionary 1990s to the Present*, Durham, NC: Duke University Press, pp. 16–53.

Yoda, Tomiko and Harootunian, Harry (eds) (2006) *Japan after Japan: Social and Cultural Life from the Recessionary 1990s to the Present*, Durham, NC: Duke University Press.

Yoshikawa, Hiroshi (trans. Charles H. Stewart) (2002) *Japan's Lost Decade*, Tokyo: The International House of Japan.

Yuzawa, Yasuhiko and Miyamoto, Michiko (2008) *Dêta de Yomu Kazoku Mondai* (Reading Family Problems through Data), Tokyo: NHK Books.

Index